COMPANY ACCOUNTS

J. O. MAGEE, F.C.A.
Senior Lecturer in Accountancy at the
North Western Polytechnic

MACDONALD & EVANS LTD
8 John Street, London, W.C.1
1967

First published November 1967
Reprinted August 1968
Reprinted April 1969

©

MACDONALD & EVANS LTD
1967

S.B.N.: 7121 0304 X

*Printed in Great Britain by Richard Clay (The Chaucer Press), Ltd.,
Bungay, Suffolk*

GENERAL INTRODUCTION

The HANDBOOK Series of Study Notes

HANDBOOKS are a new form of printed study notes designed to help students to prepare and revise for professional and other examinations. The books are carefully programmed so as to be self-contained courses of tuition in the subjects they cover. For this purpose they comprise detailed notes, self-testing questions and hints on examination technique.

HANDBOOKS can be used on their own or in conjunction with recommended textbooks. They are written by college lecturers, examiners, and others with wide experience of students' difficulties and requirements. At all stages the main objective of the authors has been to prepare students for the practical business of passing examinations.

P. W. D. REDMOND
General Editor

NOTICE TO LECTURERS

Many lecturers are now using HANDBOOKS as working texts to save time otherwise wasted by students in protracted note-taking. The purpose of the series is to meet practical teaching requirements as far as possible, and lecturers are cordially invited to forward comments or criticisms to the Publishers for consideration.

AUTHOR'S PREFACE

THE primary purpose of this HANDBOOK is to try to show the student the basic principles underlying the main aspects of accountancy in relation to limited companies. It is not intended as a replacement of any of the many excellent books on accountancy already in existence, but mainly as a supplement to them. It might be described as a "method" book, in that in a number of chapters a method or plan has been suggested for dealing with problems.

Long experience of teaching has forced me to the conclusion that accountancy is best taught by the use of very short steps. Reference to the text will show how examples have been broken down into a number of stages when working out the solution. Certain accounts are repeated again and again with the further addition of a fresh entry each time. The object of this, of course, is to enable the student to see the gradual "build up" of the account, and equally important, to see where the latest entry comes from. One further vital element in teaching the subject is that *every* account should be shown, since students' abilities vary so very much; one will grasp a point immediately whereas another will require a detailed, step by step explanation. It is for these latter students especially that this book has been written in the hope that some, at least, of their difficulties may be resolved.

Many of the examples have been taken from recent examination papers of the Institute of Chartered Accountants in England and Wales, the Association of Certified and Corporate Accountants, the Chartered Institute of Secretaries and the Corporation of Secretaries. To each of these bodies I wish to acknowledge my gratitude, and accept full responsibility for the worked solutions given.

Special Note.

At the time of going to press the *Companies Act*, 1967, had just been passed. The provisions of this Act will come into operation in respect of companies whose financial years end on or after 27th January 1968, apart from the provisions relating to turnover which will apply to financial years ending on or after 27th July 1968.

More information than has been demanded hitherto is now required to be given in respect of Balance Sheets and Profit and Loss Accounts. It is, therefore, most important that the student should take steps to familiarise himself with this recent legislation.

The main requirements affecting the accounts and Balance Sheets of limited companies are set out in Chapter VI and Appendix IV. As the 1967 Act was passed by Parliament a few weeks before the publication of this book, the publishers felt that the general provisions should be incorporated in the text so far as was possible, in spite of the difficulties which this involved. Chapter VI was therefore re-written and the rest of the text amended where necessary.

Students are further recommended to read the *Guide to the Accounting Requirements of the Companies Acts, 1948–1967*, published for the Institute of Chartered Accountants in England and Wales.

August 1967   J. O. MAGEE.

CONTENTS

CHAPTER I

THE ACCOUNTS OF LIMITED COMPANIES

INTRODUCTION

1. Companies Act. When people speak of a "company" in relation to business matters it may be taken for granted that they are referring to those business entities which are known legally as *limited liability companies*.

When the revolutionary idea of the *limitation of personal liability* was introduced a number of rules were laid down as to the manner in which these new creations (limited companies) should conduct themselves. These rules were given the force of law when passed by Parliament in the form of the *Companies Act*, 1862. Subsequently, these rules were revised and added to from time to time, the last two Acts being in 1948, and 1967, which are the only two which concern us.

2. Principle of limited liability. The essence of the *Companies Act* has always been the idea of setting a *limit* to the amount of money a *member* of a company could be called upon *by law* to subscribe towards the settlement of that company's debts. This principle is of the greatest importance for *no other business unit can obtain such protection*.

If a sole trader fails to meet his business debts he may be made bankrupt and the law may well force him to sell his private possessions so that his creditors can be paid. In exactly the same way the members of a partnership may be forced to pay the debts of the business out of their *private* means. In neither of these cases does the *protection of limited liability* apply. Sole traders and partners are exposed to all the risks there are, while, on the other hand, the members of a limited company can and do enjoy a considerable measure of protection. From the very beginning *a member of a limited company knows exactly how much money he is going to place at risk* when he invests in the shares of that company. He is thus in a position to be envied, *knowing* in advance the *maximum* amount of money he can lose.

1

THE CAPITAL STRUCTURE

There is no basic difference between the Capital Account of a sole trader, the Capital Account of any of the members of a partnership or, finally, the Capital Account of a limited company.

> NOTE: In each case the Capital Account is a record of the amount of money *invested* in the particular business by the owner or *owners*.

3. Sole traders and partnerships. The capital structure of a business is seen at its simplest when considering the case of a sole trader. The entire amount of capital which he *invests* is credited to his Capital Account.

In the case of a partnership the matter is slightly more complicated because a number of capital accounts are needed, *i.e.* a *separate* one for *each* partner must be opened and credited with the amount of capital *invested* by each individual partner.

4. Company Capital Account. Only *one* Capital Account is required in the case of a limited company even though there may be many more people sharing in it than in the case of a partnership. The reason for this is that in the eyes of the law a limited company is regarded as being a *person*, and, like a person, having an individuality of its own.

5. How a company Capital Account differs. The *capital structure* of a company differs from that of a sole trader or a partnership in the manner in which it is built up and because of the fact that many people individually may have a share in it. In substance the Capital Account is no different from that of a sole trader or a partnership, nor does it differ in its purpose or function. Its difference lies in the following factors:

(a) In the larger companies, at least, *it is built up over a period of time*, *i.e.* the entire amount of capital is not usually paid up in one lump sum.

(b) Even though many people may be contributing varying sums to the company's capital *we do not keep separate Capital Accounts for each of these individuals*.

(c) In a company *it is possible for there to be different classes of capital* (and to that extent there may be more than one Capital Account). The existence of different classes of capital is in order to distinguish between those members who are prepared to take greater *risks* and those who are not. Generally speaking, those members who are prepared to take the greater risks have the greater say in controlling the affairs of the company.

6. Share capital. The *capital* of a limited company is divided into a number of parts. Each of these parts is called a *share*, and the people who contribute the money which goes to make up the capital of the company are called *shareholders*.

Since there are likely to be a lot of people who contribute to the capital of a company, *i.e.* who become *joint owners* in the business, the total capital is divided into a *predetermined* number of shares at the time when the company is formed. Let us suppose, for example, that a company is formed having an *authorised* capital of £1000. This £1000 worth of shares might be split up into: 1000 shares of £1 each; or 2000 shares of 10s. each; or 20,000 shares of 1s. each.

The *size* (in monetary value) of each share is a purely domestic matter so far as the company is concerned and will be decided upon by the founders of the company.

7. Types of share capital. There are two basic types of share capital:

(*a*) *Ordinary* shares; and
(*b*) *Preference* shares.

Sometimes we find shares which have been given other names, such as founders' shares, participating preference shares, preferred ordinary shares, etc. These are simply variations of the two basic types. Their introduction is to be regarded as a domestic matter of the company concerned.

8. The Share Capital Account. The *capital* of a limited company *cannot be reduced* except by permission of the Court. Consequently, in the case of the vast majority of companies, the Share Capital Account will remain *intact* during its lifetime at the figure subscribed originally by the shareholders. It follows, therefore, that *no entries* will be made on the DEBIT SIDE OF THE ACCOUNT in respect of *losses* nor for any *withdrawals* in respect of *profits* as would be done in the case of a sole trader.

On the other hand there is *no restriction* on the company *increasing* its share capital provided that in doing so it conforms to the regulations of the *Companies Act*. Note, however, that it may *not* increase the total of the credit side by adding any of its *profits* thereto.

9. The register of members. Because the capital structure of a limited company is usually made up of a large number of small contributions it is necessary to keep special records relating to the personal details of the various contributors.

It must be remembered that the *total capital subscribed* must remain *intact* throughout the lifetime of the company (**8**). The *persons* who *own* the shares may change but the *total* capital must remain unaltered (except for extraordinary reasons and with special permission). Thus it becomes essential that the company keep records which are completely *separate* from the Capital Account in respect of the names and addresses of those persons who at one time or another have *contributed* capital to the company as well as details of individual amount which they have contributed.

Each company must keep a *register of members* wherein is contained all the personal information referred to above.

10. Ordinary shareholders. The ordinary shareholders of a limited company are what may be termed the *risk-takers*. As the term suggests they stand in an exposed position, the penalty of failure, at best, being that they will receive no reward for their investment, and, at worst, may well entail the loss of their capital. On the other hand, should the venture prove successful the rewards may be very high indeed.

The ordinary shareholder is gambling. The possibility of great gains *plus* lack of security must be weighed against the risks of no income and possible loss of capital. Obviously, most people who invest in ordinary shares consider that the potential advantages outweigh the disadvantages. Ordinary shares are often referred to as being the "risk capital" of companies.

11. Preference shareholders. Investors in preference shares are looking for the twin virtues of security of capital together with a modest return on their investment. They seek no more than that. They are not concerned with the *control* of the company nor with directing its policies. Those matters they are content to leave in the hands of the ordinary shareholders who, under normal circumstances, carry the control of the company by virtue of the voting rights attached to ordinary shares.

THE ISSUE OF SHARES

12. The prospectus. In order to raise sufficient capital to enable it to carry out the objectives for which it has been created a public company must issue a *prospectus*. This is a document which contains a great deal of information required by those people who may be interested in investing money in the company.

A *prospectus is not an offer* by the company to the public.

Having read the prospectus, members of the public may then make an *offer* to the company intimating that if the company is prepared to accept their offer they, the members of the public, will be prepared for their part to invest money in the company. A prospectus has been defined as being *"an invitation to offer," i.e.* inviting prospective investors to *apply* for shares on or before a certain date.

13. Allotment of shares. When all the *applications* have been received by the company they will be scrutinised by the directors who may:

(a) Accept them *in full*; or
(b) Accept them *in part* only; or
(c) *Reject* them completely.

This action by the directors is known as *allotting the shares, i.e.* they allocate to each applicant the number of shares which they consider he should have. It must be understood that they can be completely arbitrary in their decision and that there is no appeal against it; neither are they required to give any reason for refusing to allot shares to any particular individual.

THE TRANSACTIONS IN THE COMPANY ACCOUNTS

14. Before allotment. Up till the moment when shares are *allotted* the applicants are *creditors* of the company. That is to say, there is *no contract* between the parties and, consequently, the money which the applicants have sent in with their applications does not belong to the company; it is returnable in the event of shares not being allotted to the individual applicant.

15. On allotment. *Immediately shares have been allotted* the situation changes because the company has accepted the applicants' offers and *contracts* come into being. The applicants are now shareholders. The money which stood to their credit in the company's books is no longer owed to them; instead, it at once becomes part of the *share capital* of the company.

Furthermore, at the moment of allotment, the money which the applicants promised to pay in the event of shares being allotted to them, becomes payable. Thus, in the twinkling of an eye, their status is transformed from that of creditors to *debtors*, and the full amount which is payable on allotment *at once* becomes part of the share capital of the company.

In this way the Share Capital Account of the company will be credited with (*a*) the amount which was paid by the successful applicants, plus (*b*) the amount now due from them as a consequence of their having been allotted shares. The total of these two amounts at this point is spoken of as the *called-up capital*.

16. Calls on shareholders. At some later date (or dates) the company will *make calls* upon the shareholders, *i.e.* it will require that they pay further monies to the company as instalments towards the full amount which they have undertaken to pay. The amount of a *call* and the frequency (if more than one call is to be made) are matters for the discretion of the directors.

EXAMPLE 1.

DX Ltd, made an issue of 20,000 shares of £1 each payable as follows:

Stage 1: 2*s*. per share on Application
Stage 2: 4*s*. per share payable on Allotment
Stage 3: 6*s*. per share payable on First Call
Stage 4: 8*s*. per share payable on Second Call

The issue was fully subscribed and all monies were paid as they became due.

Stage 1

Bank Account

Application A/c	£2,000		

Application Account

		Bank A/c	£2,000

The Application Account is, in essence, the personal account in total of all those people who have applied for shares. As can be seen they appear as *creditors* of the company.

If a Balance Sheet was produced at this point it would show the following entries:

BALANCE SHEET

Creditors		Bank	£2,000
Sundry applicants			
for shares	£2,000		
	£2,000		£2,000

Stage 2

Allotment Account

Share Capital A/c	£4,000		

Share Capital Account

		Allotment A/c	£4,000

In its turn the Allotment Account becomes the personal account of the applicants who have *now* become shareholders. They are now seen to be *debtors*.

Now that the applicants have been transformed into shareholders the Application Account must be closed off and the credit balance on the account transferred to the Share Capital Account, as follows:

Application Account

Share Capital A/c	£2,000	Bank A/c	£2,000

Share Capital Account

		Application A/c	£2,000
		Allotment A/c	4,000
			£6,000

The position now is that:

(a) The *called-up* capital amounts to £6000.
(b) The *paid-up* capital is only £2000.
(c) The shareholders are *debtors* for £4000.

Immediately following the posting of the Letters of Allotment a Balance Sheet would read as follows:

BALANCE SHEET

Share Capital		Bank	£2,000
20,000 £1 shares		Debtors	
6s. called	£6,000	Amount due from sundry shareholders for cash payable on Allotment	4,000
	£6,000		£6,000

When the money due on allotment has been received, the Bank Account will be debited and Allotment Account credited, thus closing it off.

Stage 3

In this stage the *first call* will be made on the shareholders and the procedure followed is exactly the same as that for allotment, *i.e.* First Call Account will be debited (signifying that the shareholders are once again debtors—this time, however, for £6000) and Share Capital Account will be credited.

A Balance Sheet would now contain the following details:

BALANCE SHEET

Share Capital		Bank	£6,000
20,000 £1 shares		*i.e.* Applica-	
12*s.* called	£12,000	tion A/c £2,000	
		Allot-	
		ment	
		A/c 4,000	
		Debtors	
		Amount due from	
		sundry shareholders	
		for cash payable	
		on 1st call	6,000
	£12,000		£12,000

Stage 4

The *second call* will be made in this final stage and will follow precisely the lines of the first call. In both *Stage 3* and *Stage 4* when the cash is received the Bank Account will be debited and each Call Account credited with its respective amount, *i.e.* £6000 and £8000.

The Capital Account will be complete and will appear thus:

Share Capital Account

Application A/c	£2,000
Allotment A/c	4,000
First Call A/c	6,000
Second Call A/c	8,000
	£20,000

At this point the total on the debit side of the Bank Account will also show a figure of £20,000 representing the *paid-up* capital.

When the two amounts of cash have been received in respect of the first and second calls the Balance Sheet will appear thus:

BALANCE SHEET

Share Capital		Bank	£20,000
20,000 £1 shares			
fully paid	£20,000		
	£20,000		£20,000

FORFEITURE OF SHARES

17. Temporary reduction of capital. Shares may be forfeited for *one* reason only; *non-payment* of the money which became due when a *call* was made. This appears to be a *reduction of capital* and in one sense it is, at least temporarily.

The company is free to reissue the forfeited shares and thus bring the share capital back to its original figure.

Alternatively, if the shares are *not* reissued the amount of money received from the original shareholder will be transferred to a Forfeited Shares Account and must be separately stated in future balance sheets. In practice it is often transferred to Capital Reserve.

18. Reissue of shares. If the company reissues the forfeited shares it must take care to ensure that the *total* amount of cash received for the shares from:

(*a*) the original shareholder, and
(*b*) the subsequent purchaser,

amounts in all to the nominal value of such shares.

For example, if Mr X had paid 12*s.* per share on 100 shares of £1 each (a total of £60) and then failed to pay the final call of 8*s.* per share, the shares would be forfeited. They could then be *reissued at any price* the company decided upon so long as they were not reissued for *less* than 8*s.* per share.

If the shares are reissued and the *total* amount of money received in connection with both their issue and reissue *exceeds the nominal value*, the *surplus* received over and above the *nominal* value should be transferred to a Share Premium Account.

19. Debiting the Share Capital Account. When shares are forfeited it is vitally important that the student understands that the *amount to be debited* in the Share Capital Account is the *total* sum of money which has been **called up**, in respect of the shares being forfeited.

Thus if we take the figures in Example 1 (*see* **16**) and suppose that Mr Y had been allotted 200 shares and had paid his application and allotment money of 6*s.* per share (a total of £60) and then failed to pay the first call amounting to a further £60 (making a total of £120 *called up*) the 200 shares would be forfeited. *The figure to be debited* in the Share Capital Account would be £120 which is the **called-up** capital, and most certainly *not* £200, which is the *nominal* capital.

The student must recognise that the nominal value of the shares (in this case £200) simply represents the *total* sum which ultimately must be paid by the owner of the shares. The nominal value is only of academic interest when dealing with problems involving forfeiture of shares. The important figure is the amount which has been **called-up** on the shares which are being forfeited.

Experience has shown that this matter gives difficulty to many students. In an effort to make it clearer let us show, in the form of a chart, what happens.

EXAMPLE 2

DX Ltd issue 20,000 shares of £1 each as in Example 1, with the exception that Mr Y, who was allotted 200 shares, failed to pay the first call of 6s. per share. His 200 shares were forfeited.

	Debit entries in the Bank Account		*Credit* entries in the Share Capital Account
(1)	£2,000	Application money is received	
(2)		Shares are allotted	£4,000
(3)		Application Account is closed when shares are allotted	2,000
(4)	4,000	Allotment money is received	
(5)		First call is made	6,000
(6)	5,940	All cash is received *except* £60 from Mr Y for his 200 shares	
	£11,940		£12,000
(7)		Mr Y's 200 shares (on which £120 has been *called up*) are forfeited	
		Deduct	120
			£11,880
(8)		**Forfeited Shares Account**	60
	£11,940		£11,940

We will show the closing entries in normal double entry form. If reference is made to *Stage 3* of Example 1 we observe that the first call has been made. Let us take matters up from this point.

Stage 1

First Call Account

Share Capital A/c	**£6,000**		

Share Capital Account

	£	Application A/c	£2,000
		Allotment A/c	4,000
		1st Call A/c	6,000
			£12,000

Stage 2

First Call Account

Share Capital A/c	£6,000	Bank A/c	£5,940
		Calls in Arrears A/c	60
	£6,000		£6,000

Calls in Arrears Account

1st Call A/c	£60

Stage 3

Share Capital Account

Forfeited Shares A/c	£120	Application A/c	£2,000
(12s. per share on		Allotment A/c	4,000
200 shares)		1st Call A/c	6,000
Balance c/d	11,880		
	£12,000		£12,000
		Balance b/d	£11,880

Forfeited Shares Account

	Share Capital A/c	**£120**

Stage 4

Calls in Arrears Account is now closed by transferring the balance to Forfeited Shares Account.

Calls in Arrears Account

1st Call A/c	£60	Forfeited Shares A/c	£60

Forfeited Shares Account

Calls in Arrears A/c	£60	Share Capital A/c	£120
Balance c/d	60		
	£120		£120
		Balance b/d	£60

Bank Account

Balance b/d	£11,940		

Share Capital Account

		Balance b/d	£11,880

From the above ledger entries we see that the total of the assets, *i.e.* balance at bank, amounts to £11,940. The liabilities total is made up of Share Capital £11,880 plus Forfeited Shares £60 = £11,940.

It must be noted that the *cash* which Mr Y paid to the company on application and allotment, *i.e.* 200 × 2s. = £20 and 200 × 4s. = £40, making a total of £60, is now held by the company *in excess* of the total amount of the *issued capital*. This simply means that the company has made a *capital profit*. The money representing that profit is held in the company's bank account and the company is at liberty to use it in the *normal* manner on any of the day-to-day running expenses. It may *not*, however, use the money for the payment of *dividends*.

NOTE: The student's attention is once again drawn to the fact that the amount debited to Share Capital Account is the amount which has been *called-up*.

20. Forfeited shares reissued. Companies frequently reissue to *new* holders shares which have been previously *forfeited*. They must be careful, however, to make sure that the total amount of cash they receive in respect of these particular shares amounts, *at least*, to the *nominal* value of the shares. Reference has already been made to this point in **18** above.

Before showing an example of the procedure on reissue, let us first make the final call on the remainder of the shares. This is being done to avoid confusing the student.

EXAMPLE 3

Following the forfeiture of Mr Y's 200 shares in Example 2, the company made the second (and final) call of 8s. per share. All the members duly paid the call.

The call was in respect of 19,800 shares since 200 of the original 20,000 were no longer in issue. The money received amounted (at 8s. per share) to £7920.

Bank Account

Balance b/d	£11,940		
2nd and Final Call A/c	7,920		
	£19,860		

Second and Final Call Account

Share Capital A/c (Call on 19,800 shares at 8s. per share)	£7,920	Bank A/c	£7,920
	£7,920		£7,920

Share Capital Account

	Balance b/d (per *Stage 3*, Example 2)	£11,880
	2nd and Final Call A/c	7,920
		£19,800

Forfeited Shares Account

	Balance b/d (per *Stage 4*, Example 2)	£60

EXAMPLE 4

Following the forfeiture of Mr Y's 200 shares on each of which 6s. had been paid, the company *reissued* them all to Mr W at a price of 18s. per share *fully paid*.

Stage 1

In the first place, the shares must be *reissued* and brought into the Share Capital Account. We must remember that Mr W is buying the 200 shares as being *fully paid*, and so, the *full nominal value* must be credited to the Share Capital Account.

In this first stage the amount which Mr W is *paying* is of no significance.

The student is advised to think of the *Forfeited Shares Reissued Account* as being a *Call Account*, for this is exactly what it is.

When a call is made, the Call Account is debited and Share Capital Account credited. The circumstances are virtually the same when a number of shares which had previously been forfeited are reissued. The *only* difference is in the *name* of the account, *i.e.* Forfeited Shares Reissued Account, instead of Call Account.

The book-keeping entries then are:

> *Debit* Forfeited Share Reissued Account.
> *Credit* Share Capital Account.

NOTE: In examination work it can safely be said that the question will state that the shares are being reissued "*as fully paid*" at so many shillings per share. The *full nominal value* of the shares being reissued *must be used in the double entry* indicated above.

Forfeited Shares Reissued Account (in reality a Call Account)

Share Capital A/c	£200

Share Capital Account

	Balance b/d (per Example 3)	£19,800
	Forfeited Shares Reissued A/c	200
		£20,000

Stage 2

In Example 2 if reference is now made to *Stage 4* it will be seen that there is a credit balance of £60 standing on the Forfeited Shares Account. *This sum is a capital profit* made by the company at the expense of the original shareholder whom we are calling Mr Y. The company has this sum of £60 lodged in its bank account.

At this point we now treat this money as having been contributed towards the full payment on the reissued shares. When money is received for a call we credit the Call Account. *We do much the same in this case.*

Forfeited Shares Account

Forfeited Shares Reissued A/c	**£60**	Balance b/d	**£60**

This account is now closed by the transfer of the *credit* balance of £60 to the Forfeited Shares Re-issued Account (or Call Account).

Forfeited Shares Reissued Account

Share Capital A/c	£200	Forfeited Shares A/c	**£60**
		Balance c/d	140
	£200		£200
Balance b/d	£140		

Stage 3

The *cash* is received from Mr W.

Bank Account

Balance b/d (per Example 3)	£19,860
Forfeited Shares Reissued A/c (200 shares at 18s. per share)	**180**
	£20,040

Forfeited Shares Reissued Account

Balance b/d	£140	Bank A/c	**£180**

Stage 4

The balance on Forfeited Shares Reissued Account is now *capitalised* and transferred to Share Premium Account.

Forfeited Shares Reissued Account

Balance b/d	£140	Bank A/c	£180
Share Premium A/c	**40**		
	£180		£180

Share Premium Account

		Forfeited Shares Reissued A/c	£40

By making reference to *Stage 3* we see that the Bank balance (*debit*) amounts to £20,040. In *Stage 1*, the final balance on the Share Capital Account shows as £20,000 (*credit*). Lastly, in *Stage 4* there appears a balance of £40 (*credit*) in the Share Premium Account. Thus, the assets and liabilities are equal.

OTHER ISSUES OF SHARES

21. The issue of shares at a premium. The principles laid down for the issue of shares in the case of a *newly-formed* company apply also in those cases where an *established* company makes a public issue of shares to obtain *additional* capital.

There may well be, however, one important point of difference. If the company has done well and established a reputation for soundness as well as giving a good return in the shape of dividends, *i.e.* has proved itself as being a good company in which to *invest*, then it may well feel that when approaching the public it can ask for *more* than the *nominal* value for each share of the new issue. For example, it may offer £1 shares for, say, £1 4s. 0d. each. That is to say, £1 is the value of each share according to the company's Memorandum of Association, but owing to the fact that the company is well-regarded in the financial world it feels that it can ask *new* shareholders to pay something more than the *nominal* value. It therefore asks them to pay £1 4s. 0d. instead of £1. The extra 4s. is called a *premium*.

From the company's viewpoint this premium of 4s. on every share is a most desirable feature since it increases the *liquid funds* of the business.

22. Premiums. There are two important points to bear in mind with regard to premiums:

(a) The premium which is being charged is nearly always required to be paid *when the allotment money is paid*.

(b) The money received by the company as premium must be credited to a special account, the *Share Premium Account*. The credit balance on this account may only be used in an extremely limited way as laid down in the *Companies Act*. *No deviations* are permissible (see V, **11**). This means that, among other things, *the premium may not be distributed as a dividend*.

23. Book-keeping entries. It is also most important that the student understands the position from the practical aspect, *i.e.* from the point of view of the company receiving a considerable amount of cash from the payment of the premium. The money is received and is, therefore, debited in the Cash Book. The money is thus available to be spent, and it may be spent on any normal business expense. It does *not* have to be set aside in some special bank account or anything of that nature. It simply forms part of the ordinary assets of the business.

24. Premiums form additional capital. As has been mentioned above (**22**), the credit entry will be made in the Share Premium Account and this balance must remain as a *permanent* credit balance (with only those items mentioned in the Act as being capable of reducing it). The effect of this is that in most cases a premium is nothing other than a *contribution of additional capital* apart from the above-mentioned exceptions.

Compare what happens when capital monies are contributed to a company and when money from a premium on these same shares is received. The *capital* monies are used for *buying* things the company needs, *e.g.* stocks, new machines, motor vans. The *premium* money is paid into the company's bank account in the same way as is the money for the shares and *is there to be spent on any normal business activity of the firm*.

EXAMPLE 5

PQR Ltd made a public issue of 10,000 ordinary shares of £1 each at a premium of 8s. per share. Payments were to be made as follows:

(a) 5s. per share on Application.
(b) 12s. per share on Allotment (including the premium).
(c) 11s. per share on First and Final call.

Stage 1

Applications reach the company's office together with the money *due on application*. The cash is paid into bank.

Bank Account

Application and Allotment A/c	£2,500		

Application and Allotment Account

		Bank A/c	£2,500

Stage 2

On allotment the allotment monies as well as the amount due for the *premium* become payable. *The sum due for the premium* now takes up a *permanent* position on the *credit* side of the Share Premium Account.

Application and Allotment Account

Share Capital A/c	**£4,500**	Bank A/c	£2,500
Share Premium A/c	**£4,000**	(application money)	

Share Capital Account

		Application and Allotment A/c	**£4,500**

Share Premium Account

		Application and Allotment A/c	**£4,000**

When the money is received it will, of course, be debited in the Bank Account and credited to Application and Allotment Account.

25. The issue of shares at a discount. The *Companies Act,* 1929, gave permission for the first time for the issue of shares *at a discount, i.e.* at a figure *below the nominal value* of the particular shares. In Section 57 of the 1948 Act are laid down those matters to be observed for such an issue to be valid. The conditions are the *SAME* as in the 1929 Act and are as follows:

> *S*anction of the Court is required.
> *A*lready issued, must be of a *class*.
> *M*eeting of the members must authorise the issue.
> *E*lapsing of one year since the company started business.

The *aide memoire*, "*S A M E*" may be of some assistance in remembering the requirements of this section of the Act.

EXAMPLE 6

A company with an issued capital of 50,000 £1 ordinary shares which stand on the market at a quotation of 16s. per share requires further capital and applies to the Court for permission to issue 25,000 £1 ordinary shares at a discount of 4s. per share. The company, which had been trading for more than a year, had already agreed in general meeting to make the application which was duly granted.

The 25,000 shares were fully applied for on the terms of 3s. payable on application, 5s. on allotment and 8s. on the first and final call.

Stage 1

Bank Account

Application A/c	£3,750		

Application Account

		Bank A/c	£3,750

Stage 2

Allotment Account

Ordinary Share Capital A/c	£6,250		

Ordinary Share Capital Account

	Balance b/d	£50,000
	Application A/c	**3,750**
	Allotment A/c	**6,250**
		£60,000

Application Account

Ordinary Share Capital A/c	**£3,750**	Bank A/c	£3,750

When the allotment money is received Bank Account will be debited and Allotment Account credited with £6250.

Stage 3

First and Final Call Account

Ordinary Share Capital A/c	**£15,000**	

Ordinary Share Capital Account

	Balance b/d	£60,000
	First and Final Call A/c	**15,000**
		£75,000

Stage 4

First and Final Call Account

Ordinary Share Capital A/c	£15,000	Bank A/c	**£10,000**
		Discount on Shares A/c	**5,000**
	£15,000		£15,000

Discount on Shares Account

First and Final Call A/c	£5,000	

Bank Account

Application A/c	£3,750	
Allotment A/c	6,250	
First and Final Call A/c	10,000	
	£20,000	

NOTE

(i) Ordinary Share Capital Account is credited with the *full nominal amount* of the shares issued.

(ii) The *Companies Act* lays it down that the *discount* on the issue must be stated *separately* in all subsequent Balance Sheets *until written off*.

(iii) *In practice* it is usual for such discount to be written off *by periodical transfers* from Profit and Loss Account.

26. Oversubscription. When a public company issues a prospectus one finds that as a rule a large number of shares is involved, possibly amounting to some hundreds of thousands of pounds in terms of cash. If the prospectus is fortunate enough to receive favourable notices in the press the chances are that the issue will be *oversubscribed*, *i.e.* the applications for shares will exceed the number of shares available.

As has already been pointed out (**13**), when the directors examine the list of applications they may:

(a) accept an application in full; or
(b) accept it in part; or
(c) reject it completely.

EXAMPLE 7

A company proposed to make an issue of 10,000 shares of £1 each. 2s. per share was required on application and 4s. on allotment. Calls were to be made as and when required.

The public applied for 15,000 shares and the directors decided to deal with the applications in the following manner:

(a) Applications for the first 6000 shares were accepted *in full*.

(b) The next 8000 applications were *scaled down*, so that for each *two* shares applied for only *one* was allotted, making a total of 4000 shares.

(c) The last 1000 applications were *rejected*.

The following chart shows one way in which a problem of this type may be dealt with.

CASH RECEIVED (*at* 2s. *per share*)	SHARES APPLIED FOR	ALLOTMENTS	CASH RETAINED (*by the company*)	CASH CARRIED FORWARD (*to Allot- ment A/c*)	CASH RETURNED (*to unsuc- cessful applicants*)
£1,500	15,000				
£600		6000 shares allotted *in full*	£600	—	—
£800		*One* share allotted for every *two* applied for	£400	£400	—
£100		*None*	—	—	£100
£1,500	15,000		£1,000	£400	£100

Having ascertained the position let us now make the necessary entries in the ledger accounts.

Stage 1

Bank Account

Application A/c	**£1,500**		

Application Account

		Bank A/c	**£1,500**

Stage 2

Application Account

Transferred to Allotment A/c	**£400**	Bank A/c	£1,500

B

Allotment Account

		Application A/c	**£400**
		(Cash received from applicants who obtained *part*-allotment *only*)	

Stage 3

Application Account

Transferred to Allotment A/c	£400	Bank A/c	£1,500
Bank A/c	**100**		
(Money returned to unsuccessful applicants)			

Bank Account

Application A/c	£1,500	Application A/c	**£100**

At this point the Application Account would be closed by transferring £1000 to the credit of Share Capital Account.

As soon as the shares have been allotted the money to be paid on allotment becomes due immediately. This amounts to 4*s.* per share on 10,000 shares, a total of £2000. We must remember, however, that the £400 *excess application money* has already been placed to the credit of Allotment Account. As a result, only £1600 will be required from the shareholders as a group when the allotment letters are sent out.

Stage 4

Bank Account

Application A/c	£1,500	Application A/c	£100
Allotment A/c	**1,600**		

Allotment Account

Shase Capital A/c	£2,000	Application A/c	£400
		Bank A/c	**1,600**

The principle explained in this example will be applied in those circumstances where more cash is received than is strictly due at a particular time. For example, it might happen that a person decides to pay for his shares *in full* at the time of allotment. In such a case a simple expedient is to credit the full amount so received from this individual to a Calls Received in Advance Account. As and when any subsequent call is made the appropriate amount will then be transferred from this account to the particular Call Account.

PROGRESS TEST 1

1. What is meant by the term "risk capital"? (**10**)

2. What is the position of an applicant for shares before allotment? (**14**) and after allotment? (**15**)

3. Under what circumstances may shares be forfeited? (**17**)

4. When a number of shares are forfeited how is the amount of the debit entry in the Share Capital Account calculated? (**19**)

5. What do you understand by a Share Premium? Are there any limitations on its use? (**22–24**)

6. What requirements are placed upon a company which issues shares at a discount? (**25**)

CHAPTER II

PROFIT AND RESERVES

THE TWO ASPECTS OF PROFIT

1. Profit as a sum due. Profit may be described as the reward which becomes *due to the owner* of a business as a result of a successful period of trading. In other words we may say that profit is something which, when it has been made, is *owed* to the owner by the business.

Stated in terms of double entry book-keeping, we must:

> *Debit* Net Profit to the Profit and Loss Account.
> *Credit* The owner's Capital Account.

The effect, then, upon the Capital Account is to *increase the amount* shown as *owing to the owner*.

2. Profit as abstract or concrete. The record thus made is, in essence, of an *abstract* nature, *i.e.* that of *demonstrating* that the business owes to the proprietor a greater sum than it did before. The *concrete* aspect will be shown, although usually in a less recognisable form, by an increase in the assets. To make the point perfectly clear let us take a very simple illustration.

EXAMPLE 8

J. Snodgrass commences business on 1st January with a capital in cash of £1000. A summary of his transactions up to 31st March are as follows:

Total purchases	£3000
Total sales	£4000
Business expenses	£350

All of the transactions were for cash and there was no stock on hand at 31st March.

The results of the three months' trading would be as follows:

Cash Account

Capital A/c	£1,000	Purchases A/c	£3,000
Sales A/c	4,000	Expenses A/c	350
		Balance c/d	1,650
	£5,000		£5,000

Trading and Profit and Loss Account to 31st March

Purchases	£3,000	Sales	£4,000
Gross Profit	1,000		
	£4,000		£4,000
Expenses	350	Gross Profit	1,000
Net Profit	650		
	£1,000		£1,000

BALANCE SHEET AS AT 31ST MARCH

Capital at start	£1,000		Cash	£1,650
Add Net Profit	650	1,650		
		£1,650		£1,650

From the above figures we see that the *asset* of Cash has increased by £650 during the period. This corresponds *exactly* with the amount of the profit made.

EXAMPLE 9

Let us suppose that the business in Example 8 instead of being that of a sole trader had from the start been a *limited company.* Using exactly the same figures for the same period the Balance Sheet would have appeared thus:

J. SNODGRASS LTD—BALANCE SHEET AS AT 31ST MARCH

Share Capital	£1,000	Cash	£1,650
Profit and Loss Account	650		
	£1,650		£1,650

Here we note a subtle change from the original Balance Sheet. In that of the limited company the profit has *not been added* to the capital but is shown separately under the heading *Profit and Loss Account*, *£650.* This is set out in this fashion in order to conform with the requirements of the *Companies Act.* Turning to the assets side we see that there is no difference from the original Balance Sheet.

3. Profit and Loss Account balance. We must be clear as to what the balance of £650, standing to the credit of the Profit and Loss Account means when its appears as a separate item on the liabilities side of the Balance Sheet. This £650 is the amount of the profit which the company has made and which, therefore, is a debt due to the owners, *i.e.* the shareholders.

(*a*) It thus follows that the shareholders are now *owed*:

  (*i*) The amount of cash which they contributed as capital: and
  (*ii*) The amount of the profits earned which have *not*, as yet, been *distributed* to them.

This, then, is the *abstract* angle, and it shows the shareholders as creditors for an *additional* sum at the *end* of the training period.

(*b*) What of the *concrete* aspect?

In this simple example it is very easy to see. The asset of Cash has *increased by* £650 and this *corresponds* precisely with the amount of *profit* made. Thus we may sum the matter up by saying that:

The profit is represented in a concrete manner by the increase of the asset *Cash* by £650.

4. Profit may be spent. Taking matters a stage further let us consider another example.

EXAMPLE 10

Again using the same basic figures (*see* Examples 8 and 9) let us imagine that on 31st March J. Snodgrass Ltd purchased some shop fittings costing £130, and a motor van for £520. The Balance Sheet would then read:

BALANCE SHEET AS AT 31ST MARCH

Share Capital	£1,000	Shop Fittings	£130
Profit and Loss		Motor Van	520
Account	650	Cash	1,000
	£1,650		£1,650

In this case we would say that the *abstract* element of profit is represented in *concrete form* in the shape of the *assets* "Shop Fittings" and "Motor Van." That is to say, the *cash* which *originally* represented the profit *has now been spent* on fixed assets.

Having been spent *once* it cannot, of course, be spent a second time and the shareholders cannot, therefore, be paid a dividend. At the same time it must be recognised that, in their capacity as shareholders, they are still *owed* the profit plus their original contribution of cash as capital. The total amount owing to them is £1650 and this is covered by the value of all the assets in whatever form they are held.

NOTE: *Always remember* that when you see an item on the liabilities side of the Balance Sheet bearing the title "Profit and Loss Account" there will be found *somewhere* among the assets *items of an equivalent value* to the amount shown against the Profit and Loss Account.

REALISED AND UNREALISED PROFIT

5. The Net Profit. After passing the Trial Balance stage of book-keeping students move on to the preparation of Final Accounts.

Almost inevitably, it seems, they tend to look on the Net Profit as a *balancing* figure which emerges after they have entered all the appropriate items in the Profit and Loss Account. This misconception is not altogether surprising since so much store is set on getting the accounts and Balance Sheet to agree. Certainly the main purpose of students working so many exercises is to enable them to develop their skill in the purely mechanical operation of double entry book-keeping, but at the same time they should be taught to understand that this in itself is not everything.

The student must appreciate what happens in business and must understand that the entering of transactions in a set of books is simply a method of recording these events. It does not need the operation of double entry to ensure that a profit is made.

Profit is built up on a day-to-day basis. It does not suddenly emerge as the result of preparing the profit and loss account.

That this is so is very simply demonstrated if we consider the case of a business which starts on 1st January and completes a year of trading on 31st December. On each day that business is carried on, goods will be sold. Each sale brings with it a small proportion of profit and it therefore follows that the build-up of profit is gradual, but, at the same time, *steady*. Thus we can see that the Net Profit which appears *in total* when the Profit and Loss Account is completed is the accumulation of small amounts of profit earned day by day throughout the year.

6. Profit is nearly all "realised." In the first three examples everything was dealt with on a *cash* basis. The Net Profit amounted to £650 and this coincided with the increase in the cash balance between 1st January and 31st March in Examples 8 and 9. In Example 10 we saw that this increased amount of cash was used for the purpose of buying certain fixed assets.

In all three cases, however, the profit was *realised in cash.*

This particular fact is especially easy to see when everything is treated as a cash transaction.

7. Unrealised profit. This leads us to the question: what is the position where *credit* transactions are involved?

EXAMPLE 11

The transactions of J. Snodgrass Ltd for the three months ended 30th June were as follows:

Purchases on *credit*	£4500
Sales on *credit*	£6050
Expenses incurred on *credit* (not paid for)	£820
Stock at cost on 30th June	£246

The assets and liabilities are as shown in the Balance Sheet of Example 10.

Trading and Profit and Loss Account to 30th June

Purchases	£4,500	Sales	£6,050
Gross Profit	1,796	Closing Stock	246
	£6,296		£6,296
Expenses	£820	Gross Profit	£1,796
Net Profit to P/L			
Appropriation A/c	976		
	£1,796		£1,796

Profit and Loss Appropriation Account

Balance c/d	£1,626	Net Profit for period	£976
		Balance b/f from last	
		account	650
	£1,626		£1,626
		Balance b/d	£1,626

BALANCE SHEET AS AT 30TH JUNE

Share Capital	£1,000	Fixed Assets		
		Shop Fittings		130
Profit and Loss A/c	1,626	Motor Van		520
	2,626			
Current Liabilities		Current Assets		
For goods	4,500	Stock	246	
For expenses	820	Debtors	6,050	
		Cash	1,000	
	5,320			7,296
	£7,946			£7,946

In this example the profit has not *been realised, i.e.* it has not been turned into cash, the reason, of course, being that every transaction was on a credit basis. At the same time it must be appreciated that the profit of £976 has been *earned*. When goods are bought on credit or sold on credit they are rightly to be regarded as valid transactions. The debts thus contracted will ultimately be settled by payment in *cash*.

However, for the moment they remain unsettled and have not been converted into cash. We are therefore forced to the conclusion that the profit (for there most certainly is a profit) is an *unrealised* one. It is only a matter of *time* before this profit becomes a realised one, *i.e.* as soon as the debtors pay the company what they owe; the company, in its turn, will then be able to pay its own creditors both for goods supplied and for services rendered.

Proof: When all debts both owing to and owed by the company have been *paid*:

Cash received from debtors		£6,050
Less Cash paid to creditors for:		
Goods	£4,500	
Expenses	820	
		5,320
		730
Add Unsold Stock which has now been paid for as shown above		246
Leaving *realised profit*		£976

8. The total profit. The examples taken are, of course, extreme cases as will be appreciated, purely to show fundamentally what happens, and that profit may be either *realised* or *unrealised*. It does not matter into which of these categories it falls, it is profit. We find that in almost every business the *total* profit consists partly of *realised* profit and partly of *unrealised* profit.

This section may be summed up by saying: where *debtors* appear in the Balance Sheet there *must* be a proportion of *unrealised* profit.

9. Assessing profit. Many companies carry on business almost entirely on a credit basis. If we study the published Balance Sheets of the large public companies we will almost certainly find that the amounts owing by debtors and owed to creditors are substantial. As a rule we rarely see the trading accounts of these concerns but it is possible to make a fairly good guess as to the approximate amounts of the purchases and sales.

It is generally accepted that suppliers will require payment of their accounts in from four to six weeks from the date of invoice. Debtors, on the other hand, seem to be a little slower in paying and an average period of from six to eight weeks appears to be fairly general. If, then, we take two months as being the time-lag between the date of sale and the date on which the money is received from the debtor we can say that the sales for the year, *i.e.* for twelve months, amount to approximately six times the sum owed by the debtors at the end of the year. (The debtors owe the equivalent of the sales for the last two months.) This, of course, is a rough and ready guide and does not take into consideration such factors as seasonal trades.

The purpose of the above paragraph however is to bring to the student's notice the fact that, broadly speaking, the sales which were made during the first ten months of the year have been paid for and that the profit element contained in those sales has been realised in cash.

Thus we may say that at least five-sixths of the profit of most businesses has actually been received in the form of cash during the year.

10. The treatment of profit in Company Accounts. A feature of accounting which is peculiar to limited companies is the manner in which the net profit is dealt with.

(*a*) Consider, first of all, the cases of *sole traders and partnerships*. The net profit of a sole trader is transferred to the credit of his Capital Account. In the case of a partnership the net profit is divided into the shares to which the partners are entitled. The appropriate share is then credited to the Capital Account of each individual partner. Thus, in principle, the treatment is exactly the same both for sole traders and for partnerships.

(*b*) Now turn to the case of a *limited company*. There is in operation a system which appears to be completely different in principle from that which is in use for sole traders or partnerships. Before we begin to discuss it there is one important matter which must be mentioned. This is that by virtue of the strict rules laid down in the *Companies Act* only in exceptional circumstances may any *alteration* be made to the *capital* of a limited company. As a result of this the only entries which normally are to be found in the Share Capital Account are those which deal with money that has been subscribed by the shareholders as the *capital* of the company. *No* other entries are permitted in the ordinary way. Since this is a matter of law it follows that the *net profit* of a company *must*, of necessity, be transferred from the Profit and Loss Account to some account *other than the Share Capital Account*.

APPROPRIATION OF PROFIT

11. The Profit and Loss Appropriation Account. The *net profit* of a limited company will be transferred to the *credit* side of an account called the Profit and Loss *Appropriation* Account.

Because of its name and of the fact that it is placed immediately below the Profit and Loss Account there is a widespread misconception that it is a *part of* the Profit and Loss Account. This is *not* so. It is, in reality, a part of the *Capital Account*. A strictly more correct title would be "Appropriation of Profit Account."

12. The function of the Appropriation Account. The purpose of the Profit and Loss Appropriation Account is to *dispose of the profit* of the company in whatever manner the *proprietors* decide.

(*a*) It must be appreciated that the *proprietors* of a limited company consist of *all* the shareholders and *not* merely the directors. The directors are, in essence, those shareholders who have been appointed to manage the day-to-day business affairs of the company. Any profit which the company makes belongs to the *entire body of shareholders* and is, therefore, their property to do with as they wish.

(*b*) At least once every year the company is bound to summon all its members, *i.e.* all the shareholders, to a meeting called the *Annual General Meeting*. At this meeting a statement setting out the trading results for the past year is placed before the members and a *report* on the affairs of the company is made to the members by the chairman of the board of directors. Having reported to the *owners* (*i.e.* the shareholders) of the business the chairman then tells them what the board of directors *advises* should be done with the year's profit. These recommendations are then *voted* upon. Provided that they are passed by the members, the recommendations must then be carried out.

13. Distribution of profit. Generally, the two most important items to be voted upon at an annual general meeting are:

(a) The amount of profit which is to be transferred to *reserve*; and
(b) How much of the profit is to be paid out from the company funds by way of *dividend*.

14. Transfers to reserve. The expression "transfer to reserve" is one which is well known to students of company accounts. Its significance, however, is not so well understood.

The accounting entries to record such a matter are very simple, merely involving a debit in the Profit and Loss Appropriation Account and a corresponding credit to General Reserve Account. It is not the accounting entries which present the problem but what underlies them.

EXAMPLE 12

X Ltd commenced to trade on 1st January and made a profit of £12,000 during the first year.

(a) *Yearly profit.* We will assume that the profit of £12,000 was spread *evenly* throughout the year. That is to say, a profit of £1000 was made each month. We will also assume that the average time-lag between the date of a sale and the date on which the *money* was received from the customer was *two months*. We may therefore conclude that at the end of the year ten-twelfths of the whole year's profit has actually been received by the company in cash; *e.g.* if a sale is made in January the money will be received in March, the cash received in April is in respect of February sales, and so on.

The important point to be appreciated here is that this ten-twelfths of the profit has actually been received in the form of cash. Furthermore, it has been received steadily during the *ten months* from March to December, inclusive.

(b) *Utilisation of profit.* Now, as we can see, ten-twelfths of £12,000 (the total profit) amounts to £10,000. The company can either keep the money or it can spend it.

Profit is the reward which accrues to the owners of a business as a result of a successful period of trading. It is the surplus which remains after all expenses have been paid or provided for.

NOTE: There is a very natural tendency for a student to look at the *final* result, *i.e.* the *total* profit of £12,000. This tendency must be avoided. Let us look instead at matters *on a month-to-month basis* with special reference to the ten months of March to December. By the end of March a *realised* profit of £1000 out of a total profit of £3000 to date will be in the hands of the company. This £1000 will be *surplus* to all its immediate requirements. Now let us ask ourselves what the company proposes to do with it? It goes without saying that every business will, in normal circumstances, try to improve its position by expansion of trade leading to higher profits. How is this expansion to take place?

The policy of the firm may perhaps, in the early days be to add fresh lines of goods to its original ones. In that case the main part of the *realised* profit, *i.e.* the *cash*, would be spent on increasing the *stocks*. Alternatively, it might be decided to purchase a delivery van early in April. Later on perhaps, when further profit has been amassed, the concern might purchase the *building* in which it carries on its business. If, on the other hand, it was a manufacturing company the expansion could take the form of buying additional *machinery*. All of these things, and others besides, will generally improve the earning capacity of the business as month follows month. Thus we can see that, in the main, profit is used as and when it is realised.

(c) *Position at year end.* Coming now to the end of December the financial year is completed and the accounts will be prepared. It is at this point that the *full* profit is found to amount to £12,000.

When the members of the company meet the accounts are placed before them together with the recommendations of the board of directors. From what has been stated above it should be clear that although a large profit has been made the greater part of it *is not available* for distribution to the members of the company in the form of a dividend because the cash representing the profit is no longer there. It has been *spent* on the purchase of *stocks or fixed assets*.

15. ". . . recommended that £6000 be placed to reserve." The above phrase, or one similarly worded, appears in the annual reports of many company chairmen.

Such a phrase is always taken to indicate that profits (amounting in this particular case to £6000) are intended to be *retained in the business* or, to use another well-known phrase, *ploughed back into the business*. To express it in yet another way, it means that the directors are proposing that out of the profit of £12,000 *originally available for distribution to the members* the sum of £6000 is to be regarded as earmarked for other purposes. They are therefore suggesting that the shareholders *deny* themselves the enjoyment of splitting the full £12,000 among themselves and that the amount which may be paid out to them be *restricted to half* the total profit at the most.

It should not be difficult to understand the reason for this apparent act of self-denial.

It is simply that the directors have *already spent* a large proportion of the profit. It cannot be spent twice! Since the company (through its board of directors) had decided some months ago on a progressive policy and used a considerable part of the profits to develop the business during the course of the year, profits (in the form of cash) were used for one or other of the purposes indicated in the previous section. This, then, is the real meaning of the expressions "retaining profits in the business" or "ploughing them back."

Thus, when the board recommends that "£6000 be placed to reserve" what it is really saying to the shareholders is "we want your approval of our having spent £6000 out of the profits *during* the year to improve the prospects of the company."

16. Reserves. Some confusion may arise in the minds of students in connection with the designations Revenue Reserve and Capital Reserve and it is felt that a word of explanation may be of help at this point.

The word "reserve" is in everyday use for various purposes; it simply means that something has been *set aside* for a specific person and, as a result, that particular thing is *not available* to other people. In company accounting the same meaning attaches to profit which has been *"transferred to reserve."* That is to say, it is regarded as *not being available for distribution by way of dividend* for the present.

17. Profit from various sources. Profit may arise as follows:

(a) As a result of *trading*, in which case we refer to it as a *revenue* profit.

(b) A fixed asset realising a *greater sum* than the book value of the asset. This is called a *capital* profit.

(c) From an issue of shares, etc., at a premium, *i.e.* a sum greater than the nominal value of the shares. This premium is a *capital* profit.

(d) Should an asset such as Land and Buildings be *re-valued* and be found to have a value greater than that shown in the books the *difference* in values will be debited to the Land and Buildings Account and credited to a Capital Reserve Account, *i.e.* as a *capital* profit.

All of these profits belong to the shareholders as the owners of the business.

Generally speaking, however, only the revenue profits are available for distribution by way of dividend.

18. Capital Reserves. When a *capital* profit is made it is normally realised in *cash*. Therefore, the assets of the company are increased. To compensate, the liabilities side of the Balance Sheet must be increased by a similar sum. This is done by crediting an account headed *"Capital Reserve"* and placing it (usually) immediately below the share capital in the Balance Sheet. It thus appears in that section which shows the amount due to the shareholders of the company.

> NOTE: It must be clearly understood that even though the company is not permitted to *distribute*, in the form of a dividend, the cash so obtained, it does have the right to employ this money in its *day-to-day transactions*.

PROGRESS TEST 2

1. Describe profit in (*a*) its abstract form; (*b*) its concrete form. **(2)**, **(3)**

2. What do you understand by (*a*) realised profit; and (*b*) unrealised profit? **(5)**, **(6)**

3. From reading a company's Balance Sheet could you decide whether or not all of the profit had been realised? **(8)**

4. What is the function of the Appropriation Account? **(12)**

5. To what use does a company normally try to apply its profit? **(13** (*a*), (*b*)**)**

6. What is meant by the expression "ploughing profits back into the business"? **(15)**

CHAPTER III

SINKING FUNDS

OPERATION OF SINKING FUNDS

As we have seen in the previous chapter, the expression "transfer to reserve" is used in accountancy when a part of the profits is set aside, *i.e.* is ploughed back, or retained in the business. The effect of this is to stop the shareholders from voting that particular part of the profit to be distributed to themselves as a dividend.

1. Meaning of "fund." Sometimes we come across the expression "transfer to Reserve Fund," or "Sinking Fund."

Although in law there appears to be no significant difference in the meaning of the expressions "Reserve Account" or "Reserve (or Sinking) Fund," there is in the minds of people in the financial and the accountancy world a considerable difference in meaning. To them the use of the word "*fund*" indicates that at the same time as that portion of the profit was set aside, *an equal sum of cash* has also been set on one side and it will no longer be available for use in the company's business.

2. What a Sinking Fund is. The expression "*Sinking Fund*," is generally used to describe the *double* operation of:

(a) The setting aside of part of the profits of a limited company by transferring such part to a special account; and, *at the same time,*

(b) Buying for cash suitable investments (*e.g.* government stocks), the cost of which is exactly equal to the amount set aside out of the profits as in (a) above.

Thus we may find in the Balance Sheet of a limited company the following terms:

On the *liabilities* side   Sinking Fund   £x
On the *assets* side   Sinking Fund *Investments*   £x

From this it can be clearly seen that the action required falls into *two absolutely separate and distinct parts*. If only one part is carried out then a Sinking Fund cannot be said to exist. *Both parts* of the action are required to bring a Sinking Fund into being.

3. Purpose of a Sinking Fund.

Why do companies consider it necessary to act in this way? The usual answer is that they will require to have a specific amount of *cash* available for certain on some *known* date in the future for a *particular* expenditure.

For example, a company may have purchased a lease of its business premises. When the lease expires, in order to retain occupation of the property the firm will have to pay a large sum of money for a renewal of the lease. Therefore, to ensure that this large sum of money will be available when the lease expires, the firm may well decide to build up a *Sinking Fund* in order to *provide the cash* to purchase a renewal of the lease on that *known* date in the future. Accordingly, they calculate how much of their profits must be set aside annually, and at the same time, the amount of money which will have to be specifically invested to provide the total sum required on the expiry of the lease.

4. Creating a Sinking Fund.

The following three Examples illustrate the difference between Sinking Funds and other transfers of profit.

EXAMPLE 13

Company A makes a profit of £5000 and transfers £2000 of this to General Reserve.

Profit and Loss Appropriation Account

General Reserve A/c	**£2,000**	Net Profit	£5,000

General Reserve Account

	P/L Appropriation A/c **£2,000**

The decision of the shareholders at the annual general meeting to set aside £2000 of the profit means that they abandon their right to take £2000 cash from the company in the form of a dividend. They would, therefore, be restricting the maximum dividend to the remaining balance of £3000.

Part of the *profit* is set aside; but *no* Sinking Fund has been created.

EXAMPLE 14

Company B also made a profit of £5000. It did *not* set aside any part of that profit to General Reserve, but it did invest £2000 in cash (from the balance at the bank) in 4% Government Stock. We will assume that there is a balance of £2781 in the bank.

Bank Account

Balance b/d	£2,781	4% Govt. Stock A/c	£2,000

4% Government Stock Account

Bank A/c	£2,000		

The position now is that there are two assets where before there was only cash at bank. Thus there is no alteration in the *total* worth of the assets, merely a change in their composition.

Part of the *assets* has been set aside, but no Sinking Fund has been created.

EXAMPLE 15

Company C makes a profit of £5000. It transfers (or sets aside) £2000 of this profit to a Sinking Fund for the purpose of redeeming, at some future date, £10,000 debentures. At the *same time* it purchases in cash for £2000 some 4% Government Stock with the object of building up a sufficient fund of investment which will be capable of being realised, *i.e.* sold and turned into cash at the appropriate date in the future. The bank balance amounts to £2189.

Here we *do* have the *two* requirements for a Sinking Fund. These are carried out *in parallel*, as follows:

Profit and Loss Appropriation Account				*Debenture Redemption Sinking Fund Account*		
Debenture Redemption Sinking Fund A/c	£2,000	Net Profit for the year	£5,000		Profit and Loss Appropriation A/c	£2,000

Debenture Redemption Sinking Fund Investment Account				*Bank Account*		
Bank A/c	*£2,000*				Debenture Redemption Sinking Fund Investment A/c	*£2,000*

In this illustration we can see quite simply how the *two* requirements necessary for the creation of a *sinking fund* have been fulfilled. It should also be plain as to *how* the two accounts relating to the Sinking Fund and the Sinking Fund Investments march hand-in-hand, so to speak.

The fundamental requirement of a Sinking Fund is:

> *that the amount of money invested should never be less than the amount set aside out of profits.*

While the basic proposition is as shown above there may be, at times, small divergences from this pattern. This matter is dealt with later in this chapter (**6**).

SINKING FUNDS FOR SPECIFIC PURPOSES

5. The two usual purposes of Sinking Funds. Sinking Funds are built up over a period of time in order to meet some future demand on the finances of a company. In other words, the company is *saving up* so as to be able to *pay* for something in a few years' time.

Usually, Sinking Funds are operated for two specific purposes:

(*a*) To redeem *debentures*; and
(*b*) to replace *assets*.

The redemption of debentures will be dealt with in a subsequent chapter (*see* IV). For the present, therefore, we will confine our attentions to the use of a Sinking Fund to replace an asset.

6. Providing for the replacement of an asset. When a fixed asset is purchased this expense is called *capital expenditure*. During the lifetime of the asset we *write off* a portion of the original cost *every year* against the profits. This charge we call *depreciation*.

In acting in this way a company would be following the normally-accepted procedure and at the end of its life the value of the asset would, in theory at least, have been reduced to nil. So far as it goes this is all very well, but obviously, when the asset comes to the end of its life the business would need a *replacement*.

The act of *charging an annual sum* against the profits will have done precisely nothing to ensure that money will be available to purchase a replacement. If the cost of renewing the asset is small then it will probably not present any great problem to find the necessary money when the time comes. On the other hand it might well be that the expense of a replacement could be a crippling blow to the finances of a business. If this was likely to prove the case then some forethought on the part of the directors of a company would be expected and it would be in such circumstances that a Sinking Fund might well be set up.

EXAMPLE 16

X Ltd had acquired a lease of its premises for a period of seven years at a cost of £3500.

In this case we would expect to find the sum of £500 per annum being charged to the Profit and Loss Account by way of depreciation. The corresponding credit would be entered in the Lease Account. Thus at the end of five years the balance on the Lease Account would have been reduced to £1000. Two years later, after £500 had been written off each year, the value of the lease would be *nil*.

If the company wished to continue to use the premises it would have to find a large sum of money to renew the lease. The precise amount would depend upon the circumstances and what arrangements had been agreed upon when the original lease was entered into.

EXAMPLE 17

When X Ltd entered into the original agreement to take a seven-year lease of the premises a clause gave it the option to renew it for a further seven years on the expiration of the original lease.

In such a case when it is anticipated that the option will be taken up and the lease renewed the normal procedure is to leave the Lease Account undisturbed, *i.e.* to show it at its original cost and make no further entry in the account until it has expired.

At the same time a Depreciation Fund Account is brought into existence and at the end of every year Profit and Loss Account is debited with the appropriate annual sum, *i.e.* in this case, £500 per annum, and the Depreciation Fund Account credited.

At the end of the seventh year the accounts would appear as follows:

Lease Account

Year 1. Bank A/c	£3,500	

Depreciation Fund Account

		Year 7. Balance b/d (start)	£3,000
		Year 7. P/L A/c (end)	500
			£3,500

At this point the lease would be of no value and would be closed in the following manner:

Depreciation Fund Account

Year 7. Lease A/c	£3,500	Year 7. Balance	£3,500

Lease Account

Year 1. Bank A/c	£3,500	Year 7. Depreciation Fund A/c	£3,500

Each year as the Depreciation Fund is being built up by the annual sum of £500 *a similar amount would be taken from the bank* and invested in a Depreciation Fund *Investment Account* so that at the end of the seventh year there would be an asset of

£3500 in investments which could be encashed with a view to paying the capital cost of a renewal of the lease.

7. Providing for renewal at an increased cost. There has been considerable discussion in recent years as to the best way of providing for the replacement of assets during periods of inflation.

For example, it is not uncommon for a lease to cost considerably more than its original figure if the option to renew is taken up.

If it was anticipated that, say, £6000 would be asked for when the time came for its renewal, the company would do well to provide more than the £500 per annum which would cover the *historical* cost only. Otherwise it would find itself £2500 short.

The Councils of the various accounting bodies have discussed this matter at considerable length. The general opinion can be summarised by saying that the *historical cost*, *i.e.* in this case, the original £3500, should be debited as a charge against profits, but that any anticipated excess required for renewal or replacement should be treated as an *appropriation of profit*. That is to say, a certain sum (not necessarily the same amount each year) should be debited to the Profit and Loss Appropriation Account annually and credited to a specific *Capital Reserve for Replacement of Assets*.

It follows that each year an amount of money equal to the *total of the two amounts* should then be *invested* in the Depreciation Fund Investment Account.

8. Differences arising between the Sinking Fund and the Investment Account. Although, in theory, the credit balance on the Sinking Fund and the debit balance on the Sinking Fund Investment Account should be equal but opposite, differences may arise in practice. As a rule, these differences are comparatively small. A word of explanation may be helpful. The differences, if any, will be found most probably where a Sinking Fund is in operation for the redemption of debentures (*see* IV, **1, 2, 5**).

9. Debenture Redemption Sinking Fund. After debentures have been in existence for some years and a Sinking Fund and complementary Investment Account have been built up, some, but not all, of the debentures may be redeemed. This will entail the sale of a portion of the investments to make money available to pay off the debenture holders. When this happens it is improbable that the proceeds of the sale will be exactly equal to the amount which this portion of the investments cost.

For example, suppose that investments which originally cost £1000 were sold. In the period of time elapsing between the date of purchase and the date of sale the stocks may have moved up or down in value. Consequently, there will be a profit or a loss on the sale. This profit or loss must be accounted for on the Sinking Fund itself and the result will be that a difference equal to the amount of the profit or loss will then appear between the balances on Sinking Fund and the Investment Account.

EXAMPLE 18

X Ltd had issued £10,000 debentures some years ago and had built up a Sinking Fund by transferring £500 each year from the Profit and Loss Appropriation Account. A similar sum was invested annually.

When each of these two accounts had built up a balance of £4000 the company redeemed £1000 of the debentures. Investments which had cost £1000 originally were sold and realised £1030.

The entries in the Sinking Fund and the Sinking Fund Investment Account would be as set out below.

Stage 1

The position immediately *before* the sale:

Debenture Redemption Sinking Fund Investment Account

	Nomi-nal	£			Nomi-nal £	£
Balance b/d	£4,000	£4,000				

Debenture Redemption Sinking Fund

			Balance b/d			£4,000

Stage 2

£1000 nominal of the stocks are *sold for £1030* and the *profit* is transferred to the Sinking Fund.

Debenture Redemption Sinking Fund Investment Account

	Nomi-nal £4,000	£4,000		*Nomi-nal* £1,000	£1,030
Balance b/d Sinking Fund (profit on sale)	—	30	Bank A/c	1,000	1,030
			Balance c/d	3,000	3,000
	£4,000	£4,030		£4,000	£4,030
Balance b/d	£3,000	£3,000			

Debenture Redemption Sinking Fund

General Reserve A/c	£1,000	Balance b/d	£4,000
Balance c/d	3,030	Sinking Fund Invest-ment A/c	30
	£4,030		£4,030
		Balance b/d	£3,030

Thus we see the two accounts go slightly out of balance as a result of this operation.

10. Redemption of debentures at a discount. Another set of circumstances which could give rise to a difference would be where debentures are redeemed at a *discount, i.e.* at a price *below* their nominal value.

EXAMPLE 19

Let us suppose that the £1000 debentures redeemed in Example 18 were redeemed at £98, *i.e.* £100 worth redeemed for £98. This would give the company a profit of £20 on the £1000 redeemed.

The relevant accounts would appear as follows:

Debentures Account

Bank A/c	£980	Balance	£10,000
Sinking Fund (profit on redemption)	**20**		
Balance c/d	9,000		
	£10,000		£10,000
		Balance b/d	£9,000

Debenture Redemption Sinking Fund

Balance b/d (per Example 18)	£3,030
Debenture A/c	**20**
	£3,050

The Sinking Fund Investment Account balance would remain at £3000 as in the previous example.

PROGRESS TEST 3

1. Describe what you understand by a Sinking Fund. (**2**)
2. What are the essential requirements of a Sinking Fund? (**4**)
3. How would you make provision for the eventual replacement of an asset, at a cost which is expected to be considerably higher than the original cost? (**7**)
4. Give two reasons for the balance on the Sinking Fund Account differing from the balance on the Sinking Fund Investment Account. (**9**), (**10**)

CHAPTER IV

REDEMPTION OF DEBENTURES

DEBENTURES

1. Meaning of debentures. When a limited company *issues shares* to its members it acknowledges the payment for those shares by the issue of share certificates. These certificates are numbered and give details of the shares which they represent. In addition, to be valid, they must be impressed with the seal of the company.

When a limited company *borrows* money it commonly does so by means of *debentures*.

In return for the money which it has received and in acknowledgment of the fact that it has borrowed the money, the company issues a certificate, stamped with the official seal of the company. This *certificate* is called a *debenture*.

2. The debenture certificate. A *debenture* is a certificate which:

(a) *Acknowledges that the company owes* to the person named in the certificate a *stated sum* of money; and
(b) *Promises that a stated rate of interest will be paid* periodically to the person named in the certificate.

In addition, the document usually states:

(c) That the sum borrowed will be *repaid* by the company on or before a certain date; and
(d) Precise details of the *security* which is given to the person named in the debenture certificate.

3. What is meant by the term "security"? In practice, the debenture trust deed contains an undertaking (stated in clear and unequivocal terms) which gives the owner the right to seize assets, sell them and thus recover the amount of his loan in the event of the company failing to satisfy the obligations it has undertaken under the terms of issue of the debenture. This undertaking into which the company enters is called *"charging the assets"* or "making a charge on the assets."

The assets so charged are referred to as the *"security"* for the loan. Suppose a person lent a company £2000 and the company agreed to charge its land and buildings as security for the loan. When this had been done it would mean that the holder of the security, *i.e.* the lender, would, if the company did anything to put the asset in danger of losing its value, be able to step in legally and claim his security. That is to say, he would, under such circumstances, have the unquestionable right to sell the asset and thus obtain repayment of his loan out of the proceeds.

4. Charges on the assets of a company. There are *two* types of charges:

(*a*) *A fixed charge is a mortgage on specified assets.* That is to say, the owner of the asset will, in consideration of a loan, make a transfer of the ownership of the asset to another person. The physical transfer of ownership, however, will only take place in the event of the original owner failing to carry out any of the conditions agreed to when the loan was made to him. For example, if he failed to pay the fire insurance on a building which was the specified asset, thereby running grave risk to the security of the loan the charge would be said to "crystallise."

NOTE: The term "physical transfer" is used to distinguish it from a "legal" transfer. Quite obviously buildings could not, in the literal sense, be transferred physically.

(*b*) *A floating charge is a charge upon a class of assets.* The charge is not restricted to the particular assets which formed the class at the time the charge was entered into, *e.g.* the stock. Stock, of course, changes from day to day. A floating charge on stock would, therefore, cover the stock as it altered, day by day.

METHODS OF REDEMPTION

5. Redemption of debentures. *Most issues of debentures are redeemable.* That is to say, the company which borrows the money in the first instance, and issues debentures as an acknowledgment of the debt it owes to the lender, may, at some future date repay the loan, *i.e.* redeem the debentures.

The usual manner in which companies deal with this matter is by the establishment of a Sinking Fund, which, as we have seen, (III, (2)) means that:

(a) An *annual* amount must be set aside out of the profits; and
(b) An *equal amount of money* must be withdrawn from the business bank account and used to purchase investments, *i.e.* high class stocks or shares, or, alternatively, to pay the annual premium on an endowment assurance policy.

NOTE: This cash transaction leaves the total assets of the business unchanged; but it does mean that there is a kind of moral check upon the company which would normally prevent it from using the money so invested in its everyday business affairs.

6. The three methods of redemption. There are *three* ways in which debentures may be redeemed:

(a) *On maturity, i.e.* on the date promised as the repayment date when the debentures were issued.
(b) *By means of annual drawings, i.e.* a yearly ballot.
(c) *By the company purchasing its own debentures in the open market, i.e.* through the Stock Exchange.

7. Redemption at maturity. Many debentures, when they are first issued, are stated to be repayable on or before a certain date. The actual year is given.

This type of debenture lends itself very readily to the Sinking Fund method of redemption because the company knows precisely the amount of time it has available to *save up* the amount of money required to make the repayment. The Sinking Fund investment is specifically earmarked for the purpose of repaying the debenture-holders on the appointed date, and will *not* be available for the business should it find itself short of money for its normal trading purposes.

8. Alternative form of investment. An alternative to the purchase of stocks or shares is for the company to take out an endowment assurance policy, a method with two important virtues:

(a) *It produces the required sum on the date* it will be needed; and
(b) Since the policy is only kept alive by the payment of the yearly premium, there is *less temptation to "let it slide"* should times be difficult financially.

If money is scarce when the time comes to make the annual purchase of investments there is undoubtedly a great temptation to put off buying. There is always the hope that things will be easier in two or three months' time. This way disaster lies, for the chances are that the money will never be spent in the way that it should.

The insurance method has much to commend it (especially in respect of the prompt payment of premiums):

(i) Non-payment means that the policy will lapse and only the *surrender value* will be payable. This surrender value, as it is called, is very much less than the amount which has been paid by way of premiums, particularly in the early years of a policy.

(ii) One further advantage is that when a certain number of premiums have been paid the insurance company will be prepared to give a *loan* on the policy.

Book-keeping entries. The yearly picture.

> *Debit*   Profit and Loss Appropriation Account
> *Credit* Sinking Fund Account

with the yearly amount *set aside* from the profit.

> *Debit*   Sinking Fund Investment Account
> *Credit* Bank Account

with the amount of cash paid in the purchase of investments *or* for the payment of the insurance premium.

9. Annual interest. This matter will only arise *where income has been received from investments* (*i.e.* it will *not* apply where an insurance policy has been taken out).

(a) Where the interest (or dividend) is received, either quarterly, half-yearly or yearly, it will normally come in the form of a warrant which will have to be paid into the company's bank account. This will entail the normal debit entry in the Bank Account.

(b) What of the corresponding credit? Here we have to deal with a point of considerable importance.

When the calculations of the *yearly sum* to be invested were made from actuarial tables the *annual amount of interest* formed a vital part of those calculations, because this interest must be reinvested and so become, itself, a part of the capital invested. In other words, as *this interest is automatically turned into capital* by being reinvested it means that the yearly extraction of cash from the business assets will be *less* than if the interest were to be treated as normal income and used in the day-to-day business operations, or be paid away in turn as a dividend.

EXAMPLE 20

Z Ltd required a sum of £1000 in ten years' time and made an annual investment of £100.

In ten years' time the company would have amassed a total of £1000 in invested capital. The interest received each year would have been treated as normal income and credited to Profit and Loss Account.

EXAMPLE 21

Instead of dealing with the matter as in Example 20 the company looked at the problem from a different angle. It decided to ascertain what amount of money would have to be invested at, say, 3% compound interest to produce £1000 in ten years' time.

The answer (obtained from tables) is that the company would have to make an annual investment of £84 13s. 4d. each year for ten years to produce £1000 at the end of that time. The yearly saving is £15 6s. 8d. which is a considerable amount.

The interest at 3% on £84 13s. 4d. would be £2 10s. 10d. and this sum would be *added* to the annual appropriation of £84 13s. 4d. making a total of £87 4s. 2d. This amount would then be spent in the purchase of further investments, making the total capital £171 17s. 6d.

In order that the position may be clearly seen in terms of accounting entries let us look at a full example.

EXAMPLE 22

T Ltd borrowed £2625 on 31st December 1964 under a debenture which was to be redeemed three years later, *i.e.* on 31st December 1967. An annual sum of £832 13s. 6d. was set aside from profits at the end of each year and credited to a Sinking Fund. A similar amount was invested each year at 5% compound interest.

1ST YEAR

Stage 1

Profit and Loss Appropriation Account
Year ended 31st December 1965

	£ s. d.		£
Debenture Redemption Sinking Fund	832 13 6	Net Profit for year 1965	x

Debenture Redemption Sinking Fund Account

£		£	s.	d.
	Transferred from			
	P/L Appropriation			
	A/c	**832**	**13**	**6**

Stage 2

At the same time as the above entries are made a similar sum of money is invested in some stocks which yield 5% per annum.

Bank Account

	£	1965	£	s.	d.
		Dec. 31			
Balance b/d	*y*	Sinking Fund			
		Investment A/c	**832**	**13**	**6**

Sinking Fund Investment Account

1965	£	s.	d.	
Dec. 31				
Bank A/c	**832**	**13**	**6**	

The above entries complete matters for 1965. At the end of 1966 a like set of entries will be made with *one significant difference*. There will be additional entries which deal with the *interest received* on the first year's investments.

2ND YEAR

Stage 1

At the end of 1966, *i.e.* on 31st December 1966, the interest on the investment will be received and entered as follows:

Bank Account

	£	s.	d.	
Sinking Fund A/c				
(Interest received				
from investment)	**41**	**12**	**6**	

Debenture Redemption Sinking Fund Account

		£	s.	d.
	1966			
	Jan. 1			
	Balance b/d	832	13	6
	Dec. 31			
	Bank A/c	41	12	6
		874	6	0

Stage 2

Following the entries recording the receipt of the interest the next step is to transfer the annual *appropriation* of profit to the Sinking Fund.

Profit and Loss Appropriation Account
Year ended 31st December 1966

	£	s.	d.		£
Debenture Re-				Net Profit for 1966	*x*
demption					
Sinking Fund	832	13	6		

Debenture Redemption Sinking Fund

	1966		£	s.	d.
	Dec. 31	Balance from *Stage 1*			
		(above)	874	6	0
	Dec. 31	Profit and Loss			
		Appropriation A/c	832	13	6
			1,706	19	6

Stage 3

The company will now purchase some more investments. The amount to be spent will be the *equivalent* of:

	£	s.	d.
(a) The yearly appropriation of	832	13	6
(b) The interest *received* which must now be			
reinvested	41	12	6
	£874	6	0

c

The entries will be as follows:

Bank Account

			1966	£	s.	d.
			Dec. 31			
			Sinking Fund			
			Investment A/c	**874**	**6**	**0**

Sinking Fund Investment Account

1965	£	s.	d.				
Dec. 31							
Balance b/d	832	13	6				
(from 1st Year,							
(Stage 2)							
1966							
Dec. 31							
Bank A/c	**874**	**6**	**0**				
	£1,706	19	6				

Thus we see that the Sinking Fund and its corollary, the Investment Account, continue to have balances which are *equal* but *opposite*.

3RD YEAR

Moving into the third year, *i.e.* 1967, the year of *maturity*, we again have a series of entries similar to those for 1966.

These appear below and have not been broken down into various stages as was done for the sake of clarity in the second year. Using the second year's entries as a pattern, they should be followed without difficulty.

Profit and Loss Appropriation Account
Year ended 31st December 1967

	£	s.	d.		£
Debenture Re-				Net Profit for year 1967	x
demption					
Sinking Fund	832	13	6		

Debenture Redemption Sinking Fund Account

		£	s.	d.
1967				
Jan. 1	Balance b/d	1,706	19	6
Dec. 31	Bank A/c—(Interest on Investment)	85	7	0
Dec. 31	P/L Appropriation A/c	832	13	6
		£2,625	0	0

Bank Account

1967	£ s. d.	1967	£ s. d.
Jan. 1		Dec. 31	
Balance b/d	x	Sinking Fund Investment A/c	918 0 6
Dec. 31			
Sinking Fund A/c	85 7 0		

NOTE
(*i*) The item "Sinking Fund A/c—£85 7*s*." is the amount of interest received on 31st December 1967, on £1,706 19*s*. 6*d*., the total sum invested *one year ago*.
(*ii*) The item "Sinking Fund Investment A/c—£918 0*s*. 6*d*." is made up of cash equal to:

	£	s.	d.
The annual appropriation of profit	832	13	6
Reinvestment of interest received	85	7	0
	£918	0	6

Sinking Fund Investment Account

1967	£	s.	d.
Jan. 1			
Balance b/d	1,706	19	6
Dec. 31			
Bank A/c	918	0	6
	£2,625	0	0

NOTE: In practice it is not likely that the sum of £918 0s. 6d. would have been reinvested because the date of redemption has arrived. It is shown here as being reinvested in order to demonstrate the important principle that the balance on the Sinking Fund Investment Account should be equal (but opposite) to the Sinking Fund Account balance.

10. The closing entries. The Debenture Account will have remained unchanged since the date on which the debentures were first issued. The credit balance of £2625 will indicate that this sum is owing to the debenture holders.

On the date upon which the debentures become redeemable (or, more probably a day or two before) the investments must be sold for cash to enable the company to have sufficient funds in hand to make the repayment. Thus continuing with Example 22:

Sinking Fund Investment Account

1967			1967		
Dec. 31	Balance b/d	£2,625	Dec. 31	Bank A/c	£2,625

The Sinking Fund Investment Account will be closed by transferring the amount of cash realised from the sale from the debit side of the Bank Account.

Bank Account

1967			1967		
Dec. 31	Sinking Fund Investment A/c	£2,625	Dec. 31	Debentures A/c	£2,625

With sufficient cash now in the bank, payment can be made to the debenture holders.

Debentures Account

1967			1957		
Dec. 31	Bank A/c	£2,625	Dec. 31	Balance b/d	£2,625

11. The closing balance. The above entries show that the liability is now cancelled and, at the same time, the assets of the company have diminished by £2625.

On the other hand, the company is still showing a surplus on the Sinking Fund Account. This balance represents profit which has accumulated during the past three years and, as has already been explained in the chapter on Profit (II, (3)) there *must* be assets of an equivalent amount standing in the company's books.

To explain it another way, the company has actually **saved** £2625 during the past three years. The company had the choice of saving up the money or of giving it away (in the form of dividends). It chose to save.

If it had chosen to pay its profit out year by year in the form of dividends, when the time came to repay the debenture-holders, it would have had to raise £2625 in some way (probably by obtaining another loan from someone). By taking £832 13s. 6d. out of the profits each year the shareholders were prevented (by their own action, of course) from *withdrawing* that much money *from the cash funds* of the business. If they had withdrawn that amount of cash each year then quite clearly the assets would have been reduced by precisely the same amount. Thus it can be seen that the company has indeed saved £832 13s. 6d. for each of the three years and, in addition, has gained the compound interest thereon.

As a result, the balance of £2625 standing to the credit of Sinking Fund Account (*i.e.* the saving referred to above) can now be transferred to General Reserve Account since it is now a "free" balance of profit. That is to say, it is no longer earmarked for a *specific purpose* because the purpose for which it was originally set aside has now been fulfilled. This saving may, in the future, be used as the members of the company please, including the payment of dividends.

The final entries in Example 22 would be as follows:

Sinking Fund Account

1967		1967	
Dec. 31		Dec. 31	
Transfer to General			
Reserve	£2,625	Balance b/d	£2,625

General Reserve Account

	1967 Dec. 31 Transfer from Sinking Fund A/c £2,625

Some students may still not understand too clearly how it comes about now that there is, indeed, at this point, a fund of profit which belongs to the shareholders. In an effort to make the matter clearer consider the following example.

EXAMPLE 23

Brown decided to set up in business on his own account and invested all of his savings, £1000, in a company called Brown Ltd. He found that he required more capital and persuaded his friend Green to lend £500 to the business.

The balance sheet of the company *before* trading began was as follows:

BALANCE SHEET 1

Share capital	£1,000	Cash at Bank	£1,500
Loan A/c, Green	500		
	£1,500		£1,500

During the first month of trading the company made a profit of £175 and the balance sheet appeared thus:

BALANCE SHEET 2

Share Capital	£1,000	Cash at Bank	£1,675
Profit and Loss A/c	175		
Loan A/c, Green	500		
	£1,675		£1,675

Suppose the company now decided to repay £175 to Green. After this had been done the balance sheet would show the following position:

BALANCE SHEET 3

Share Capital		£1,000	Cash at Bank	£1,500
Profit and Loss A/c		175		
Loan A/c,				
Green	£500			
Less Repaid	175			
		325		
		£1,500		£1,500

Now if we compare Balance Sheet 1 with Balance Sheet 3 we find that the amount of cash at bank is the same, *i.e.* £1500, in each case. On the other hand on Balance Sheet 1 the company *owed* £500 to Green. On Balance Sheet 3 it only owed him £325, *but* the company *still possessed* £1500 Cash at Bank.

It follows therefore, that the company's position so far as cash is concerned is:

Cash strictly belonging to the company	£1,175
Cash owed to Green	325
	£1,500

The company is thus £175 better off than it was when it started and the balance of £175 on Profit and Loss Account is reflected on the assets side of the Balance Sheet which shows (as broken down above) that the company now owns £1175 whereas at the beginning of its life it owned only £1000.

To help clear another possible doubt let us suppose that before the £175 was repaid to Green the company decided to transfer this profit to a Loan Redemption Account. This, of course, is simply a book-keeping entry and would replace the item "Profit and Loss A/c—£175" on the Balance Sheet.

When the £175 was repaid to Green this balance on Loan Redemption Account would be freed and become available to the shareholders. As can be seen above there is £1175 belonging to the company now. Think of the situation as one where Green's *own particular £500* has been partly repaid to him.

12. Redemption of debentures at a premium. When debentures are offered to the public the terms on which they will be redeemed are stated. Frequently, one of the terms of redemption is that they will be repaid at a price *higher than their nominal value*. The reason for this is to attract investors.

Suppose, for example, some 6% debentures are offered as being redeemable at 105 ten years after the date of issue. This simply means that for every £100 subscribed now, £105 will be paid to the holder at the time of redemption.

The £5 excess represents a capital profit at the end of the term *in addition to* the yearly interest of £6 for every £100 invested.

Since interest on the debentures must be paid every year by the company whether profits are made or not, an investment of £100 would produce income amounting to £60 during the ten year period plus the capital profit of £5 when the debentures are redeemed, a total return of £65 on the investment. In addition, it must be remembered that the debentures will almost certainly be secured by a charge on some of the company's assets, thus adding to the safety of the investor's money.

13. Dealing with the premium payable on redemption. From the company's point of view the premium which is payable on redemption becomes an additional charge on the funds of the company, *i.e.* for every £100 borrowed £105 will have to be found at the time of redemption. This means, of course, that where there was a liability of £100 before the redemption date an extra liability of £5 will have to be added as soon as the time for repayment arrives.

Put into book-keeping terms it means that we would credit the Debenture Account with £5 and debit an account called "Premium on Redemption Account" as follows:

6% Debentures Account

	Balance b/d	£100
	Premium on Redemption A/c	5
		£105

Premium on Redemption Account

6% Debentures A/c	£5

The premium which is payable on redemption will now be written off by transferring it to the debit of Sinking Fund Account. Thus, if there were a balance of £100 on the credit side of the Sinking Fund Account before redemption took place we would transfer the £5 from the credit of Premium on Redemption Account to the debit of Sinking Fund Account, thereby reducing the balance on this account to £95. This balance would then be transferred to General Reserve.

14. Redemption of debentures at a discount. Should debentures be redeemed at a discount, *i.e.* if for any reason they are to be repaid at an amount which is lower than *the par* figure, this will mean that a profit will be made on the redemption.

When payment is made in such cases the sum of cash to be debited to Debenture Account will be *less* than the credit balance standing on the account. The difference, representing the discount, will be debited to the account in order to close it and a corresponding credit will be made in the Sinking Fund Account. Thus, the credit balance which will ultimately be transferred to General Reserve will be greater by the amount of the discount.

If it is so desired an intermediate step may be taken whereby the discount is credited to a Discount on Redemption Account. This account would finally be closed by a transfer to the credit of Sinking Fund Account.

15. Profit or loss on sale of Sinking Fund investments. As will already have been appreciated the balance on the Sinking Fund represents *undistributed profit*.

The proceeds of the sale of the investments will almost certainly amount to either *more than* or *less than* the balance standing on the Sinking Fund Investment Account. (It is extremely unlikely that investments held for any length of time will be sold for exactly the same amount as was paid for them.) That being so, there will be either a profit or a loss on realisation.

NOTE: This profit or loss on the sale of the investments will be transferred to the Sinking Fund Account.

16. Items in the Sinking Fund Account. We thus find that there are several items which can affect the Sinking Fund Account. These may be summarised as follows:

(a) Redemption at a *premium*:   *Debit* Sinking Fund with the *premium*

(b) Redemption at a *discount*:   *Credit* Sinking Fund with the *Discount*

(c) *Profit on sale* of investments: *Credit* Sinking Fund with the *Profit*

(d) *Loss on sale* of investments: *Debit* Sinking Fund with the *Loss*

(e) *Interest* received on *investments*:   *Credit* Sinking Fund with the *Interest*

(f) *Close* Sinking Fund by transferring the balance to the credit of *General Reserve*

17. Redemption by means of an insurance policy. Some companies prefer to build up the cash funds which will ultimately be required to redeem debentures by taking out an endowment assurance policy rather than by investing the money in securities.

An insurance company will be asked to quote for the premium which will have to be paid every year for a stated number of years, *i.e.* to coincide with the date on which the debentures are due to be redeemed, in order to produce the capital sum needed on redemption.

This method has both advantages and disadvantages:

(a) *Advantages:*

    (i) *There is no danger of loss of capital* as there is with investments.

    (ii) *If necessary a loan can be obtained* during the lifetime of the policy based on the surrender value of the policy.

(b) *Disadvantages:*

    (i) *The annual rate of interest* will almost certainly be *lower* than that obtainable from investments.

    (ii) *If the policy should lapse*, *i.e.* be cancelled owing to non-payment of premiums, the surrender value will be considerably less than the amount which has been paid by way of annual premiums.

The book-keeping entries will be the same as for those made under the "Investment" method except that Debenture Redemption *Policy* Account will take the place of Debenture Redemption *Investment* Account.

18. Redemption by purchase of a company's own debentures.

A company can buy its own debentures.

This statement frequently puzzles students because at first sight it appears to them to be a contradiction. The matter has, however, a simple enough explanation. First of all, it is necessary to look somewhat farther than the company's own books.

Debentures are commonly issued by public companies, usually in the form of what is called "debenture stock." Units of this debenture stock are quoted on the Stock Exchange and, therefore, if a person has some money to invest and wishes to purchase a quantity of a particular debenture stock all he has to do is to contact a stockbroker and instruct him to purchase whatever amount he requires. The procedure is similar to that employed when purchasing shares.

(a) Let us take the case of a *purchase of shares* first of all (as a simple way of understanding what happens) through the medium of the Stock Exchange. Suppose that you, the reader, have £100 which you wish to invest. You choose the shares of the particular company in which you are interested and give your broker the necessary instructions to purchase as many shares as your £100 will buy. Just at this time a man whom we will call Alexander Wotherspoon has a number of these same shares which he wishes to sell. He, in his turn, notifies his broker, who duly places them on the market. Your broker then buys some of these shares in accordance with your instructions. Thus, you become a shareholder in the company through this *private transaction* with Alexander Wotherspoon.

The important point to appreciate is that no entries whatsoever will be made in the company's financial books, *i.e.* there will be *no* entry in the Capital Account of the company.

(b) In precisely the same way a company's *debentures may be purchased* in the open market, *i.e.* the Stock Exchange. The matter is purely a *private transaction* between a buyer and a seller. It follows, therefore, that if a company has, in the past, issued some debentures, and if those debentures are freely available to be purchased through the Stock Exchange, then that company is at liberty to use any surplus cash it may have to buy a quantity of its own debentures.

19. The advantage to a company buying its own debentures.
Most debentures which are issued today are *redeemable*. That
is to say, at the time they are issued the company undertakes
to repay the money so borrowed at a certain date in the future.
This being so the company can, in certain circumstances, make
a considerable saving by purchasing its own debentures at any
date *before* the date on which it has undertaken to redeem them.

As a general rule when the debentures are issued the company expressly states in the Debenture Deed that it may, if it
so wishes, purchase its own debentures in the open market.
It is usual to add "should the debentures be quoted at a
discount." This means that should a £100 unit of the debentures be quoted at, say, £98, then the company may enter
the market and buy this unit for £98.

There would thus be:

(a) An immediate saving of £2, plus
(b) A future saving of the amount of any premium which was
promised at the date on which they were due to be redeemed.
(c) In addition, there is, of course, the saving of annual interest
payable on the debentures in the future, *i.e.* the interest
which would be payable if the debentures had not been
purchased in the open market.

20. Dealing with accrued interest. As a rule interest on
debentures is payable half-yearly.

Should a company purchase its own debentures it is almost
certain that the purchase will be made on some date *between*
two interest dates and, therefore, the *accrued interest* will have
to be taken into consideration. The reason for this is that
debentures are what is known as a "fixed interest" security
and each month there is added to the *nominal* value that
particular month's interest, *i.e.* in the Stock Exchange
quotation.

21. Illustration. The following Examples and worked
examination problem illustrate accounting entries where debenture interest is involved.

EXAMPLE 24

LS Ltd made an issue of £20,000 6% debentures seven years
ago. Interest dates were 1st January and 1st July. On 30th April
in the present year they were quoted at 96, *i.e.* a block of £100
of these debentures could be purchased for £96.

It is important that the student understands the principle underlying such a quotation. The last time a payment of interest was made was on 1st January. Between 1st January and 30th April, a period of four months, interest amounting to £2 would have accrued, *i.e.* a 6% rate of interest amounts to ten shillings per month throughout the year and so four months' interest amounts to £2. Thus the quotation of 96 means that *the basic capital value* of £100 nominal would be 94. To this would be added the £2 of interest which has accrued since 1st January, making the total worth £96 at 30th April. This is referred to as being the "cum div" value.

From this it can be seen that if the company paid £96 for £100 of debentures through a purchase on the open market it would, in fact, be *paying for the accrued interest* of £2.

This will require an adjustment in the company's books.

The nominal value of the debentures, *i.e.* £100, will be debited to the 6% Debentures Account and credited to Redemption of Debentures Account. Cash Account will be credited with £96 and the corresponding debit will be made in Redemption of Debentures Account. The £2 interest will be debited to Debenture Interest Account and credited to Redemption of Debentures Account. This last account would then appear as follows:

Redemption of Debentures Account

Cash A/c	£96	6% Debentures A/c	£100
Balance c/d	6	Debenture Interest A/c	2
	£102		£102
		Balance b/d	£6

The account will now be closed off by transferring the balance of £6 to the credit of Sinking Fund Account as representing the profit on the transaction.

EXAMPLE 25

DK Ltd had issued £10,000 of 6% debentures four years ago. The debenture interest is payable on 1st January and 1st July each year. On 31st August in the present year the company purchases £1000 nominal of its own debentures when they were standing at 98 but it decides not to cancel them, *i.e.* the debentures so purchased are to be retained as an asset of the company.

Show the position at 31st December.

Stage 1

Bank Account

	6% Debentures A/c	**£980**

6% Debentures Account

	Balance b/d	£10,000

Investment Capital Account (own 6% debentures)

	Nominal	*Capital*		
Bank A/c	£1,000	**£980**		

Here we see the purchase being effected and the amount so purchased appearing in the books *as an asset.*

Stage 2

On 31st December the debenture interest for six months falls due and is paid.

Bank Account

	Debenture Interest A/c (6% on £10,000 for ½ year)	£300

Debenture Interest Account

Bank A/c	£300	

Stage 3

When the company made the purchase at the end of August *two months' interest had accrued, i.e.* the company bought the debentures *cum div.* The amount of interest included in the purchase price would be calculated as follows:

$$\frac{6}{100} \times £1{,}000 \times \frac{2}{12} = £10$$

Thus *the basic price* of the debentures purchased amounted to £970, *i.e.* £980 — £10.

This must now be adjusted.

Investment Capital Account

	Nominal £1,000	Capital £980		Nominal	Capital
Bank A/c			Transfer to Debenture Interest A/c		**£10**
			Balance c/d	£1,000	970
	£1,000	£980		£1,000	£980
Balance b/d	£1,000	£970			

Debenture Interest Account

Bank A/c	£300
Investment Capital A/c	10
	£310

Stage 4

Since the company *owns* £1000 of the 6% Debentures (*i.e.* one-tenth of the total amount of debentures in issue) it follows that it is entitled to *receive* one-tenth of the total amount of debenture interest paid, *i.e.* we should, therefore, in theory at least, debit the Bank Account and credit Debenture Interest Account with £30 in order to correct matters.

NOTE: In practice, of course, the company would not pay the interest to itself, but would simply pay out the *net* amount of interest to the outside holders of the debenture stock.

Bank Account

Debenture Interest A/c (*received*)	£30	Debenture Interest A/c (*paid*)	£300

Debenture Interest Account

Bank A/c	£300	Bank A/c	£30
Investment Capital A/c	10	Profit and Loss A/c	280
	£310		£310

The *net* amount of £280 will be transferred to the Profit and Loss Account at 31st December, the end of the company's financial year, together with the £300 of interest which would have been paid on 1st July.

The *true charge* in respect of debenture interest for the six months is:

$$\frac{6}{100} \times £10,000 \times \frac{2}{12} = £100 \quad i.e. \text{ interest for 2 months on £10,000}$$

$$\frac{6}{100} \times £9000 \times \frac{4}{12} = \underline{£180} \quad i.e. \text{ interest for 4 months on £9000}$$

$$\underline{\underline{£280}}$$

NOTE: For the purposes of this illustration it is assumed that the payment of interest has been made on 31st December and not on the following day, *i.e.* 1st January.

SPECIMEN QUESTION

(C.A.)

In 1953, Alpha Ltd issued £200,000 6% debentures at par which were redeemable at 102 on 30th June 1964. Annual appropriations had been made out of profits to a Sinking Fund set up under the terms of the debenture trust deed. The appropriations were invested annually on 30th June, together with the Sinking Fund investment income received in the year ended on that date. The trustees have power to purchase, for immediate cancellation, any debenture available at a market price below par, and to realise investments of the Sinking Fund for this purpose.

The following balances appeared in the company's books on 1st July, 1963:

    (a) Sinking Fund Account £117,490, represented by investments at cost of an equal amount.
    (b) 6% debentures £120,000.

The undermentioned transactions took place during the year ended 30th June 1964:

    (a) Half-year's debenture interest to 31st December 1963, was paid on that date.
    (b) Investments costing £9750 were sold, and realised £10,050 on 1st January 1964, in order to provide funds for purchase of debentures. On the same date, £10,000 debentures were purchased at 98 (inclusive of expenses) on the market, and cancelled.
    (c) The remaining investments of the Fund were sold, and the proceeds amounting to £110,200 were received on 29th June 1964.
    (d) Income amounting to £6950 received in the year from the Sinking Fund investments was not invested in view of the impending debenture redemption.

(e) On 30th June 1964, the debentures were repaid together with the half-year's interest thereon.

You are required to write up the following ledger accounts for the year ended 30th June 1964:

(a) 6% Debentures, showing capital and interest entries;
(b) Sinking Fund Investments;
(c) Sinking Fund; and
(d) Debenture Redemption.

Ignore income tax.

SUGGESTED ANSWER

ALPHA LTD

6% *Debentures Account*

	Capital		*Capital*
1964		1963	
Jan. 1		July 1	
Debenture Redemption A/c (debentures purchased for cancellation)	£10,000	Balance, b/f	£120,000
Debenture Redemption A/c (debentures redeemed on maturity)	110,000		
	£120,000		£120,000

Debenture Interest Account

1963		1964	
Dec. 31		June 30	
Cash A/c—Interest for six months	£3,600	Profit and Loss A/c	£6,900
1964			
June 30			
Cash A/c—Interest for six months	3,300		
	£6,900		£6,900

Sinking Fund Investments Account

1963			**1964**		
July 1			Jan. 1		
Balance b/f		£117,490	Cash: proceeds of sale		£10,050
1964					
Jan. 1			June 29		
Sinking Fund A/c—profit on realisation (£10,050 — £9,750)		300	Cash: proceeds of sale		110,200
June 30					
Sinking Fund A/c—profit on realisation		2,460			
		£120,250			£120,250

Sinking Fund Account

1964			**1963**		
June 30			July 1		
Premium on redemption of debentures		£2,200	Balance b/f		£117,490
Balance transferred to General Reserve A/c		125,200	**1964**		
			Jan. 1		
			Profit on realisation of investments		300
			Profit on redemption of debentures		200
			July 30		
			Income from investments		6,950
			Profit on realisation of investments		2,460
		£127,400			£127,400

Debenture Redemption Account

1964		1964	
Jan. 1		Jan. 1	
Cash A/c Purchase for cancellation	9,800	6% debentures cancelled	£10,000
Sinking Fund A/c: (Profit on redemption)	200	June 30 6% debentures redeemed	110,000
June 30		Sinking Fund A/c:	
Cash: A/c Re-demption at 102	112,200	(Premium on redemption)	2,200
	£122,200		£122,200

PROGRESS TEST 4

1. What do you understand by the term "debenture"? (**2**)

2. What is meant by "charging the assets"? Distinguish between a fixed and a floating charge. (**4**)

3. In what ways may debentures be redeemed? (**6**)

4. How should a premium payable on the redemption of debentures be dealt with? (**13**)

5. Summarise those items which must be either debited or credited in the Sinking Fund Account. (**16**)

6. What do you understand by the statement that a company can purchase its own debentures? (**18**)

a company can buy its own debentures,
for immediate cancellation
or investment.

CHAPTER V

REDEEMABLE PREFERENCE SHARES

REGULATIONS COVERING REDEMPTION

1. Maintaining the capital structure. One of the basic principles of the law relating to limited companies has always been that the capital which has been contributed by the shareholders should form a permanent fund. This means that, in theory, at least, the *net worth* of the business (total assets less creditors of all kinds) must be equal to the subscribed capital. In practice, of course, the book value of the assets does not always match up to this requirement.

The idea underlying the principle of the permanent fund of capital is that the worth of the assets (for which the capital was originally subscribed) would provide a fund of cash sufficient, in the last resort, to satisfy the debts due to the company's creditors. Since this was, and is, the legal viewpoint, it follows that only in extreme cases and under very careful safeguards will the law permit any *reduction* of the issued capital.

2. Redeemable preference shares. When the *Companies Act* was revised in 1929 a new principle was enacted whereby a company was permitted to issue a special class of shares called *Redeemable Preference Shares*. This type of share has now become a regular feature of the capital structure of limited companies and many of them do issue such shares. Basically, the idea is that investors may purchase redeemable preference shares in the knowledge that they will be redeemed, *i.e.* the company will repay those shareholders the money they subscribed and cancel the shares, at some fixed date in the future. When an issue of redeemable preference shares has been made, a strict code of regulations is laid down which must be followed most carefully when redemption is to take place.

3. The regulations to be followed on redemption. It is quite surprising how the letter "*P*" dominates the whole of this section of the *Companies Act*, but it has the great advantage of making the memorising of the main features comparatively easy.

(a) The Act gives *power* to issue *preference* shares which may, if the company so wishes, be redeemed.

(b) *Power* must be taken in the company's articles to *permit* redemption.

(c) The shares must be *fully paid* before it is possible to redeem them.

(d) The shares may be redeemed *only*:

    (i) out of *profits* earned *prior* to redemption which would otherwise have been available for distribution as dividends; or

    (ii) out of the *proceeds* of an issue of shares made specifically to provide the company with sufficient money to *pay* the *preference* shareholders.

(e) If shares are to be redeemed at a *premium*, *i.e.* at a price higher than the nominal value of the shares, the premium must be *provided from the following sources*:

    (i) out of *profits* otherwise available for dividends; or,

    (ii) from the credit balance standing on an *existing share Premium Account.*

NOTE: This last point with regard to redemption at a premium is one on which students frequently experience some difficulty. Fuller details are given in **4** below.

ORGANISING THE PROBLEM

In order to deal with examination problems relating to redeemable preference shares it is suggested that a logical sequence should be followed.

There are *six* points to be dealt with in building up the answer and the sequence of moves is set out in subsequent paragraphs (**4–10**).

4. Set out the full amount of issued capital. The entire capital which has previously been issued, regardless of the *type* of shares, *e.g.* ordinary, preference, preferred ordinary, etc., should be written down on a piece of paper.

(a) The total of the issued capital is a most important matter because this *effective total*, must *not*, under ordinary circumstances *be reduced.* The total of the issued capital *as it stands before any redemption takes place* was originally represented by a certain amount of cash. This is the *effective* total of the issued capital and the cash was used to purchase assets of various kinds. The *Companies Act* requires that *this effective total be maintained*.

(b) If, therefore, a certain amount of money is to be paid away by the company (in the redemption of preference shares) and the total of the effective share capital is thus reduced, it follows that something must be introduced to *replace the sum deducted from the* **original** *issued capital*. This *replacement* is carried out by one of two alternatives:

(i) by the issue of new share capital for cash; or

(ii) by transferring into the "Capital section" of the Balance Sheet the appropriate amount from the General Reserve, the Profit and Loss Account or other account carrying a balance of *undistributed* profit which would *otherwise* be available for distribution to the members as dividend.

(c) If this second alternative is used the profit so appropriated must be transferred to a *Capital Redemption Reserve* and placed immediately beneath the remaining issued capital on the Balance Sheet. This act has the effect of "freezing" this part of the profit thus making it no longer available for distribution to the shareholders. We call this *capitalising* the profit. It is more usual, however, for companies to go one step further and to make an issue of *bonus shares*. This is dealt with in more detail below.

NOTE: The student is referred back to Chapter II, Profit and Reserves, for a full explanation of what profit is and how it is dealt with in the Balance Sheet of a company.

5. Decide how much money is required. Calculate the amount of money needed to pay off the preference shareholders whose shares are to be redeemed.

The total amount required will be made up of:

(a) the *nominal value* of the preference shares to be redeemed; and

(b) any *premium* to be paid on *redemption*.

6. Decide what is to be made available for the redemption. When considering this part of the problem we have to bear two main points in mind:

(a) The fact that a *payment in cash* has to be made. The money for this will have to come from:

(i) *Present funds available.* The Balance Sheet (assets side) will tell us what sums are available from the two items: Cash at Bank, and Investments (if any).

(ii) *Future funds.* The question will tell us whether any cash is to be raised from a fresh issue of shares.

(b) The provisions of the *Companies Act* as regards the *non-reduction of the effective issued capital.* We have to consider what is available in the shape of reserves which have been set aside out of the profits of earlier years. These will normally consist of any or all of the following items, under the heading: *Past profits.*

(i) General Reserve;

(ii) Profit and Loss Account balance; and

(iii) Any specific reserve previously set aside to a Capital Redemption Reserve Fund.

The Balance Sheet (liabilities side) will tell us what sums stand to the credit of these three items.

7. Take steps to raise the money. Having decided how much *extra* cash is needed the next step is to raise it and so place the company in the position of being able to pay to the preference shareholders the sum they require. This money will normally be raised by one of two methods:

(a) *By a new issue of shares.* Usually the question indicates that the full amount of cash is payable on allotment. This means that only an Application and Allotment Account will have to be opened. It is unusual for any Call Accounts to be involved.

(b) *By the sale of investments.* In some cases the assets of the company will consist, in part, of investments. If these have to be sold to provide funds to pay out the preference shareholders the book-keeping presents no difficulty:

> *Investment account* will be *credited;* and
> *Bank account* will be *debited.*

It is unlikely that when the investments are sold the amount realised will be *precisely* the figure at which they stand in the books. In other words, there will be either a profit or a loss on the sale. Any such profit or loss must be transferred to the Profit and Loss Account, thus closing off the Investment Account.

8. Pay off the preference shareholders. With sufficient money now in the bank the company is in a position to pay off the preference shareholders, and thus redeem the preference shares.

In many cases the payment will include a *premium* on redemption. That is to say, the arrangement was made originally that the company should, on redemption of the preference shares, pay more than the nominal value of the shares, *e.g.* if £1 Preference shares are to be *redeemed at a premium of 2s. 6d. per share* the company will have to pay £1 2s. 6d. for every share it redeems.

The procedure on redemption will usually be on the following lines:

(a) *Close the Redeemable Preference Shares Capital Account* by transferring the balance to the credit of Redeemable Preference *Shareholders* Account (*i.e.* this is to be regarded as being a *personal* account for these shareholders as a group).

(b) *Enter the amount of the premium* which has to be paid as follows:

> *Debit* Share Premium Account.
> *Credit* Redeemable Preference Shareholders Account.

(c) *On making the payment:*

> *Debit* Redeemable Preference Shareholders Account.
> *Credit* Bank Account.

9. Capitalising undistributed profits of past years. When profit is set aside to, let us say, General Reserve, all that happens in fact is that a book-keeping entry is made *debiting* Profit and Loss Appropriation Account and *crediting* General Reserve. This is simply the double entry which becomes necessary as a result of the shareholders' decision to restrict the amount of dividend to be paid to themselves out of the company's assets, *i.e.* the retention of profits in the business. By doing this the asset of cash remains at a higher figure than would have been the case had it paid away the available profit in the form of dividends.

10. Book-keeping entries on redemption. Now, when redemption of the preference shares actually takes place *sufficient cash must be there* to pay the preference shareholders, as has already been explained.

It follows, therefore, that when they are paid the *assets* of the company are diminished by the amount of the payment. At the same time the *liabilities* of the company are diminished by an equal amount, *i.e.* the preference shares are eliminated from the Balance Sheet. But, as has already been shown, the *Companies Act* will not permit a reduction of the effective capital of the company.

(a) Therefore, if the redemption has been completely achieved by a *fresh issue of capital*, *i.e.* if all the money required is received from that source, the new capital simply cancels out the capital which is being redeemed and both assets and liabilities remain, in total, the same as before. And, of course, the issued capital also remains, in total, at the same figure as before, thus conforming to the requirements of the Act.

(b) If, however, part of the redemption (or, the whole of it, for that matter) is to be achieved *by using past profits* which have been set aside to reserve then an amount must be transferred from General Reserve account (or some other similar fund) to an account called "*Capital Redemption Reserve*." By this means, those past profits become frozen and can never be used in the future except for the purpose of issuing bonus shares. Thus they become a part of the effective capital of the company.

EXAMPLE 26

BALANCE SHEET

Issued Capital:			Fixed Assets	£20,000
10,000 £1 ordinary shares		£10,000	Cash at Bank	1,000
5000 redeemable preference shares of £1 each		5,000		
		£15,000		
General Reserve		4,800		
Creditors		1,200		
		£21,000		£21,000

The £5000 preference share capital is to be redeemed at par, *i.e.* at £1 per share. *For the purpose of raising sufficient cash* a further 4000 ordinary shares of £1 each are to be issued (since the company has at present only £1000 but requires £5000 to pay out the preference shareholders).

Stage 1

If a new Balance Sheet was prepared when the new issue of shares has been made and the cash received by the company it would appear as under:

BALANCE SHEET

Issued Capital:		Fixed Assets	£20,000
10,000 *plus* 4,000		Cash at Bank	
£1 ordinary		£1,000 *plus* £4,000	
shares	£14,000	from the new issue	5,000
5,000 redeemable			
preference shares			
of £1 each	5,000		
	———		
	19,000		
General Reserve	4,800		
Creditors	1,200		
	———		———
	£25,000		£25,000

Stage 2

When the preference shareholders are paid, the £5000 of redeemable preference shares disappear from the Balance Sheet. At the same time the asset of cash, £5000, also disappears. A Balance Sheet prepared at this point would look like this:

BALANCE SHEET

Issued Capital:		Fixed Assets	£20,000
14,000 £1 ordinary			
shares	£14,000		
General Reserve	4,800		
Creditors	1,200		
	———		———
	£20,000		£20,000

Stage 3

The original Balance Sheet, *i.e.* the one appearing in the example, shows a total of issued capital amounting to £15,000. The Balance Sheet at *Stage 2*, above, shows the total issued capital as being £14,000, *i.e.* a decrease of £1000.

We know that this state of affairs is not permitted by the *Companies Act*, and so we must now capitalise £1000 of the profits which were earned in previous years, *i.e.* out of the £4800 standing to the credit of General Reserve. We therefore debit £1000 to General Reserve account and credit it to Capital

Redemption Reserve. When this is done our final Balance Sheet would appear thus:

BALANCE SHEET

Issued Capital		Fixed Assets	£20,000
14,000 £1 ordinary shares	£14,000		
Capital Redemption Reserve	1,000		
	15,000		
General Reserve	3,800		
Creditors	1,200		
	£20,000		£20,000

11. The Share Premium Account. The *Companies Act* states that:

(a) *Where shares are issued at a premium* this premium shall be transferred to a Share Premium Account; and

(b) *That the amount standing to the credit of this account* shall be treated in the same way as is the share capital of the company in so far as any reduction of this balance is concerned. That is to say, *the Share Premium Account must not be reduced* in ordinary circumstances.

12. Exceptions. This prohibition is subject to the following exceptions:

(a) If the company has *not* issued all of its authorised capital, the balance on the Share Premium Account may be used for an issue of *fully paid bonus shares.*

(b) The Share Premium Account may be used for the purpose of *writing off preliminary expenses.*

(c) If the company makes either: *an issue of shares,* or, *an issue of debentures* the Share Premium Account may be used to write off:

    (i) The *expenses* incurred in making the issue.

    (ii) Any *commission, e.g.* underwriters' commission, which may have to be paid.

    (iii) Any *discount* which was granted to the subscribers to the issue (of shares or debentures).

NOTE: The student must note especially that *under no circumstances is goodwill allowed to be written off* out of the balance on Share Premium Account.

(*d*) If the company should redeem at a premium:

   (*i*) any redeemable preference shares; or
(*ii*) any debentures;

then it may use the balance, if any, standing to the credit of the Share Premium Account to provide for the premium payable on redemption.

BONUS SHARES

After a company has made the necessary provision for taxation on its profits the remainder of those profits are the property of the shareholders. If they so wish they are at liberty to withdraw the entire sum in the form of a dividend payable in cash. It is not usual, however, for such a thing to happen since financial prudence demands that some of the profits, at least, be ploughed back into the business.

13. Liquidity of profit. The profit which a business makes is either:

(*a*) *Realised*, *i.e.* goods or services have been sold and cash has been received, and therefore, the profit element in such sales comes into the business in the form of cash; or
(*b*) *Unrealised*, *i.e.* goods or services have been sold to the customers on credit, and as a result the profit on such sales is locked up temporarily in the form of debts due to the business. In such cases it is expected that the cash due from the debtors will be received during the course of the next few weeks.

Thus, *profit can be regarded as being liquid,* or very nearly so, provided that the business has not used any of it to purchase assets or to dispose of it in any way, such as in the payment of interim dividends.

14. General Reserve. If profits have been ploughed back into the business in purchases of extra stock or fixed assets, this amount at least should be "transferred to General Reserve" by the shareholders' vote at the annual general meeting (*see* II, **14, 15**).

Under normal circumstances the credit balance on General Reserve is *built up over a number of years* until it reaches a substantial sum. It shows on the Balance Sheet as a liability and is represented on the assets side somewhere among the *general total* of all the assets. That is to say, *we will not find any specific item* (under ordinary circumstances) listed among the assets which agrees with the balance on General Reserve.

15. Capitalising reserves. As a direct consequence of all this the true amount of capital which has been invested by the shareholders in the company does not show up as plainly as it might. The capital which they have contributed for shares is clearly visible since this was contributed in cash, but the capital which they have *contributed out of past profits* tends to be obscured because this was not a direct contribution in cash. In order to rectify this (and sometimes for other reasons as well) *a portion of the reserves is sometimes capitalised, i.e.* past profits are converted into shares.

16. Entries in the accounts. The book-keeping entries to record such matters would be:

(*a*) *Debit* General Reserve and/or Profit and Loss Account, etc.
     Credit Bonus Issue Account.
(*b*) *Debit* Bonus Issue Account.
     Credit Share Capital Account.

NOTE: In the above text reference has been made to General Reserve. It must be pointed out that this has been done as a matter of convenience and the student must recognise that *any fund of undistributed profit* such as the balance on Profit and Loss Account *may be utilised for this purpose*. Note also that, as was pointed out in **11** and **12**, any credit balance on Share Premium Account may also be used to make a *bonus issue* of shares.

SPECIMEN QUESTION

(C.A. (adapted))

The Balance Sheet of Green Pastures Ltd at 31st December 1965, is as follows:

Share Capital			Fixed Assets		
Issued and fully paid:			Land and Buildings		£100,000
50,000 £1 redeemable			Plant		25,000
preference shares		£50,000	Fixtures and Fittings		5,000
90,000 £1 ordinary shares		90,000	Motor Vans		2,000
		140,000			132,000
Share Premium Account		10,000	Current Assets		
Revenue Reserves			Stock	£33,000	
General Reserve	£20,000		Debtors	12,000	
Profit and Loss A/c	25,000		Investments	30,000	
		45,000	Bank	18,000	
Current Liabilities		30,000			93,000
		£225,000			£225,000

The company exercised its option to redeem all the preference shares at a premium of 5% on 1st January 1966.

To finance the redemption all the investments were sold realising £28,000. A fresh issue of 10,000 ordinary shares of £1 each was made at 24s. per share, payable in full on 1st January 1966. These were duly subscribed for and the full amount was received on that date.

The directors wish that only the minimum reduction should be made in the revenue reserves.

You are required to draft journal entries, including those relating to cash, to record the above transactions and to set out the Balance Sheet of the company as it would then appear.

SUGGESTED ANSWER

Stage 1

Set out the *full* amount of the issued capital.

The total amount of the issued capital, regardless of type, is £140,000. The figure which must be *effectively maintained* is, therefore, *£140,000.*

Stage 2

How much money is required?
We need £52,500 made up as follows:

(a) To pay off the nominal value of the preference shares	£50,000
(b) To pay the premium	2,500
Total amount of cash required	£52,500

Stage 3

What is to be made available for the redemption?

(a) *Present funds:*

(i) Cash at Bank	£18,000
(ii) Investments (realised at market value)	28,000

(b) *Future funds:*

New share issue		
10,000 £1 shares	£10,000	
Premium of 4s. per share	2,000	
		12,000
Total available cash		£58,000

(c) *Past profits* for statutory needs:

(i) General Reserve	£20,000
(ii) Profit and Loss Account	25,000
	£45,000
(iii) Share Premium Account	£10,000

NOTE: Since the Share Premium Account, by its nature, has not been built up out of past *trading* profits it can only be used in respect of the premium payable on redemption.

Stage 4

Raising the money.

(a) The investments will be sold realising £28,000 in cash, *i.e.* £2000 less than their book value. The journal entries will therefore be:

Bank Account	Dr. £28,000	
To Investment Account		£28,000
Being cash realised on sale		

Profit and Loss Account	Dr. £2,000	
To Investment Account		£2,000
Being loss written off investments		

(b) The fresh issue of shares is now made and the full amount of cash received immediately. The journal entries will be:

Application and Allotment A/c	Dr. £12,000	
To Ordinary Share Capital Account		£10,000
To Share Premium Account		2,000
Being issue of 10,000 ordinary shares at 24s. each		

Bank Account	Dr. £12,000	
To Application and Allotment Account		£12,000
Being cash received on issue of shares		

The company now has a total of £58,000 cash at bank as a result of these transactions, *i.e.* £18,000 as per the Balance Sheet plus £28,000 from the sale of investments and £12,000 from the issue of shares.

Stage 5

Paying off the preference shareholders.

(*a*) The first step is to close the Redeemable Preference Share Capital Account. Journal entry will be:

Redeemable Preference Share Capital Account Dr.	£50,000	
To Preference Shareholders Account		£50,000
Being transfer of the sum due on redemption		

(*b*) Next, the *premium* to which these shareholders are entitled is credited to their account, the journal entry being:

Share Premium Account Dr.	£2,500	
To Preference Shareholders Account		£2,500
Being provision of premium on redemption of redeemable preference shares		

(*c*) Finally, the payment of £52,500 is made to the shareholders. The journal entry will be:

Preference Shareholders Account Dr.	£52,500	
To Bank Account		£52,500
Being discharge of amount payable on redemption		

Stage 6

Capitalising undistributed profits of past years.

At this point we must refer to *Stage 1* in order to refresh our memory as to the full amount of the Issued Capital *before* redemption took place.

The amount was £140,000. What is the position now?

The Issued Capital at present consists only of ordinary shares (since the redeemable preference shares have now disappeared).

The ordinary share capital consists of:

(*a*) The original 90,000 shares of £1 each	£90,000
(*b*) The *new* issue of 10,000 £1 shares	10,000
Total	£100,000

We need, therefore, a further £40,000 to make the total of the *effective capital* up to *£140,000*. This must be made up from the various funds of undistributed profit which may be available.

The problem stated that the directors wish that only the minimum reduction shall be made in the *revenue* reserves. On consulting **11** and **12** above, we see that the company has used part of the Share Premium Account on the redemption *i.e.*, as permitted by the Act, but apparently it is not intended to make a bonus issue. Consequently, the company is *not* permitted to use any of the remaining credit balance on this account in this final section of the problem. It must turn to the *revenue reserves* in order to complete matters. This means that it will take the entire £20,000 standing to the credit of General Reserve and a further £20,000 from the balance on the Profit and Loss Account. The final journal entry will then be:

General Reserve Account	Dr.	£20,000	
Profit and Loss Account		20,000	
To Capital Redemption Reserve Fund			40,000
Being transfer of available profits to Capital Redemption Reserve Fund			

The Balance Sheet of the company after the redemption has taken place would appear as follows:

Issued Capital			*Fixed Assets*		
100,000 ordinary shares			Land and Buildings		£100,000
of £1 each		£100,000	Plant		25,000
Capital Redemption Reserve			Fixtures and Fittings		5,000
Fund		40,000	Motor Vans		2,000
		140,000			132,000
Share Premium Account		9,500	*Current Assets*		
Revenue Reserves			Stock	£33,000	
Profit and Loss			Debtors	12,000	
A/c	£5,000		Bank	5,500	
Less Loss on sale					50,500
of investment	2,000				
		3,000			
Current Liabilities		30,000			
		£182,500			£182,500

Bank Account

Balance b/d	£18,000	Pref. Shareholders A/c	£52,500
Investment A/c	28,000	Balance c/d	5,500
Application and			
Allotment A/c	12,000		
	£58,000		£58,000

Share Premium Account

Pref. Shareholders		Balance b/d	£10,000
A/c	£2,500	Application and	
Balance c/d	9,500	Allotment A/c	2,000
	£12,000		£12,000

D

PROGRESS TEST 5

1. Set out the main requirements of the *Companies Act*, regarding the issue and redemption of preference shares. **(3)**

2. What are the six points to be remembered when dealing with a problem involving redeemable preference shares? **(4–9)**

3. In what circumstances may a Share Premium Account be used? **(11)**

4. What do you understand by "liquidity of profit"? **(13)**

5. Explain what is meant by capitalising reserves. **(15)**

CHAPTER VI

PUBLISHED ACCOUNTS

INTRODUCTION

1. Items to be disclosed. Those particulars which *must be disclosed* by any company whose accounts have, by law, to be published, are set out in the 2nd Schedule to the *Companies Act, 1967*, together with certain matters brought forward from the 1948 Act.

From the point of view of the student of accountancy paragraph 12 (1), subsections (*a*) to (*h*), might have been better drafted. This criticism is in respect of the directions given relating to those items which are *required* to be disclosed in the Profit and Loss Account. No attempt appears to have been made to set out in an orderly manner the following *three* clear divisions:

(*a*) Items of expense, *i.e.* which are normally regarded as being *charges against the profit*;
(*b*) Items of income; and
(*c*) Appropriations made *out of* profit.

2. Dividing the net profit. When preparing the accounts of a company we do not regard the net profit as having been correctly ascertained until *all items of expense* have been charged against the gross profit. As a consequence, the net profit cannot be divided up until the amount of that profit is, in fact, known.

This being so, the first task is to create order in place of disorder.

THE PROFIT AND LOSS ACCOUNT

3. Items of expenditure. The following schedule, with the letters "*D*" and "*C*" as the principal aides-memoire, sets out those *items of expense* which must be shown in the published Profit and Loss Account (*see* **1**(*a*)).

(*a*) **D**epreciation of fixed assets.
(*b*) **D**ebenture interest and other loan interest (including bank loans and overdrafts) repayable within *five years* of the first day of the *next* financial year.

(c) *AuDitors' remuneration* (paragraph 13) including any sums paid in respect of their expenses.

(d) **D**irectors' *emoluments*. These fall into seven subsections, namely:

  (*i*) salary for services; (1948, *s*.196)

  (*ii*) fees, as a member of the Board; (1948, *s*.196)

  (*iii*) benefits in kind, the cash value of which must be disclosed; (1948, *s*.196)

  (*iv*) prior year adjustments arising from the disallowance of expenses for United Kingdom tax; (1948, *s*.196)

  (*v*) the number of directors whose emoluments (under (*i*) to (*iii*) above) fall in each bracket of a scale in multiples of £2500; (1967, *s*.6)

  (*vi*) the emoluments of the highest paid director(s) (under (*i*) to (*iii*) above) if exceeding those of the chairman during the financial year; (1967, *s*.6)

  (*vii*) the number of directors who have waived rights to receive emoluments (under (*i*) (to *iii*) above) during the year and the aggregate amount thereof; (1967, *s*.7).

(e) **D**irectors' *pensions*, but not including pensions from contributory schemes.

(f) **D**irectors' *compensation* for loss of office.

(g) **C**hairman's *emoluments* during the year. (1967, *s*.6.)

(h) **C**harges for hire of plant and machinery. (1967, 2 Sch. 12.)

(i) **C**harges and **C**redits relating to prior years. (1967, 2 Sch. 12A.)

(j) **C**ash *emoluments* of employees who receive more than £10,000 per annum. The number of employees who fall in this category must be stated showing the numbers in each group, commencing at £10,000 per annum and ascending in steps of £2500.

NOTE: (*i*) Items (*d*)(*v*) and (*d*)(*vi*) do not apply to directors whose duties were wholly or mainly outside the United Kingdom.

(*ii*) Tax-free payments to directors are not permitted (except under contracts in force on 18th July 1945).

TURNOVER

4. Turnover for the financial year. The *turnover* (*i.e.* sales or main source of income) of a company for any financial year must be stated, either in the published accounts or by way of a note.

The *method* by which the *turnover* is arrived at must also be disclosed. Banks and discount houses are exempted from this disclosure.

The Jenkins Committee have suggested that *turnover* might be described as the total amount receivable by a company in the ordinary course of its business for goods sold or supplied by it as a principal and for services provided by it. The Act itself does not give any definition of turnover.

If the *total turnover* of a company does *not exceed* £50,000, disclosure is not required except in the cases of holding or subsidiary companies.

5. Income receivable. On the credit side of the published Profit and Loss Account details of the following *income* must be shown:

(a) **D**ividends and interest received from *quoted* investments.
(b) **D**ividends and interest from *unquoted* investments.
(c) **D**etails of income from *rents of land* (if substantial) after deduction of rates and other outgoings.

APPROPRIATIONS OF PROFIT

This section involves no difficulty since it covers the normal appropriations which are made after the net profit has been established.

NOTE: Experience has shown that a surprising number of students experience some difficulty in deciding whether or not some items are *appropriations of profit* or *charges against profit*. For instance, directors' fees, salaries, etc., appear to confuse many students, and they place them in the appropriation section. This is quite wrong, of course, since the directors' emoluments are a charge *against* the profits in exactly the same way as are employees' salaries. The directors are employees, too.

6. Taxation in the Profit and Loss Account. The first *appropriation* to be dealt with is taxation. Most companies place this in a section on its own, the procedure being to bring down the net profit from the first section of the published Profit and Loss Account to the credit side of what may be described as the taxation section.

The amounts required are transferred from the respective Taxation Accounts and debited in this section of the Profit and Loss Account.

The balance of profit now remaining, and which is usually referred to as "Balance *after* taxation," is then carried down to the credit side of the final section. (*See* Appendix IV.)

THE CREDIT SIDE OF THE ACCOUNT

7. Other appropriations. It is usual to find only two items on the credit side of this final section:

(a) Balance of net profit *after* taxation; and
(b) The balance of *undistributed* profit which has been *brought forward* from the previous year.

NOTE: If the balance brought forward from the previous year is a *debit* balance then, of course, it must be brought in on the debit side.

8. Requirements of the Acts as regards appropriations of profit. Those *appropriations of profit* which must be shown are set out in Appendix IV.

9. A true and fair view. The 1967 Act has laid down as a general principle that the Profit and Loss Account shall show *a true and fair view* of the profit or loss for the financial year.

In particular, the company must show, either in the account itself or by way of a note, factors which materially affect items shown in the Profit and Loss Account. These are specifically stated as being:

(a) transactions of a sort not usually undertaken by the company;
(b) circumstances of an exceptional or non-recurrent nature; and
(c) any change in the basis of accounting.

10. Corresponding figures. The corresponding amounts for the immediately preceding financial year must be shown in the Profit and Loss Account.

11. Adjusting the net profit on trading. A point of considerable difficulty with many students is deciding how to set matters out and how to arrive at the *opening balance of profit* which should appear as the first item in the published Profit and Loss Account.

In the first place it is vital that the wording of the question be studied carefully so that it is clearly understood *which items of expenditure have already been debited* before arriving at the figure of net profit on trading given in the problem. Usually, the wording of the questions is phrased on the following lines: "The net profit on trading has been arrived at after charging. . . ." Then follow the amounts charged in respect of a number of items, some of which are required by the Act to be published. It is in regard to these that some guidance may be of help.

EXAMPLE 27

The net profit on trading of Splintex Ltd. amounted to £25,000, after charging: depreciation £3000; interest on debentures £8000; advertising £2500; directors' salaries £6000; loss on sale of motor lorry £200; and auditors' remuneration £750, in respect of a special investigation the need for which had arisen since the last annual general meeting.

Of the above listed items the company is required to show the amounts charged in respect of depreciation, debenture interest, directors' salaries and auditors' remuneration. In arriving at the figure of net profit those items have already been debited in the Profit and Loss Account. It follows, therefore, that they must be *added back* to the profit of £25,000.

For the sake of absolute clarity it is suggested that the following method will assist the student to arrive at the adjusted figure of profit.

Profit and Loss Account (for Publication)

General section			
Net profit on trading			£25,000
Add:			
Depreciation	£3,000		
Debenture interest	8,000		
Directors' salaries	6,000		
Auditors' remuneration	750		
			17,750
Adjusted profit			£42,750

Having increased the net profit by £17,750 we now employ the adjusted profit of £42,750 as our starting figure and debit the Profit and Loss Account with the items which, by law, are bound to be published.

Depreciation	£3,000	Net profit on trading	
Debenture interest	8,000	*as adjusted*	£42,750
Directors' salaries	6,000		
Auditors' remuneration	750		
Balance c/d (Profit *before* taxation)	25,000		
	£42,750		£42,750

12. The taxation section. Using the same details as in Example 27 we proceed to the second section of the Profit and Loss Account and deal with the taxation aspect.

EXAMPLE 28

The amount to be debited in respect of United Kingdom Corporation Tax was £9000.

Profit and Loss Account (for Publication)

Taxation section			
Corporation Tax	£9,000	Balance b/d (from	
Balance c/d (Profit		Example 27)	£25,000
after taxation)	16,000		
	£25,000		£25,000

13. The appropriation section. We continue using the same details as in the above two examples.

EXAMPLE 29

The profit brought forward from the previous year was £1800. It was decided to transfer £5000 to General Reserve; to set aside £4000 towards the redemption of debentures; to provide for a dividend of £6000 (gross) and to carry forward the balance.

Profit and Loss Account (for Publication)

Appropriation section			
General Reserve	£5,000	Balance b/d (from	
Debenture Re-		Example 28)	£16,000
demption		Balance brought	
Reserve	4,000	forward from last	
Provision for		account	1,800
dividend (gross)	6,000		
Balance c/f	2,800		
	£17,800		£17,800

14. The account in vertical form. From the above examples it can be seen that there are three clearly defined sections to the published Profit and Loss Account: general, taxation and appropriation sections.

The account has been broken down for the purpose of emphasising this. When working problems the sections would follow each other in unbroken succession, but, and let this be quite clear, they *must* be shown as *three distinct parts of the same account*. If they are not so shown marks are liable to be lost in examination work.

When answering examination questions the present-day method of showing the Profit and Loss Account in vertical form will almost certainly be expected. Students, when unfamiliar with this form of presentation, tend to get confused. When looking at the long column of figures with its insets and the words "*add*" and "*deduct*" liberally spread about, the effect on their minds is one of confusion and muddle, in spite of the fact that this method of presentation is *supposed* to make things clearer to the uninitiated. The probable explanation is that the student of accountancy has become accustomed to seeing and thinking in terms of debit and credit whereas the man who has had no training in this form of expressing figures finds it easier to add and subtract.

In view of this it is recommended that *until the student has become accustomed* to presenting the Profit and Loss Account in vertical form he should prepare it along the lines suggested above and then *convert it* into vertical form. His basic work will thus be produced by a method with which he is familiar.

EXAMPLE 30

Using the details of Examples 27 to 29 we will now show the completed Profit and Loss Account in *vertical* form.

Profit and Loss Account (for Publication)

Net profit on trading as adjusted		£42,750
Less: Depreciation	£3,000	
Debenture interest	8,000	
Directors' salaries	6,000	
Auditors' remuneration	750	
		17,750
Profit *before* taxation		25,000
Less: United Kingdom Corporation Tax		9,000
Profit *after* taxation		16,000
Add: Balance of undistributed profit brought		
forward from last year		1,800
Net *divisible* profit		17,800
Less: General Reserve	5,000	
Debenture Redemption Reserve	4,000	
Provision for Dividend (gross)	6,000	
		15,000
Balance carried forward to next account		£2,800

The conversion is a very simple matter and after working a few exercises the student should have gained sufficient confidence to deal with future problems in vertical form without having to worry about the debit/credit presentation.

DISCLOSURES IN THE BALANCE SHEET

15. The Balance Sheet. The 1948 Act laid down certain minimum requirements with regard to the information to be disclosed in the Balance Sheets of limited companies. As a result, the practice of setting out both assets and liabilities under broad sectional headings has developed.

The 1967 Act has extended these requirements. Time will be required, however, before an accepted mode of "good practice" becomes the established routine conforming with the additional requirements, just as some years were to pass after the introduction of the 1948 Act before a more or less "standard" form of presentation came to be regarded as the accepted practice.

Under the 1967 Act the main headings required appear to be:

(*a*) Share capital and reserves.
(*b*) Liabilities and provisions.
(*c*) Fixed assets.
(*d*) Current assets.
(*e*) Assets that are neither fixed nor current.
(*f*) Certain expenditure so far as is not written off.

16. Share capital and reserves. The following details must be shown where appropriate:

(*a*) Authorised and issued share capital.
(*b*) Redeemable preference shares stating the earliest and latest dates of redemption. The *premium payable* on redemption (if any) must also be stated.
(*c*) Shares held by subsidiary companies *in the parent company*. Such holdings were not permitted under the 1948 Act.
(*d*) Reserves classified under appropriate headings.
(*e*) Capital Redemption Reserve Fund.
(*f*) Share Premium Account.
(*g*) Movements on reserves stating the source of any increase and application of any decrease in the aggregate.

Two further items of information must be disclosed: details of options on unissued shares, and arrears of fixed cumulative dividends. Details of interest on shares which has been paid out of capital during the financial year must also be given.

17. Revenue reserves. Revenue reserves can be either *general* or *specific*.

(a) *A general reserve* is usually taken to mean that part of the profit which has been ploughed back into the business. The balance on Profit and Loss Account which has not been distributed as dividend but carried forward to the following year is sometimes spoken of as a "free reserve." Both of these balances should be shown under the first heading on the liabilities side, *i.e.* the section headed Capital and Reserves.

(b) *A specific reserve* is the name given to amounts set aside out of profits with a *particular object in mind*. Examples of specific reserves would be a Dividend Equalisation Reserve or a Debenture Redemption Reserve.

LIABILITIES AND PROVISIONS

18. Loans made to a company. In the case of a limited company these almost always take the form of *debentures*. If a liability of this nature is *secured* by a charge on certain assets the fact that it is so secured *must be stated*.

Sometimes, particularly in examination problems, a loan called *"Notes"* is brought into the Balance Sheet. A loan of this kind is a simple form of indebtedness and is *not* a debenture. Interest at a fixed rate is payable, *e.g.* "£10,000 5% Notes." (*See* Appendix IV.)

19. Taxation. With the introduction of Corporation Tax the Institute of Chartered Accountants in England and Wales has suggested that the information shown in the Balance Sheet should be treated in a different manner than hitherto. (*See also* XVII.)

The following extract, for which suitable acknowledgment is made, is from their booklet entitled *Notes on the Treatment of Taxation in Company Accounts after the Finance Act, 1965.*

"Corporation tax on the profits of each accounting period is a liability at the balance sheet date; it is not a reserve or an amount set aside. It should therefore be classified as a creditor or, if its amount cannot be determined with substantial accuracy, as a provision.

Where a company's accounting year ends between April and December, there may, depending on the due date for payment of corporation tax in each company's circumstances, be accrued corporation tax liabilities for two accounting periods, that for the later not falling due for payment for a period of up to twenty months from the date of the balance sheet.

The following suggestions are made:

(*a*) The liability for corporation tax on the profits of the period covered by the accounts should be disclosed either as an item of current liabilities or as a separate item but not grouped with corporation tax equalisation account, and the due date for payment should be shown. Corporation tax for earlier periods not yet paid should normally be shown as such under current liabilities.

(*b*) Corporation tax recoverable should be included in the balance sheet either as a current asset or as a deduction from the liability to corporation tax."

Amounts set aside for the purpose of preventing undue fluctuations in charges for taxation as well as any amounts transferred from such provision *for another purpose* (and the fact that they have been transferred), must be stated. Unless otherwise shown a note must state the basis on which any amount set aside for United Kingdom Corporation Tax is computed.

20. Current liabilities. The most usual liabilities falling under this sub-heading are:

(*a*) Trade creditors.
(*b*) Expense creditors.
(*c*) Recommended dividends (gross).
(*d*) Debenture interest due but unpaid.
(*e*) Bank overdrafts and loans in aggregate.
See Appendix IV for further details.

21. Fixed assets. The *different types* of fixed assets must be clearly shown. The Act does not lay down specific headings under which they are to be shown, but, by implication, differentiation is necessary. As a result, the standard practice is to show under separate headings the following, among others:

(*a*) Land and Buildings.
(*b*) Plant and Machinery.
(*c*) Fixtures and Fittings.
(*d*) Office Furniture and Equipment.
(*e*) Motor vehicles.
(*f*) Goodwill.
(*g*) Patents and Trade Marks.

The Act, however, makes it obligatory for a company to disclose the methods used to arrive at the amount of fixed assets under each heading.

For further information see Appendix IV.

22. Current assets. Current assets fall under the following broad headings:

(a) Stock.

(b) Debtors.

(c) Cash at Bank and Cash in Hand.

The Act does not require any special methods to be employed in valuing current assets beyond stating that if the directors are of the opinion that any of these assets are of a lower value than that shown in the Balance Sheet this fact must be disclosed.

The manner in which stock in trade or work in progress is computed is to be shown (by way of note) if the amount is material, in order that the members may appreciate its effect upon the company's profit and state of affairs.

23. Loans made by a company. Details must be given of:

(a) *loans to employees* granted for the purpose of purchasing fully paid shares in the company, or in its holding company;

(b) *loans to officers of the company* together with particulars of any repayments during the year.

24. Quoted investments. There shall be shown under a separate heading:

(a) the aggregate amount of the company's quoted investments;

(b) quoted investments which have been granted a quotation or permission to deal on a recognised Stock Exchange; they must be distinguished from those which have not been granted such permission.

Where the aggregate *market value* differs from the amount stated in the Balance Sheet and is taken as being of a *higher* value than the Stock Exchange quotation, this fact must be shown by way of a note.

25. Unquoted investments. The aggregate amount of unquoted investments is to be shown as a separate heading. The following information must be given:

(a) The cost or valuation as shown in the books of the company.

(b) The aggregate amount of depreciation provided or written off.

(c) The difference between (a) and (b) above.

26. Sundry minor points. Certain other items must be disclosed.

(*a*) The following items must be shown *separately* in every Balance Sheet until they have been written off:

    (*i*) Preliminary expenses.

    (*ii*) Discount on the issue of shares or debentures.

    (*iii*) Commission paid in respect of shares or debentures.

    (*iv*) Expenses incurred on any issue of share capital or debentures.

(*b*) If a company has entered into any *contracts for capital expenditure* involving expenditure of a substantial amount the fact that such an obligation has been undertaken must be disclosed even though at the date of the Balance Sheet no expenditure has as yet been incurred.

(*c*) Similarly, if there are any *contingent liabilities*, their nature and amount must be shown, usually by way of a note.

(*d*) Finally, the relevant *figures for the previous year* must be set out on every Balance Sheet for the purposes of comparison.

SPECIMEN QUESTION

(c.s. (adapted))

The following list of balances has been extracted from the draft accounts of J. Snodgrass Ltd for the year ended 31st December 1965:

Profit and Loss Account balance 1st January, 1965 (Cr.)	£9,000
Stocks	52,000
Ordinary share capital: 100,000 £1 shares	100,000
Machinery at cost	230,000
Delivery vehicles, at cost	30,000
Provisions for depreciation:	
Machinery	69,000
Delivery vehicles	12,000
5% Debentures	80,000
Debenture redemption sinking fund	45,000
Debenture redemption sinking fund investments	45,000
General reserve	29,000
Debtors	38,000
Creditors	28,000
Cash at Bank	30,000
Net profit	53,000

The following items have been charged before arriving at the net profit:

Office wages	£17,000
Transfer to general reserve	6,000
Debenture interest (gross)	4,000
Administrative expenses	27,000
Directors' salaries	8,000
Debenture redemption sinking fund transfer	5,000

Adjustments are to be made in the final accounts for the following items which were overlooked in preparing the draft accounts:

(a) Audit fee outstanding (not agreed at the annual general meeting) £1,000

(b) Depreciation for the year:
Machinery 10% of cost
Delivery vehicles 20% of cost

(c) Tax liability on the profit of the year: £9,000
(all tax on the profit of the preceding year has been paid)

(d) The company has agreed to pay a former director £6000 as compensation for loss of office.

(e) A dividend of 8%, less income tax, is proposed for the year. Assume the standard rate of income tax to be 7s. 6d. in the £.

Required: the annual accounts and balance sheet in a form suitable for publication.

SUGGESTED ANSWER

NOTE: Before drawing up the Profit and Loss Account in a form suitable for publication we must adjust the profit given in the question by adding back the revenue items already charged, *i.e.* items (b) and (c) on the right below, since these *must* be published. In addition, we must also add back appropriations of profit, *i.e.* items (a) and (d), below.

J. Snodgrass Ltd, Profit and Loss Account for the year ended 31st December 1965

Debenture Interest	£4,000	*Net Profit on trading*		£53,000
Directors' Salaries	8,000	*Add back:*		
Audit Fee	1,000	(a) Transfer to		
Depreciation:		General Reserve	£6,000	
Machinery £23,000		(b) Debenture interest	4,000	
Delivery vehicles 6,000		(c) Directors' Salaries	8,000	
	29,000	(d) Transfer to Re-		
Director's Compensation	6,000	demption Deben-		
		ture sinking fund	5,000	
	48,000			23,000
Profit *before* taxation c/d	28,000			
		Adjusted Net Profit		£76,000
	£76,000			
Provision for Taxation	9,000	Profit *before* taxation b/d		28,000
Profit *after* taxation c/d	19,000			
	£28,000			£28,000
Transfer to General Reserve	6,000	Profit *after* taxation b/d		19,000
Transfer to Debenture Redemp-				
tion Sinking Fund	5,000			
Provision for Dividend (8% gross)	5,000			
Balance carried forward	12,000	Balance brought forward from last account		9,000
	£28,000			£28,000

J. SNODGRASS LTD, BALANCE SHEET AS AT 31ST DECEMBER 1965

Capital and Reserves			Fixed Assets		
Share Capital—Authorised and Issued: 100,000 £1 ordinary shares fully paid		£100,000	Machinery at cost	£230,000	
			Less Depreciation provision	92,000	
					£138,000
General Reserve		29,000	Delivery Vehicles at cost	30,000	
			Less Depreciation provision	18,000	
Profit and Loss Account		12,000			12,000
		£141,000			£150,000
Loans					
5% Debentures		80,000			
Revenue Reserves					
Debenture Redemption Sinking Fund		45,000	Investments		
			Debenture Redemption Sinking Fund Investments		45,000
Current Liabilities					
Creditors	£28,000				
Audit Fee	1,000		Current assets		
Director's compensation	6,000		Stocks	52,000	
Provision for taxation	9,000		Debtors	38,000	
Provision for dividend	5,000		Cash at Bank	30,000	120,000
		49,000			
		£315,000			£315,000

Several points arise which require discussion and explanation. First of all, however, let us convert the Profit and Loss Account into *vertical form* so that the student may compare this with the debit/credit form.

(a)
Profit and Loss Account for the year ended 31st December 1965

Net Profit on trading		£76,000
Deduct: Debenture interest	£4,000	
Directors' salaries	8,000	
Audit fee	1,000	
Depreciation	29,000	
Director's compensation	6,000	
		48,000
Profit before taxation		28,000
Less Taxation provision for the year		9,000
Profit after taxation		19,000
Add Balance of undistributed profit brought forward from last year		9,000

Total *disposable* profit		£28,000
Deduct: Transfer to General Reserve	£6,000	
Transfer to Debenture Redemption		
Sinking Fund	5,000	
Provision for Dividend (less tax)	5,000	
		16,000
Balance carried forward		£12,000

(b) The second point relates to the two appropriations, *i.e.* the transfer to (i) General Reserve £6000, and (ii) the transfer to Debenture Redemption Sinking Fund £5000.

The question states that these two items have been charged before the net profit has been ascertained. This means that the double entry has been made in each case, and, therefore, both General Reserve and Debenture Redemption Sinking Fund have been credited with their respective transfers. It follows that *no further additions* will have to be made in the Balance Sheet.

(c) Similarly, we should make no adjustment to the Debenture Redemption Sinking Fund investments. We are entitled to assume that this has already been done because the total of the investments is equal to the total of the Sinking Fund.

(d) On the other hand, adjustment *is* required in the case of the Depreciation Provisions appearing in the Balance Sheet since no account had been taken for depreciation in arriving at the net profit.

PROGRESS TEST 6

1. Make a list of those items of expense which must be disclosed in a company's published Profit and Loss Account. **(3)**

2. What are the provisions of the 2nd Schedule as regards appropriations of profits? **(7, 8)**

3. Certain items should appear under the heading "Capital and Reserves" in the Balance Sheet. What items do you consider fall within this category? **(16)**

4. Define: (a) Revenue reserves; (b) Capital reserves. **(II, 16, 17, 18)**

5. What are current liabilities? Give examples of five. **(20)**

6. What information concerning investments must be shown in the Balance Sheet? **(24, 25)**

CHAPTER VII

THE PURCHASE OF A BUSINESS

SELLER AND PURCHASER

An existing business may be bought or sold as a "going concern" and the same principles which apply to the purchase or sale of goods will also apply to the purchase or sale of *a complete business*.

1. Book-keeping entries. We know that when goods are sold on credit the customer's account will be debited with the selling price, the corresponding credit being made in the Sales Account. In the case of the sale of a business the purchaser will be shown as a debtor in the first place and a Sales Account will take up the corresponding credit. In this case, however, the proper title of this account will be Sale of Business Account.

2. The selling price. When goods are offered for sale each individual item will have its recognised selling price. In exactly the same way, if a complete business is being sold that business as a whole will have its proper selling price. That price will almost certainly be reached by negotiation, since in a transaction of this kind there are many factors to take into consideration. For example, it may well be that the value of an asset as shown in the books of the seller (*i.e.* the figure appearing in the last Balance Sheet) has no relation to present-day values. In such a case it would be usual to call in an expert in order to obtain an up-to-date valuation which was fair to both the buyer and the seller.

In examination work we will, of course, be given all information of this kind which may be required for the solution of the problem.

3. Sale of a business illustrated. This example shows the accounting procedure to be followed when a business is sold.

EXAMPLE 31

John Sweet agrees to sell his business to Arthur Lowe as on 1st July. The Balance Sheet set out below forms the basis of the sale.

BALANCE SHEET AS AT 30TH JUNE

Capital Account			Fixed Assets	
John Sweet	£5,000		Land and Buildings	£1,920
Creditors	1,450		Motor Van	600
			Current Assets	
			Stock	£810
			Debtors	3,070
			Bank	50
				3,930
	£6,450			£6,450

It was agreed that the present-day value of the land and buildings should be taken as £3520

Sweet was to retain the balance at the bank and Lowe agreed to pay off the creditors. The purchase price was settled at £12,000 and Lowe paid this on 1st July out of £15,000 which he had paid into a bank account opened for the purpose.

Before starting to deal with the entries the student's attention is called to the following most important point:

Although this subject is normally referred to as "the purchase of a business" it could equally well be called "the sale of a business," as it is in this section. We must, therefore, be ready to look at the matter from both aspects. By so doing it will be found that most of the apparent difficulties are resolved comparatively simply.

Stage 1

The first thing to be done is to *adjust the value of any asset* which is considered to be in need of revaluing, in order to bring it to its present-day value. In this example the only item which requires adjustment is the asset Land and Buildings, the value of which is to be increased from £1920 to £3520. We must, therefore, debit the Land and Buildings Account with £1600 (the difference between the two valuations) and credit John Sweet's Capital Account with a similar sum. Thus, the balance on Land and Buildings Account will now become £3520.

NOTE: If adjustments have to be made to more than one of the assets it is usual to open a Revaluation Account and to transfer all adjustments to it. When these have been completed the *final difference* between the two sides will be transferred to the owner's Capital Account.

The entries adjusting the value of Land and Buildings will be:

Land and Buildings Account

Balance b/d	£1,920		
Capital A/c, increase in valuation	1,600		
	£3,520		

Capital Account

		Balance b/d	£5,000
		Land and Buildings A/c	1,600
			£6,600

Stage 2

Having made the above entries we must now *open a ledger account* for each item appearing on the Balance Sheet, *i.e.* for both assets and liabilities.

We then close off the ledger account of each asset which is being taken over, making the corresponding debit entries in a Sale of Business Account, or, as it is more commonly called, Realisation Account.

Land and Buildings Account

Balance b/d	£3,520	Transfer to Sale of Business A/c	£3,520

Motor Van Account

Balance b/d	£600	Transfer to Sale of Business A/c	£600

Stock Account

Balance b/d	£810	Transfer to Sale of Business A/c	£810

Debtors Account

Balance b/d	£3,070	Transfer to Sale of Business A/c	£3,070

Sale of Business Account (or Realisation Account)

Transfer from: Land and Building A/c	£3,520	Balance c/d	£8,000
Motor Van A/c	600		
Stock A/c	810		
Debtors A/c	3,070		
	£8,000		£8,000
Balance b/d	£8,000		

Stage 3

There are now *no* asset accounts standing open in John Sweet's books *except* the Bank Account. There is, however, a credit balance of £1450 on the Creditors Account. Lowe, the purchaser, has arranged, as part of the general agreement, to be responsible for this sum. We must, therefore, close the Creditors Account by transferring the balance of £1450 to the Sale of Business Account since it is to be no longer regarded as a liability of Sweet, *i.e.* he is not going to be called upon to pay his creditors.

Creditors Account

Transfer to Sale of Business A/c	£1,450	Balance b/d	£1,450

Sale of Business Account

Balance b/d (from *Stage 2*)	£8,000	Transferred from Creditors A/c	£1,450
		Balance c/d	6,550
	£8,000		£8,000
Balance b/d	£6,550		

Stage 4

The *balance* on the Sale of Business Account, £6550, represents the *net worth* of the business. Lowe has agreed to pay £12,000 for this business, *i.e.* £5450 more than its net worth. This amount over and above the net worth must be regarded as the *cost of the goodwill*, which is, of course, Sweet's profit on the sale.

Sale of Business Account

Balance b/d (from *Stage 3*)	£6,550	Arthur Lowe A/c (purchase consideration)	£12,000
Profit on sale (*i.e.* Goodwill) transferred to Capital A/c	**5,450**		
	£12,000		£12,000

Capital Account—John Sweet

	Balance b/d	£5,000
	Land and Buildings A/c	1,600
	Sale of Business A/c (Goodwill)	**5,450**
		£12,050

Arthur Lowe Account

Sale of Business A/c £12,000

Note particularly at this stage that Lowe appears in Sweet's books as a *debtor* for the agreed value of the business. We can see that, basically, there is no difference between Lowe and any other debtor of the business: *both owe money to Sweet.*

Stage 5

The final matter remaining is the *payment of the purchase consideration* of £12,000 by Lowe to Sweet.

Arthur Lowe Account

Sale of Business A/c	£12,000	Bank A/c	**£12,000**

Bank Account

Balance b/d	£50		
Arthur Lowe A/c	**12,000**		
	£12,050		

There is now £12,050 in the Bank Account. This is precisely the sum required to pay out John Sweet. The books of Sweet will now be closed when he withdraws this sum from the bank account of the business and transfers it to his private account.

The attention of the student is drawn to the fact that the *capital profit consists of two quite separate parts*:

(a) *Profit on the sale of the assets*
Assets sold for £12,000
Deduct:

Land and Buildings (revised)	£3,520	
Motor Van	600	
Stock	810	
Debtors	3,070	
		8,000

	Profit	£4,000

(b) *Profit made as a result of the creditors* (amounting to £1,450) *being taken over* by Arthur Lowe   1,450

Total profit on sale, *i.e.* Goodwill   £5,450

4. Purchase of a business. Example 32 continues the transaction given in Example 31, this time showing the accounting procedure in the purchaser's books.

EXAMPLE 32

We now turn to the entries which have to be made in the books of Arthur Lowe.

From the information given in Example 31 we know that he has a capital of £15,000 represented by cash at bank.

Let us look, first of all, to the assets which he has acquired from Sweet. The usual way of recording matters *in the books of the purchaser* is to open an account called Business Purchase Account. In this example the entries will be as follows:

Business Purchase Account

Sundry Liability A/cs:		Sundry Asset A/cs:	
Creditors	£1,450	Land and Buildings	£3,520
John Sweet—		Motor van	600
Vendor	12,000	Stock	810
		Debtors	3,070
		Goodwill	5,450
	£13,450		£13,450

Each of the above items will now be entered in its appropriate account.

John Sweet—Vendor Account

Bank A/c	**£12,000**	Business Purchase A/c	£12,000

Land and Buildings Account

Business Purchase A/c	£3,520		

Motor Van Account

Business Purchase A/c	£600		

Stock Account

Business Purchase A/c	£810		

Debtors Account

Business Purchase A/c	£3,070		

Goodwill Account

Business Purchase A/c	£5,450		

Creditors Account

		Business Purchase A/c	£1,450

Bank Account

Capital A/c— Arthur Lowe	£15,000	John Sweet A/c	£12,000
		Balance c/d	3,000
	£15,000		£15,000
Balance b/d	£3,000		

Capital Account—Arthur Lowe

		Bank A/c	£15,000

From the accounts set out above it is a simple matter to construct a Balance Sheet.

BALANCE SHEET

Capital Account— Arthur Lowe	£15,000	Land and Buildings	£3,520
Creditors	1,450	Motor Van	600
		Stock	810
		Debtors	3,070
		Goodwill	5,450
		Bank	3,000
	£16,450		£16,450

5. Sale of Business and Purchase of Business Accounts compared. If the details which appear in the Sale of Business Account are compared with those in the Business Purchase Account it will be seen that they are *identical*, but that they appear on *opposite* sides in their respective ledgers. Since the Sale of Business Account has been built up section by section in Example 31 the fact that the accounts are absolutely identical (though opposite) may not be immediately apparent. So that the student may appreciate this point the Sale of Business (or Realisation) Account is shown below as a complete account.

Sale of Business Account

Land and Buildings		Creditors A/c (as per	
A/c	£3,520	*Stage 3*)	£1,450
Motor Van A/c	600	Arthur Lowe A/c (as	
Stock A/c	810	per *Stage 4*)	12,000
Debtors A/c (as per			
Stage 2)	3,070		
	8,000		
Goodwill to Capital			
A/c (as per *Stage 4*)	5,450		
	£13,450		£13,450

The important point is that when dealing with examination problems once the *Sale of Business* Account has been prepared it only has to be *reversed* and it can immediately be used as the *Business Purchase* Account in the books of the buyer, whether he be a private individual or a limited company. In questions of this type a favourite requirement of the examiner is for the production of the "journal entries relating to the purchase and the opening Balance Sheet of the new business."

The principal journal entries will come from the Business Purchase Account and the Vendor's Account as a general rule.

PLAN OF WORK

When dealing with examination problems it is suggested that the plan of work set out below is followed. As is the case with so many problems in accountancy *method* is the key to the solution.

6. Entries in the seller's books. There are ten rules:

   (*a*) Open a *separate ledger account* for *each balance* appearing in the Balance Sheet of the seller.

This rule applies equally for problems involving sole traders, partnerships and limited companies.

(*b*) Should there be a *Provision for Bad Debts* standing in the seller's Balance Sheet an account must be opened and the "provision" entered as a *credit*. The account which is opened for debtors must be *debited* with the gross total of debtors.

(*c*) If the value of any of the *assets* is to be *increased*, make the entries which are necessary by *debiting* the asset account concerned. Then open a new account called *Revaluation Account* and post the corresponding credit thereto.

Should the value of any *asset* have to be *reduced*, *credit* the asset account concerned and debit Revaluation Account.

(*d*) Close off the accounts of those *assets* which are being *taken over* by the purchaser. *Credit* the asset accounts and *debit* Sale of Business Account.

(*e*) If the *creditors* are being *taken over* by the purchaser, *debit* Creditors Account and *credit* Sale of Business Account.

(*f*) If there are any *Provision accounts* which are *no longer required*, *i.e.* by the *seller*, such as Provision for Bad Debts or Repairs Equalisation Reserve, these must be closed off and credited to Sale of Business Account. The reason for this treatment is that *during past years* these sums had been *debited* in the seller's Profit and Loss Account thus reducing his profit *at that time*. Now that he no longer has to provide for such matters he is entitled to receive the benefit.

(*g*) Open an *account for the purchaser* (or the purchasing company) and make him (or it) a *debtor* for the agreed amount of the *purchase price*. *Credit* the Sale of Business Account with the corresponding entry.

(*h*) The Sale of Business Account will now be closed, *the difference between the two sides* being inserted as appropriate. If the credits exceed the debits the difference will be entered on the debit side, the corresponding entry being a credit in the Capital Account of the seller (representing a profit on the sale). This is, in fact, *the value of the goodwill* and it should be entered as such in the Sale of Business Account.

If, on the other hand, there is a loss on the sale, the Sale of Business Account will be credited, the entry reading "Loss on sale transferred to Capital Account."

(*i*) *When the purchaser pays* the purchase money, *debit* Bank Account and *credit* the personal account of the purchaser, thus closing off his account, thereby eliminating his debt.

(*j*) Sometimes we find that *certain adjustments are called for* by the examiner. An example of an adjustment of this type would be some discount allowed to the debtors on payment of their accounts. No absolute hard and fast rules can be laid down with regard to these adjustments but, as a general rule, one finds that the *Capital Account of the seller* is affected by them. No matter what the adjustment may happen to be, always remember that a *double* entry will be required to deal with the item. It is, therefore, advisable to open any accounts which appear necessary and make the required entries therein. In this way the double entry feature is kept in front of one and is not liable to be overlooked in the final result.

7. Entries in the books of the buyer. Five rules apply:

(*a*) *Open a Business Purchase Account* and credit it with all assets taken over. Debit it with all liabilities assumed by the purchaser including the amount due to the seller.

(*b*) *Post each item from the Business Purchase Account* to the *opposite side* of the appropriate account, thus completing the double entry.

(*c*) *Write up the Capital Account of the purchaser* (or, if a limited company, the Share Capital Account). The corresponding debit entries will be either to the Bank Account, or (if a limited company, with the seller being paid in shares rather than in cash) the vendor's personal account.

(*d*) *Close off the Vendor's Account.* If he is being paid in cash then credit the Bank Account. If he is taking all, or part, of his payment by means of shares (if a limited company is the purchaser) then the credit will be to Share Capital Account.

(*e*) *Prepare the opening Balance Sheet* of the new business from the balances on the open accounts.

A "TAKE-OVER"

8. Payment otherwise than in cash. We sometimes hear it said that a sole trader has "turned himself into a limited company." By this phrase is meant that he has, in fact, *sold his business to a limited company* which has been created deliberately for the purpose of taking over his business. Note particularly the use of the words "taking over."

In circumstances such as this the use of the word "buy" would hardly be correct since the newly-formed company, as a general rule, has no money with which to buy anything. What happens is that shares in the company are issued to the owner of the business *in consideration* of the owner transferring the assets of his business to the limited company. Thus the company becomes *the owner of the assets* and the *ex-proprietor* becomes the owner of the company's *shares.*

EXAMPLE 33

John Snodgrass sold his business to a limited company, Snodgrass Products Ltd. The purchase price was agreed at £4000 to be satisfied by the issue of 4000 shares of £1 each.

JOHN SNODGRASS—BALANCE SHEET

Capital	£4,000	Fixtures	£920
Creditors	840	Stock	2,160
		Debtors	1,290
		Cash at Bank	470
	£4,840		£4,840

The company was to take over the assets at their book values and to assume responsibility for the creditors.

It must be clearly understood that in cases of this kind *the company owns no assets* at this moment. It is, therefore, unable to pay anything to John Snodgrass.

The only thing that the company *can* do is to *issue shares* in exchange for the value of the things which are being transferred to its ownership. This, of course, amounts to a form of payment as the shares issued to Snodgrass represent the worth of the business. He could, if he so wished, sell his shares thus converting their worth into cash.

ENTRIES IN THE BOOKS OF SNODGRASS

Stage 1

Sale of Business Account

	Snodgrass Products Ltd (the amount of the purchase con- sideration) **£4,000**

Snodgrass Products Ltd Account

Sale of Business A/c **£4,000**	

Note well that *the new company is here shown to be a debtor.*

Stage 2

When settlement of this debt is made by the new company issuing shares the entries will be:

Snodgrass Products Ltd Account

Sale of Business A/c	£4,000	Investment A/c (4,000 £1 shares in Snodgrass Products Ltd)	**£4,000**
	£4,000		**£4,000**

Investment Account (Shares in Snodgrass Products Ltd)

Snodgrass Products Ltd A/c	**£4,000**

ENTRIES IN THE BOOKS OF SNODGRASS PRODUCTS LTD

A personal account for J. Snodgrass (the vendor) will be opened in the company's books and *credited with the purchase consideration*, the corresponding debit being made in the Business Purchase Account.

J. Snodgrass Account

	Business Purchase A/c £4,000

When the shares are issued to J. Snodgrass the following entries will be made:

J. Snodgrass Account

Share Capital A/c	**£4,000**	Business Purchase A/c **£4,000**

Share Capital Account

	J. Snodgrass A/c **£4,000**

In this way the sum owed by the company to Snodgrass is satisfied.

SPECIMEN QUESTION

Preston Products Ltd was formed with an authorised capital of 40,000 ordinary shares of £1 each and 10,000 5% preference shares of £1 each. The company agreed to purchase the goodwill, plant, fittings and stock of Frank Preston as at 31st December. The agreed consideration was £25,000 to be satisfied by the allotment of 8000 preference shares and 17,000 ordinary shares, both fully paid. Frank Preston's Balance Sheet as at 31st December was as follows:

Capital Account	£26,400	Plant	£10,000
Creditors	4,800	Fittings	2,000
		Stock	4,000
		Debtors £7,300	
		Less Provision 400	
			6,900
		Cash at Bank	8,300
	£31,200		£31,200

The purchase consideration was satisfied on 10th January following the agreement and on this date Preston paid a further sum of £3000 from his business bank account for an additional 3000 ordinary shares.

The company took over Preston's bought and sales ledgers as a matter of convenience and collected book debts and paid creditors on his behalf. All the sums due from the debtors were collected, with the exception of £95 bad debts and £209 allowed as cash discounts. The creditors as shown on the Balance Sheet had omitted an amount of £360 by error. This sum was paid together with the amount of £4800 after deducting cash discounts of £124. The company, by agreement, took credit for a "collection charge" of £365, and then paid over the remainder to Frank Preston.

Write up the accounts *in the company's ledger* recording the above transactions and show the closing entries in Frank Preston's ledger so as to provide a full record of these matters.

SUGGESTED ANSWER

Method: Section 1.

(a) *Open* an account for each item in Frank Preston's Balance Sheet.

(b) *Open* a Sale of Business Account (or Realisation Account).

(c) *Close off* the accounts of those assets which are being acquired by the company, *i.e.* Plant Account, Fittings Account and Stock Account.

(d) *Open* an account for Preston Products Ltd and debit it with the sum agreed upon as the purchase consideration. Enter the corresponding credit in the Sale of Business Account.

(e) The Sale of Business Account will have been debited with the assets which are being taken over by the company, per item (c) above. Now *close off* the Sale of Business Account by entering the difference between the two sides. The figure required is £9000 and it represents the profit on the sale, or more shortly, *goodwill*. Credit the goodwill to Frank Preston's Capital Account.

(f) The company now *settles its debt* to Frank Preston. *Credit the company's personal account* with the shares which it is issuing to Preston and *open* an account for "Shares in Preston Products Ltd" (or Investment Account) which must be debited with the value of these shares.

(g) *Record the purchase of 3000 shares* by Preston by crediting Bank Account and debiting "Shares in Preston Products Ltd."

The more important accounts are shown below.

Sale of Business (or Realisation) Account

Plant A/c	£10,000	Preston Products Ltd	£25,000
Fittings A/c	2,000		
Stock A/c	4,000		
	16,000		
Goodwill (being profit on sale transferred to Capital A/c)	9,000		
	£25,000		£25,000

Preston Products Ltd Account

Sale of Business A/c	£25,000	Investment A/c: (Shares in Preston Products Ltd)	
		Ordinary shares	£17,000
		Preference shares	8,000
	£25,000		£25,000

Investment Account (Shares in Preston Products Ltd)

Preston Products Ltd:		
Ordinary Shares	£17,000	
Preference Shares	8,000	
	25,000	
Bank A/c	3,000	
	£28,000	

Bank Account

Balance b/d	£8,300	Investment A/c	£3,000
		Balance c/d	5,300
	£8,300		£8,300
Balance b/d	5,300		

Capital Account

		Balance b/d	£26,400
		Sale of Business A/c	
		(profit on sale)	9,000
			£35,400

Method: Section 2

(a) Frank Preston must suffer the losses in respect of the Bad Debts £95, and Discount Allowed £209. We therefore debit his Capital Account with both these items and credit the Debtors Account.

The remaining balance on Debtors Account will now be transferred to the debit of Preston Products Ltd and the Debtors Account will be closed.

(b) The item of £360 in respect of those *creditors which were omitted* will be debited to Preston's Capital Account and credited to Creditors Account. The reason for this is that the company has to pay out £360 more than was shown in Preston's books.

E

Discounts received £124, are a profit for Preston and will be credited to his Capital Account; Creditors Account will be debited. The remaining balance on Creditors Account will then be transferred to the credit of Preston Products Ltd.

(c) The commission of £365 due to Preston Products Ltd will be credited to the company's *personal* account in Preston's books and his Capital Account Debited. The balance to the debit of the company will now be £1595 and this is now cleared by a payment of cash.

(d) The Provision for Bad Debts Account will be closed by transfer to Preston's Capital Account as being a gain to him. (He originally suffered a reduction in his profit when the provision was made in the first place.)

(e) The credit balance on Preston's Capital Account will now be exactly equal to the combined balances on the Bank Account plus Investment Account and his books will finally be closed off by the necessary transfers.

The following are the relevant accounts:

Capital Account—Frank Preston

Debtors A/c:		Balance b/d	£35,400
Bad Debts written		Creditors A/c:	
off	95	Discounts Received	124
Discounts Allowed	209	Bad Debts Provision	
Creditors A/c:		A/c	400
Creditors omitted	360		
Preston Products Ltd:			
Commission	365		
Balance c/d	34,895		
	£35,924		£35,924
		Balance b/d	34,895

Debtors Account

Balance b/d	£7,300	Capital A/c:	
		Bad Debts written	
		off	£95
		Discounts Allowed	209
		Preston Products Ltd	6,996
	£7,300		£7,300

Preston Products Ltd

Debtors A/c	£6,996	Creditors A/c		**£5,036**
		Capital A/c Commission		**365**
		Bank A/c		1,595
	£6,996			£6,996

Creditors Account

Capital A/c Discount		Balance b/d	£4,800
Received	**£124**	Capital A/c Creditors	
Preston Products Ltd	**5,036**	omitted	360
	£5,160		£5,160

Bank Account

Balance b/d	£5,300	
Preston Products Ltd	1,595	
	£6,895	

Bad Debts Provision Account

Capital A/c	£400	Balance b/d	£400

Investment Account (Shares in Preston Products Ltd)

Balance b/d	£28,000	

The balance on the Capital Account amounting to £34,895 can now be settled by the payment of:

Cash	£6,895
Shares in Preston Products Ltd	28,000
	£34,895

This will complete the entries in Frank Preston's books, all the accounts now being closed.

THE ENTRIES IN THE LEDGER OF THE COMPANY, *i.e.* PRESTON
PRODUCTS LTD:

Business Purchase Account

Vendor's A/c		Plant A/c	£10,000
F. Preston	£25,000	Fittings A/c	2,000
		Stock A/c	4,000
		Goodwill A/c	9,000
	£25,000		£25,000

Plant Account

Business Purchase A/c	£10,000

Fittings Account

Business Purchase A/c	£2,000

Stock Account

Business Purchase A/c	£4,000

Goodwill Account

Business Purchase A/c	£9,000

Vendor's Account—F. Preston

Ordinary Share Capital		Business Purchase A/c	£25,000
A/c	£20,000	Bank A/c	3,000
Preference Share			
Capital A/c	8,000		
	£28,000		£28,000

Bank Account

Vendor's A/c	
(F. Preston)	£3,000

Ordinary Share Capital Account

	Vendor's A/c	£20,000

Preference Share Capital Account

	Vendor's A/c	£8,000

PRESTON PRODUCTS LTD—BALANCE SHEET

Share Capital:			Fixed Assets:		
Authorised and Issued			Goodwill		£9,000
20,000 £1 ordinary			Plant		10,000
shares		20,000	Fittings		2,000
8,000 £1 preference					
shares		8,000			21,000
			Current Assets:		
			Stock	£4,000	
			Bank	3,000	
					7,000
		£28,000			£28,000

PROGRESS TEST 7

1. What two important accounts must be opened when a person sells his business? (1)

2. Compare the Business Purchase Account in the buyer's books with the corresponding account in the seller's books. (6, 7)

3. Set out in a logical manner the sequence you would follow in recording the details of the sale of a person's business. (6, 7)

4. Name the accounts you would open in the purchaser's books so that an opening Balance Sheet may be prepared. (6, 7)

5. Explain clearly in words exactly what happens when the claim of the seller of a business is settled in whole or in part otherwise than by a payment in cash. (8)

CHAPTER VIII

COMPANY RECONSTRUCTIONS

INTRODUCTION

1. What makes a company reconstruction necessary. If a limited company should be so unfortunate as to suffer heavy losses extending, possibly, over a number of years, it is almost certain that its reserves of undistributed profits will have been consumed. This means that there will be no credit balance on the liabilities side of the Balance Sheet for either "Reserves" or "Profit and Loss Account." On the contrary, it is almost certain that a debit balance will appear on the assets side under the heading "Profit and Loss Account." This debit balance is the measure of the amount of the capital of the company which has been lost.

Should this loss of capital be considerable it may be that *the only alternative to liquidation* may be "surgery" of a drastic nature.

In order to cope with such a situation it will be necessary that all of the interested parties should, firstly, be *consulted* as to what should be done, and secondly, that they should then agree on the manner in which the reconstruction should be carried out.

2. The meaning of the debit balance. To make quite certain that the significance of the debit balance on the Profit and Loss Account is properly understood the following simple example may be of assistance.

EXAMPLE 34

Queer Street Ltd was formed with a capital of £100 on 1st January. All purchases, sales and expenses were for cash, *i.e.* there were no credit transactions. A summary of the Bank Account for the year ended on 31st December is set out below.

Bank Account

Share Capital	£100	Fixtures and Fittings	£40
Sales	4,155	Purchases	3,500
		Expenses	690
		Balance	25
	£4,255		£4,255

Stock on hand at 31st December amounted to £18 at cost.

Trading and Profit and Loss Account

Purchases	£3,500	Sales	£4,155
Gross Profit	673	Closing Stock	18
	£4,173		£4,173
Expenses	690	Gross Profit	673
		Net loss	17
	£690		£690

BALANCE SHEET AS AT 31ST DECEMBER

Share Capital	£100	Fixtures and Fittings	£40
		Stock	18
		Bank	25
		Profit and Loss A/c (net loss)	17
	£100		£100

The *shareholders, in the first place,* contributed £100 *in cash.*

What is their position at the end of the year's trading? What assets are available to repay to them their investment? They are:

Fixtures and Fittings	£40
Stock	18
Cash at Bank	25
	£83

It is quite clear that £17 of their investment has been lost and that the debit balance on the Profit and Loss Account has to be imported into the assets side of the Balance Sheet in order to balance the two sides.

3. An alternative way of showing the loss. In recent years there has been a tendency to show the position in the following manner:

BALANCE SHEET AS AT 31ST DECEMBER

Share Capital	£100	Fixtures and Fittings	£40
Less adverse balance on		Stock	18
Profit and Loss A/c	17	Cash at Bank	25
	——		
	83		
	——		——
	£83		£83

There can be no denying that showing the position in this fashion has much merit.

The fact that a *part of the company's capital has been lost* is indicated quite clearly and anyone who reads the Balance Sheet scarcely requires a knowledge of accountancy to comprehend the true position.

Under the first method shown this fact was, to some degree, obscured, and as a result a student might have difficulty in appreciating the realities of the situation.

It should be noted that there can be no serious quarrel with the second method on the grounds that the *Companies Act* forbids (under normal circumstances) a company to *reduce* its capital. In the Balance Sheet set out above the loss is merely shown as a deduction from the capital which was originally subscribed. This is simply a *method of presentation*. If one were to refer to the Capital Account in the company's ledger one would find the share capital standing at £100.

4. Types of reconstruction. Company reconstructions fall into two categories:

(a) *External* reconstructions; and
(b) *Internal* reconstructions.

Internal reconstructions are dealt with separately in the chapter dealing with reduction of capital (*see* IX). External reconstructions form the subject matter of this chapter.

EXTERNAL RECONSTRUCTIONS

For an external reconstruction to be contemplated as a means of extricating a company from its financial difficulties a number of factors have to be considered.

5. Persons affected: ordinary shareholders. As has already been demonstrated *invested capital* has been lost and, as a result, *the shares of the company are no longer worth their face value*. This state of affairs is a matter of prime consideration for the ordinary shareholders. If they were the only people to be considered an internal reconstruction, *i.e.* reduction of capital, would probably be sufficient to meet the needs of the case.

6. Other persons affected. In the bigger companies, however, there are, as a rule, other *interested parties* who have all, in one way or another, contributed to the financing of the company in its trading affairs. They are detailed in their order of priority:

(a) *The outside creditors* have supplied goods or services *without payment* for the time being. If they were not willing to do this it is obvious that *more cash capital* would have had to be subscribed by the shareholders to enable the company to carry on its business, since payment for goods or services would be required at the time of delivery.

(b) *The debenture holders* have lent money to the company on a *long-term* basis. The direct result of this is that the shareholders have not had to find so much money in the form of share capital.

(c) *The preference shareholders*, although members of the company, are in a completely different category from the ordinary shareholders. They have no say in the *control* of the company but they do have the *right to receive dividends* before the ordinary shareholders qualify for any reward. Furthermore, and this is *a matter of especial importance* in reconstructions, they have the right to receive any arrears of dividend which may have *accumulated* during the bad years.

NOTE: Each of these groups of interested parties will almost certainly be introduced into most examination problems.

7. Conditions favouring reconstruction. The reconstruction of a company will normally only be contemplated when the company has emerged from a succession of bad trading years and appears to have turned the corner. If the future prospects appear to be favourable and it is anticipated that reasonable profits will be made it may then be that a reconstruction is the best possible solution.

8. Restraining factors. Even if a company has every hope and expectation of making profits in the immediate future it does not follow that the shareholders will receive dividends as soon as those profits have materialised. Should the company have a large debit balance on Profit and Loss Account it is unlikely that the directors would recommend a dividend until this has been eliminated, *i.e.* written off out of future profits. The creditors may have been very patient in the past but there comes a time when patience is exhausted. For example, the debentures may be due for redemption and the situation of the company is such that it would be useless to attempt to raise money to pay them off as the public response would almost certainly be negligible. Furthermore, it would be most unlikely that the bank would be prepared to advance the money in view of the company's history. If there were preference shares it is almost certain that there would be considerable arrears of preference dividend.

All of these factors would combine to make the outlook unpromising even though modest future profits were anticipated.

9. Agreement of interested parties. In the light of this the only sensible solution would be to *obtain the agreement of all the interested parties* to a scheme of reconstruction. Each group would, to a lesser or greater degree, be called upon to make some sacrifice. Inevitably, the greatest sacrifice would have to be borne by the ordinary shareholders, who are, of course, the risk takers.

NOTE: Sometimes, however, examiners frame the question in such a way that the creditors or debenture holders receive *more* than their entitlement.

Once the decision to reconstruct has been taken by the directors a scheme of reconstruction will be prepared which *must be agreed to by all the interested parties*. These, in order of priority, are:

(a) Outside creditors;
(b) Debenture holders;
(c) Preference shareholders; and finally
(d) Ordinary shareholders.

It sometimes happens in practice that the original scheme does not meet with the approval of one or other of the interested parties. If this is the case a new scheme will have to be devised. This process will be repeated, if necessary, until at last all parties agree. It must be emphasised that *agreement must be unanimous*.

10. An equitable scheme. In formulating the scheme it is necessary to consider the rights and interests of the various parties to the scheme and to prepare one which will, so far as is possible in the circumstances, *preserve the equities between them*. To this end one frequently finds that, for instance, the outside creditors may agree to accept a certain number of shares in part-settlement of their debt.

11. Method of external reconstruction. Every external reconstruction requires:

(a) *The winding-up of the old company.*
(b) *The formation of a new company to replace it.*

The old company transfers its assets to the new company at agreed valuations (some of which will probably differ from the values standing in the books of the old company).

The new company undertakes to satisfy the claims of the various interested creditors of the old company.

12. Method of dealing with examination problems. It is advisable to follow a set pattern in working out reconstruction problems.

In the first place it is necessary to realise that two companies are involved, *each of which will have its own set of books*.

The key to the solution lies in the *closing entries* in the books of *the company which is being liquidated.* The following Specimen Question will illustrate the method which, it is suggested, should be adopted.

SPECIMEN QUESTION

Clean Break Ltd had suffered substantial losses for some years past. Its Balance Sheet at 30th June was as follows:

Share Capital		Freehold Property	£6,500
30,000 £1 ordinary		Fixtures and Fittings	6,000
shares	£30,000	Motor Vans	4,000
6% debentures	8,000	Stock	13,000
Creditors	12,000	Debtors	3,000
		Bank	2,000
		Profit and Loss A/c	15,500
	£50,000		£50,000

The following scheme of reconstruction was agreed upon:

(*a*) A new company, New Deal Ltd, was to be formed with an authorised capital of £40,000 in £1 shares to take over the assets and liabilities of Clean Break Ltd.

(*b*) The ordinary shareholders of Clean Break Ltd were to be issued with five shares in the new company for every ten held in the old company.

(*c*) The debenture holders of Clean Break Ltd were to surrender their debentures and, in return, were to be credited with £10,000 of 5% debentures in the new company.

(*d*) The creditors were to receive 6000 £1 shares in New Deal Ltd and a cash payment of £7800 in settlement of their claims.

(*e*) The directors of New Deal Ltd were to introduce £15,000 in cash for 15,000 £1 shares in New Deal Ltd.

(*f*) The costs of winding up Clean Break Ltd were to be borne by New Deal Ltd. These amounted to £1000.

(*g*) New Deal Ltd decided to adopt the following values for the tangible assets acquired from Clean Break Ltd:

Fixtures and Fittings	£5,000
Motor Vans	2,500
Stock	10,000

The balance on freehold property was to be adjusted by the amount made available as a result of the reconstruction.

The balances due from the debtors and the bank are unchanged.

Show the closing balances in the books of Clean Break Ltd and the opening Balance Sheet of New Deal Ltd.

NOTE

(*i*) The student's attention is particularly drawn to the fact that *in actual practice* the purchase consideration would be known and that nothing would be done until full arrangements had been made and the amounts involved agreed to by all parties. In examination problems, however, one of the main considerations of the examiner is to test the student's ability to reason matters out. Hence, it is not usual for the purchase consideration to be given in the question.

(*ii*) When building up the personal account of New Deal Ltd it thus becomes necessary to deal with the credit side first. As a result, this account appears *temporarily* as a creditor instead of, as in real life, a debtor, *i.e.* the normal procedure would be to debit the account with the purchase consideration, *since this would be known*, and then to make the required credit entries prior to transferring them to the accounts of the interested parties.

SUGGESTED ANSWER

Method:

(*a*) Open a ledger account for each item on the Balance Sheet of Clean Break Ltd and enter therein the appropriate balance.

(*b*) Since the question does not state the amount of the purchase consideration this *must* be ascertained before further progress can be made.

The manner in which this is to be done is to open an account for New Deal Ltd. Then, by referring to *the details of the scheme of reconstruction* build up, on the credit side of this account, the amount which the new company is going *to give to each of the interested parties*.

Thus, the ordinary shareholders of Clean Break Ltd are to receive 15,000 £1 shares in New Deal Ltd; the debenture holders in Clean Break Ltd are to be compensated with £10,000 of debentures in New Deal Ltd; while the creditors are to be given £6000 in shares *plus* £7800 in cash. Finally, New Deal Ltd has agreed to pay the costs of the reconstruction amounting to £1000.

The total of all these items adds up to £39,800 (as will be seen from the account) and this is the amount of the *purchase consideration*.

(*c*) Having ascertained the purchase consideration the next step is to *complete the double entry* and debit the account of *each of the interested parties* with the appropriate figure.

A Reconstruction Account must now be opened and debited with the *costs of reconstruction*. The corresponding credit entry will be made in the account of New Deal Ltd.

(d) The account for New Deal Ltd must now be closed by debiting the full amount of the purchase consideration thereto and crediting a similar sum to a Realisation Account.

(e) If reference is now made to the accounts of the interested parties, *i.e.* Share Capital Account, 6% Debentures Account and Creditors Account, it will be seen that either a debit or a credit balance remains on each. These accounts must now be closed by transfer of the appropriate amounts to the debit or credit of the Reconstruction Account.

The credit balance on the Reconstruction Account which results from these transfers is *the amount which has been made available* by the scheme of reconstruction *to write off the Losses* which had accumulated as well as *to reduce certain assets* to their true worth.

(f) To complete the closure of the books of Clean Break Ltd we now turn to the asset accounts. Those assets which are being either *reduced or eliminated* will be credited with the appropriate sums and the Reconstruction Account debited.

The balances remaining on all of the asset accounts, with the exception of Freehold Property Account, must now be *transferred to the Realisation Account*.

When this has been done it will be seen that the Realisation Account shows a debit total of £22,500 and a credit total of £39,800. The difference between these totals is £17,300.

The problem states that "the balance on freehold property was to be *adjusted* by the amount made available as a result of the reconstruction." It is clear that this sum of £17,300 is required to be entered on the debit side of Realisation Account in order to close the account. Since Freehold Property Account is the only asset which has not been transferred to the Realisation Account we are bound to assume that £17,300 is to be taken as being the *revised* value of the property.

As a result of doing this we are now faced with a *credit* balance on Freehold Property Account amounting to £10,800. This has arisen as a result of the revision in the value of the property and this gives rise to the introduction of a *capital reserve*. (If the property had been *re-valued* and if it had been decided to bring the new figure into the books the Freehold Property Account would have been debited with £10,800 and the Capital Reserve credited.) This capital profit is now regarded as being available for the reconstruction and is therefore credited to Reconstruction Account.

Note, particularly, what would have happened had this amount *not* been made available. The ordinary shareholders would have had to bear this extra burden and instead of getting shares to the value of £15,000 they would only have received £4,200 in shares, *i.e.* the Share Capital Account would have been debited with £15,000 plus £10,800.

NOTE: The student's attention is drawn particularly to the special and separate functions which the Reconstruction Account and the Realisation Account, respectively, have.

RECONSTRUCTION ACCOUNT. Those assets which are considered to be *of no value* are debited to Reconstruction Account, *i.e.* written off in whole or in part.

REALISATION ACCOUNT. Those assets which are considered to have *some value* are debited to Realisation Account and are *taken over* by the new company.

Stage 1

The first thing which must be done is to open a ledger account for each asset and each liability which appears in the Balance Sheet of Clean Break Ltd and to enter therein the appropriate balance.

Check that the *total* of all the debit balances amounts to the same figure as does the *total* of all the credit balances.

Stage 2

We must now ascertain the amount of the *purchase consideration*. To enable us to do this we open an account for New Deal Ltd and build up the credit side of this account.

The entries will be as follows:

New Deal Ltd

Ordinary Share Capital	
A/c	£15,000
(Shares in New Deal Ltd)	
6% Debentures A/c	10,000
(5% Debentures in New Deal Ltd)	
Creditors A/c	13,800
(Shares in New Deal Ltd £6,000)	
(Cash £7,800)	
Reconstruction A/c	1,000
Costs	
	———
	£39,800

NOTE: The credit entries above show:

(*i*) In italics: *the account* in the books of Clean Break Ltd which accepts the corresponding debit.

(*ii*) In brackets: the *items receivable* from New Deal Ltd by each of the interested parties.

(*iii*) The *costs* of the reconstruction which are to be borne by New Deal Ltd.

Stage 3

The corresponding *debits* which are required to complete the double entry in respect of the above items credited to New Deal Ltd should next be dealt with, as shown below:

Ordinary Share Capital Account

New Deal Ltd A/c	£15,000	Balance b/d	£30,000

6% Debentures Account

New Deal Ltd A/c	£10,000	Balance b/d	£8,000

Creditors Account

New Deal Ltd A/c	£13,800	Balance b/d	£12,000

Finally, we must open a completely new account:

Reconstruction Account

New Deal Ltd A/c £1,000	
(costs of reconstruction)	

Stage 4

In this stage we close off the New Deal Ltd Account by transferring to the credit of Realisation Account the balance which represents the purchase consideration.

New Deal Ltd Account

Transfer to Realisation A/c	£39,800	Balance b/d from *Stage 2*	£39,800

Realisation Account

	Transfer from New Deal Ltd A/c	**£39,800**

Stage 5

As can be seen from *Stage 3* above the ordinary shareholders are to be the sufferers in that they are sacrificing £15,000 to provide a fund whereby the reconstruction may be carried out. We will therefore close the Ordinary Share Capital Account by Debiting it with £15,000 and making the corresponding credit entry in the Reconstruction Account as under.

Ordinary Share Capital Account

New Deal Ltd A/c	£15,000	Balance b/d	£30,000
Reconstruction A/c	**15,000**		
	£30,000		£30,000

Reconstruction Account

New Deal Ltd A/c	£1,000	Ordinary Share Capital A/c	**£15,000**

Stage 6

In this particular example the debenture holders and the creditors have required compensation in order to obtain their agreement to the scheme. The debenture holders are to receive £10,000 in shares in New Deal Ltd for the £8000 they had originally loaned to Clean Break Ltd, while the creditors are to receive a total of £13,800 made up of £6000 in shares and £7800 in cash in satisfaction of the £12,000 owing to them.

6% Debentures Account

New Deal A/c	£10,000	Balance b/d	£8,000
		Reconstruction A/c	**2,000**
	£10,000		£10,000

Creditors Account

New Deal Ltd A/c	£13,800	Balance b/d	£12,000
		Reconstruction A/c	**1,800**
	£13,800		£13,800

Reconstruction Account

New Deal Ltd A/c	£1,000	Ordinary Share Capital	
6% Debentures A/c	**2,000**	A/c (per *Stage 5*	
Creditors A/c	**1,800**	above)	£15,000
Balance c/d	10,200		
	£15,000		£15,000
		Balance b/d	£10,200

Stage 7

The seventh stage is devoted to writing off the amounts on certain of the assets as has been agreed.

Fixtures and Fittings are to be reduced by £1000, *i.e.* from £6000 to £5000.

Motor Vans are to suffer a £1500 reduction in value, *i.e.* from £4000 to £2500.

Stock is to be revalued at £10,000 instead of the figure of £13,000 as shown in the Balance Sheet.

Fixtures and Fittings Account

Balance b/d	£6,000	Reconstruction A/c	**£1,000**

Motor Vans Account

Balance b/d	£4,000	Reconstruction A/c	**£1,500**

Stock Account

Balance b/d	£13,000	Reconstruction A/c	**£3,000**

Reconstruction Account

Fixtures and Fittings A/c	**£1,000**	Balance b/d (per *Stage 6* above)	£10,200
Motor Van A/c	**1,500**		
Stock A/c	**3,000**		
Balance b/d	**4,700**		
	£10,200		£10,200
		Balance b/d	£4,700

Stage 8

The assets which are being taken over by New Deal Ltd should now be transferred to Realisation Account.

Fixtures and Fittings Account

Balance b/d	£6,000	Reconstruction A/c	£1,000
		Realisation A/c	**5,000**
	£6,000		£6,000

Motor Vans Account

Balance b/d	£4,000	Reconstruction A/c	£1,500
		Realisation A/c	**2,500**
	£4,000		£4,000

Stock Account

Balance b/d	£13,000	Reconstruction A/c	£3,000
		Realisation A/c	**10,000**
	£13,000		£13,000

Debtors Account

Balance b/d	**£3,000**	Realisation A/c	**£3,000**

Bank Account

Balance b/d	£2,000	Realisation A/c	£2,000

Realisation Account

Fixtures and Fittings A/c	£5,000	New Deal Ltd A/c (per *Stage 4*)	£39,800
Motor Vans A/c	2,500		
Stock A/c	10,000		
Debtors A/c	3,000		
Bank A/c	2,000		
Balance c/d	17,300		
	£39,800		£39,800
		Balance b/d	£17,300

Stage 9

At *Stage 7* the Reconstruction Account finished with a credit balance of £4700. As explained in (*f*) above, the capital profit on the revaluation of freehold property must now be credited to Reconstruction Account which will raise the credit balance to £15,500. This is precisely the amount needed to eliminate the debit balance on Profit and Loss Account, which is now done.

The closing entries in the books of Clean Break Ltd will be:

Realisation Account

Transfer to Freehold Property A/c	£17,300	Balance b/d (per *Stage 8*)	£17,300

Freehold Property Account

Balance b/d	£6,500	Realisation A/c	£17,300
Transfer to Reconstruction A/c	10,800		
	£17,300		£17,300

Reconstruction Account

Balance c/d	£15,500	Balance b/d (per *Stage 7*)	£4,700
		Freehold Property A/c	10,800
	£15,500		£15,500
		Balance b/d	£15,500

All that now remains to be done is to eliminate the debit balance on Profit and Loss Account.

Profit and Loss Account

Balance b/d	£15,500	Transfer to Reconstruction A/c	£15,500

Reconstruction Account

Profit and Loss A/c	£15,500	Balance (as above) b/d	£15,500

Stage 10

The question asks us to show the opening Balance Sheet of New Deal Ltd. Before doing this we will *set out the opening accounts* of this company so that the details may be checked and the contents of the Balance Sheet understood.

We will begin by opening an account which we are calling Asset Acquisition Account. It is, in effect, the Purchase of Business Account. That is to say, the entries to be made in it are the *reverse* of those found in the Realisation Account of Clean Break Ltd.

Asset Acquisition Account

Clean Break Ltd A/c	£39,800	Fixtures and Fittings A/c	£5,000
		Motor Van A/c	2,500
		Stock A/c	10,000
		Debtors A/c	3,000
		Bank A/c	2,000
		Freehold Property A/c	17,300
	£39,800		£39,800

An account should now be opened for each asset which has been acquired and debited with the amounts shown against each item in the above account.

Similarly, *a personal account* for Clean Break Ltd must also be opened and credited with the sum of £39,800.

It is not considered necessary to show the asset accounts here with the exception of the Bank Account since no further entries have to be made in them.

Stage 11

The details to be entered in the account of Clean Break Ltd are as follows:

Clean Break Ltd Account

Share Capital A/c:		Asset Acquisition A/c	£39,800
Ordinary shareholders of Clean Break Ltd	£15,000		
Creditors of Clean Break Ltd	6,000		
5% Debentures A/c:			
6% debenture holders of Clean Break Ltd	10,000		
Bank A/c:			
6% debenture holders of Clean Break Ltd	7,800		
Costs of reconstruction	1,000		
	£39,800		£39,800

Bank Account

Asset Acquisition A/c	£2,000	Clean Break Ltd 6% debentures A/c	£7,800
Share Capital A/c	15,000	Costs (C.B. Ltd A/c)	1,000
(Cash introduced by the directors of New Deal Ltd)		Balance c/d	8,200
	£17,000		£17,000
Balance b/d	£8,200		

Share Capital Account

Balance c/d	£36,000	Clean Break Ltd A/c Ordinary share-	
		holders	£15,000
		Creditors	6,000
		Bank A/c	15,000
	£36,000		£36,000
		Balance b/d	£36,000

5% Debentures Account

	Clean Break Ltd A/c	£10,000

Stage 12

BALANCE SHEET OF NEW DEAL LTD

Share Capital		Fixed Assets:		
Authorised: 40,000		Freehold property		£17,300
£1 shares	£40,000	Fixtures and		
		fittings		5,000
		Motor vans		2,500
				24,800
Issued: 36,000 £1		Current Assets:		
shares fully paid	36,000	Stock	£10,000	
5% Debentures	10,000	Debtors	3,000	
		Bank	8,200	
				21,200
	£46,000			£46,000

PROGRESS TEST 8

1. What is the most usual course which forces a company into a reconstruction? (**1**)

2. What do you understand by the statement that "the Profit and Loss Account is in debit"? (**2**)

3. The debit balance on the Profit and Loss Account can be shown in two different ways. What are these? (**3**)

4. Name the two main categories into which reconstructions may fall. (4)

5. Who are deemed to be "interested parties" in a company reconstruction? (6)

6. Under what circumstances will a reconstruction normally only be contemplated? (7, 8)

7. By what method will an external reconstruction be carried out? (11)

CHAPTER IX

REDUCTION OF CAPITAL FOR INTERNAL RECONSTRUCTIONS

THE ACCOUNTING PROCEDURE

Where a company is forced to resort to a reduction of its issued capital following a period of adverse trading the accounting requirements are, generally, rather more simple than those which have to be followed for an external reconstruction.

1. The capital reduction scheme must be approved. The interested parties, *i.e.* the various types of shareholders, debenture holders and creditors, all have to be consulted and their agreement obtained to the scheme of capital reduction. This is then submitted to the Court for its approval. When the sanction of the Court has been obtained the accounting procedures may be put into operation.

2. The accounting procedures. The important account in this instance is the *Capital Reduction Account*. This can be compared with the *Reconstruction Account* in an external reconstruction. Its function is much the same, *i.e.* to be credited with that amount of paid-up capital *which has already been lost* and to accept, on the debit side, the amounts being written off certain of the assets *as well as* the *Debit Balance* on Profit and Loss Account. The *total* of the amounts so written off will equal the amount credited from the Share Capital Account by virtue of the fact that *the Capital Reduction Scheme* will have been purposely designed to reduce the capital to a certain pre-determined figure. This will normally be exactly sufficient to write off certain so-called assets and to reduce others to realistic figures.

The following examples should be sufficient to demonstrate the basic simplicity of problems of this nature.

SPECIMEN QUESTION 1

(C.A.)

The Balance Sheet of XY Ltd as on 31st December 1965, was as follows:

Capital			Goodwill at cost	£3,000
Authorised:			Patents and trade marks at cost	5,000
100,000 6% cumulative			Freehold land and buildings at cost	15,000
preference shares of			Plant and machinery at cost less	
£1 each	£100,000		depreciation	46,000
200,000 ordinary shares			Stock	29,600
of 10s. each	100,000		Sundry debtors	50,300
	————		Profit and Loss Account	51,100
	£200,000			
Issued:				
100,000 6% cumulative				
preference shares of				
£1 each fully paid	100,000			
150,000 ordinary shares				
of 10s. each fully paid	75,000			
	————	175,000		
Sundry Creditors		20,600		
Bank Overdraft (secured by a charge				
on the freehold buildings)		4,400		
		————		————
		£200,000		£200,000

NOTE: The preference dividend is in arrear since 31st December 1961.

The company passed a special resolution to reduce its capital, and application was made to the Court for an order to confirm the reduction.

Sanction (with effect from 31st December 1965) was obtained to the following:

1. The preference shares to be reduced to 15s. each, fully paid, and the arrears of dividend to be cancelled.
2. The ordinary shares to be reduced to 5s. each, fully paid.
3. The authorised ordinary share capital to be increased to 400,000 shares of 5s. each.
4. The debit balance on Profit and Loss Account to be written off.
5. The goodwill to be written off.
6. Plant and machinery to be reduced by £4000.
7. Of the book debts £2400 known to be bad, to be written off.
8. Any available balance to be utilised in writing down patents and trade marks.

On the reduction being confirmed the chairman of the company agreed to advance the sum of £10,000 to be secured by a mortgage at 4% per annum on the freehold land and buildings, the cash to be applied in paying off the bank overdraft and providing additional working capital.

You are required (*a*) to show the entries giving effect to the above and (*b*) to prepare a revised Balance Sheet.

SUGGESTED ANSWER

(*a*) Open a ledger A/c for each item on Balance Sheet.
(*b*) Open a Capital Reduction A/c.

(*c*)	Dr.	Preference Share Capital A/c	£25,000		Note 1
	Cr.	Capital Reduction A/c		£25,000	
(*d*)	Dr.	Ordinary Share Capital A/c	£37,500		Note 2
	Cr.	Capital Reduction A/c		£37,500	
			£62,500	£62,500	
(*e*)	Dr.	Capital Reduction A/c	£51,100		Note 4
	Cr.	Profit and Loss A/c		£51,100	
(*f*)	Dr.	Capital Reduction A/c	£3,000		Note 5
	Cr.	Goodwill A/c		£3,000	
(*g*)	Dr.	Capital Reduction A/c	£4,000		Note 6
	Cr.	Plant A/c		£4,000	
(*h*)	Dr.	Capital Reduction A/c	£2,400		Note 7
	Cr.	Debtors A/c		£2,400	
(*i*)	Dr.	Capital Reduction A/c	£2,000		Note 8
		Patents and Trade Marks		£2,000	
			£62,500	£62,500	

XY LTD—REVISED BALANCE SHEET

Capital (after reduction authorised by Court)			*Fixed Assets as re-valued on reduction of capital:*		
Authorised:			Patents and Trade		
100,000 6% cumula-			Marks	£3,000	
tive preference			Freehold Land and		
shares of 15s. each	£75,000		Buildings (at		
400,000 ordinary			cost)	15,000	
shares at 5s. each	100,000		Plant and Mach-		
		£175,000	inery	42,000	
					60,000
Issued:			*Current Assets:*		
100,000 6% cumula-			Stock	29,600	
tive preference			Sundry Debtors	47,900	
shares of 15s. each			Bank Balance	5,600	
(reduced from £1					83,100
each)	75,000				
150,000 ordinary					
shares of 5s. each					
(reduced from 10s.)	37,500				
		£112,500			
4% mortgage (secured on					
Freehold Land and					
Buildings)		10,000			
Sundry Creditors		20,600			
		£143,100			£143,100

The second example set out below is a more advanced type of problem and is worked in some detail in order to show fully how the matter may be dealt with.

SPECIMEN QUESTION 2

(c. of s. (adapted))

The Balance Sheet of D. Clyne Ltd is as follows:

Share Capital		*Fixed Assets*	
Authorised and		Goodwill	£50,000
Issued 400,000		Freehold property	295,000
6% £1 cumulative		Plant	215,000
preference shares	£400,000	*Current Assets*	
500,000 £1		Stocks	178,600
ordinary shares	500,000	Debtors	113,500
	————	Bank	27,650
	900,000	*Profit and Loss*	
Share Premium Account	60,000	*Account*	208,750
7% Debentures	100,000		
Current liabilities			
Creditors	28,500		
	————		————
	£1,088,500		£1,088,500

A scheme for a reduction of capital has been approved and sanctioned which provides for the reduction of the capital to £600,000, divided into 400,000 £1 ordinary B shares and 400,000 5% cumulative preference shares of 10s. each to be allocated as follows:

    (a) Debenture holders to receive ten 5% cumulative preference shares of 10s. each and one ordinary B share of £1 each for every £5 of debentures held, all debentures being cancelled.

    (b) 6% preference shareholders to receive one 5% cumulative preference share and one ordinary B share for every two shares now held.

        Ordinary shareholders to receive nine ordinary B shares for every 25 shares now held.

The book value of the company's assets after writing off the Share Premium Account is to be written down as follows: Goodwill Account is to be eliminated and £136,052 is to be written off the plant. The balance available is to be used to write down the value of the freehold property.

Prepare journal entries to record these transactions and show the Balance Sheet as it would appear after the capital reduction has been completed.

SUGGESTED ANSWER

Stage 1

The *total* share capital of £900,000 is to be *reduced* to £600,000. Dealing with the details of the scheme of reconstruction in the order in which they appear in the question the 7% debentures are first on the list. To obtain their agreement to the scheme the shareholders are forced to give them a "bonus" amounting to £20,000 in ordinary B shares.

7% Debenture Account

5% Cumulative Pre-ference Shares A/c (200,000 shares of 10s. each)	£100,000	Balance b/d	£100,000	
Ordinary B Shares A/c	*20,000*	Capital Reduction A/c	**20,000**	
	£120,000		**£120,000**	

5% Cumulative Preference Shares Account

	7% Debentures A/c	£100,000

Ordinary B Shares Account

	7% Debentures A/c	*£20,000*

Capital Reduction Account

7% Debentures A/c	**£20,000**		

Stage 2

The 6% preference shareholders are to lose £100,000, as follows:

6% Cumulative Preference Shares Account

5% Cumulative Pre-ference Shares A/c (200,000 shares of 10s. each)	**£100,000**	Balance b/d	£400,000
Ordinary B Shares A/c (200,000 shares of £1 each)	**200,000**		
Capital Reduction A/c	*100,000*		
	£400,000		**£400,000**

5% Cumulative Preference Shares Account

		From *Stage 1*	£100,000
		6% Cumulative Preference Shares A/c	**100,000**
			£200,000

Ordinary B Shares Account

		From *Stage 1*	£20,000
		6% Cumulative Preference Shares A/c	**200,000**
			£220,000

Capital Reduction Account

From *Stage 1*	£20,000	6% Cumulative Preference Shares	*£100,000*
Balance c/d	80,000		
	£100,000		£100,000
		Balance b/d	£80,000

Stage 3

As is usual in reconstructions *it is the ordinary shareholders who are the chief sufferers*.

Ordinary Shares Account

Ordinary B Shares A/c	**£180,000**	Balance b/d	£500,000
Capital Reduction A/c	320,000		
	£500,000		£500,000

Ordinary B Shares Account

		From *Stage 2*	£220,000
		Ordinary Shares A/c	**180,000**
			£400,000

Capital Reduction Account

	From *Stage 2*		£80,000
	Ordinary Shares A/c		**320,000**
			£400,000

Stage 4

In addition to the direct sacrifices made by both groups of share-holders the credit balance on the Share Premium Account is to be given up in the interests of all parties.

Share Premium Account

Capital Reduction A/c	**£60,000**	Balance b/d	£60,000

Capital Reduction Account

	From *Stage 3*		£400,000
	Share Premium A/c		**60,000**
			£460,000

Stage 5

The balances on Goodwill Account *and* Profit and Loss Account are to be eliminated. It should be noted that no mention was made in the question as regards the Profit and Loss Account balance. These accounts will, therefore, be credited and the corresponding debits will be made in the Capital Reduction Account. Only a part of the values standing on Freehold Property and Plant Accounts is to be written off. The position will then be:

Freehold Property Account

Balance b/d	£295,000	Capital Reduction A/c	**£65,198**
		Balance c/d	229,802
	£295,000		£295,000
Balance b/d	229,802		

Plant Account

Balance b/d	£215,000	Capital Reduction A/c	£136,052
		Balance c/d	78,948
	£215,000		£215,000
Balance b/d	78,948		

Capital Reduction Account

Goodwill A/c	£50,000	From *Stage 4*	£460,000
Profit and Loss A/c	208,750		
Freehold Property A/c	65,198		
Plant A/c	136,052		
	£460,000		£460,000

Stage 6

In this stage we come to the first of the requirements of the question, namely, the journal entries.

Journal

Capital Reduction A/c	Dr.	£480,000	
To Goodwill A/c (see *Stage 5*)			£50,000
7% Debentures A/c (see *Stage 1*)			20,000
Profit and Loss A/c (see *Stage 5*)			208,750
Plant A/c (see *Stage 5*)			136,052
Freehold Property A/c (see *Stage 5*)			65,198
		£480,000	£480,000
Sundries:	Dr.		
6% Cumulative Preference Shares A/c (see *Stage 2*)		100,000	
Ordinary Shares A/c (see *Stage 3*)		320,000	
Share Premium A/c (see *Stage 4*)		60,000	
To Capital Reduction A/c			480,000
		£480,000	£480,000

Being adjustments in connection with capital reduction scheme.

Stage 7

The second, and last, requirement is the presentation of the Balance Sheet *after* the reduction.

BALANCE SHEET

Share Capital—		Fixed Assets:		
Authorised and		Freehold property		£229,802
Issued:		Plant		78,948
6% cumulative				
preference				
shares	£200,000			
Ordinary B				
shares	400,000			
	£600,000			£308,750
Current Liabilities:		Current Assets:		
Creditors	28,500	Stock	£178,600	
		Debtors	113,500	
		Bank	27,650	
				319,750
	£628,500			£628,500

FORMULATING A SCHEME OF RECONSTRUCTION

3. The "accountancy" problem. In the previous section we were able to see that the book-keeping aspect of capital reductions is not unduly complicated. It is one thing to place a "cut and dried" scheme in front of a student and ask him to deal with, say, the journal entries. It is quite another matter to ask him to devise a scheme for acceptance by all the interested parties. This calls for a rather deeper knowledge than one of the book-keeping procedures only.

4. Purpose of a company reconstruction. No company would bother about a reconstruction, either internal or external, involving as it would a considerable amount of trouble and expense, unless it was going to prove worthwhile. If, for example, such reconstruction was expected to prolong the life of the company by a year or two only, after which it would

F

have to go into liquidation, it is obvious that there would be very little point in carrying out the reconstruction. Liquidation now rather than later would almost certainly be preferable in such circumstances.

(a) There is virtually only one criterion by which the situation can be judged: *can the company be expected to earn profits in the future?*

(b) If the answer to this is affirmative, the next important question is: *how much profit can be expected each year?*

5. Importance of a company's future earning capacity. Should the future earning capacity, based on a sober and conservative estimate, be regarded as satisfactory then a scheme of capital reduction (or reconstruction) may be built up from this point. It must be emphasised that *the future ability of any company to earn profit,* and so its ability to *pay dividends is of paramount importance.* One must recognise that when people invest their money in a company they are looking for *two* things:

(a) *A return on their investment* in the form of a yearly *dividend;* and

(b) *The security of their investment, i.e.* that the money employed in buying shares will not lose its value but preferably *appreciate* in the course of time.

Unfortunately, it does not always work out this way. If, however, it appears to be reasonably certain that the bad time has passed and that reasonable profits in the future may be expected, then a reduction of capital may be proceeded with.

6. A scheme which is equitable. When devising the scheme the really important matter to concentrate on is *the preservation of the equities* as between the preference and ordinary shareholders. It must never be forgotten that the ordinary shareholders are the risk-takers, whereas the preference shareholders prefer to take less risk but will be satisfied with a smaller share of the "cake" when it is cut up. It follows, therefore, that the preference shareholders should be treated with consideration and not be called upon to make undue sacrifices. In most cases of this nature they will probably not have received their preference dividend for some years past and this fact must certainly be taken into account.

7. A scheme of reconstruction.

The following Specimen Question will give the student an idea how a scheme of capital reduction might be dealt with.

SPECIMEN QUESTION

The balance sheet of Fighting Back Ltd at 30th September, was as follows:

Share Capital Authorised and Issued			Fixed Assets:			
40,000 8% cumulative preference shares of £1 each		£40,000	Patents			£10,000
			Premises			32,000
60,000 ordinary shares of £1 each		60,000	Plant Cost		45,000	
			Less Depreciation		18,000	
		£100,000				27,000
Current Liabilities:			Fixtures Cost		5,000	
Creditors	£28,000		Less Depreciation		3,000	
Accrued Expenses	430					2,000
Bank Overdraft	1,570					71,000
		30,000	Current Assets:			
			Stock		7,000	
			Debtors		12,000	
						19,000
			Profit and Loss Account Accumulated loss			40,000
		£130,000				£130,000

When the company was first formed it was expected that the annual profits would be sufficient to permit a distribution of £10,000 on average by way of dividend to the shareholders.

For the past few years trade has been bad and heavy losses have been sustained. The preference dividend is four years in arrear and patents are regarded as being worthless. A valuation of the fixed assets has been made with the following results:

(a) Plant should be written down by £12,000.
(b) Fixtures are to be reduced to £1500.
(c) The current value of the premises is estimated to be £60,000.
(d) A great deal of the stock is obsolete and should be reduced to half its book value.
(e) Of the debtors £2000 are considered doubtful and a provision should be made for that amount.

The preference shares have priority as to repayment of capital. Future profits are expected to be maintained at a figure which will permit £5000 per annum to be distributed by way of dividend.

You are required to draw up a scheme of reconstruction which will be equitable to both classes of shareholders.

SUGGESTED ANSWER

Before consideration can be given to any scheme of reconstruction it will be necessary to give effect to the suggested revaluations of the assets.

New value of Plant (a)	£15,000
New value of Fixtures (b)	1,500
New value of Premises (c)	60,000
New value of Stock (d)	3,500
New value of Debtors (e)	10,000
Patents are to be eliminated	—
Profit and Loss Account	—
	90,000
Less Current Liabilities	30,000
Net worth	£60,000

The issued share capital of the company is:

Preference shares	£40,000	
Ordinary shares	£60,000	
		£100,000

The reconstruction scheme must therefore be based upon a reduction of capital amounting to £40,000.

To arrive at an equitable reconstruction:

(a) Originally, the company had anticipated that *£10,000 per annum would be available for dividends.* This would have meant:

(i) The preference shareholders would receive 8% on £40,000	£3,200
(ii) The ordinary shareholders would receive the remainder	£6,800
	£10,000

The dividend ratio would thus be roughly 1 : 2.

(b) Next, we must look at the *amount of money invested by each group* of shareholders.

£40,000 was invested in 8% preference shares.

For every £100 invested the yield amounts to £8 0s. 0d., *i.e.* in £40,000 there are 400 × £100 and so a dividend of £8 per £100 would amount to £8 × 400 = £3200.

£60,000 was invested in ordinary shares.

For every £100 invested the yield amounts to approximately

£11 6s. 0d., i.e. in £60,000 there are 600 × £100 and so a dividend of £11 6s. 0d. per £100 would amount to £11 6s. 0d. × 600 = £6780.

In this case the ratio is roughly 1 : 1½ that is 8 : 12. (Actually £8 : £11 6s. 0d.)

(c) *We must not be overgenerous to the ordinary shareholders* because we have to bear in mind that the preference shareholders have due to them arrears of dividend amounting to £3200 each year for the past four years. Admittedly the ordinary shareholders have had nothing either but it must be remembered that they are the *risk takers*. If we were to plan to give the preference shareholders *shares* equivalent to the amount of two years' preference dividend this would increase their holding by 6,400 shares, giving a total of 46,400 preference shares. At the same time, since the anticipated profits are now only expected to run at half the original figure, *i.e.* £5000 instead of £10,000, the *rate* of preference dividend should also be halved. Therefore the rate may be reasonably fixed at 4% in place of the original 8%. On a total dividend of £5000 the preference shares would qualify for £1856, or say, £1850, which would leave £3150 for the ordinary shares.

(d) *With the information converted into figures* we can now sum up the position as follows:

From (a) above we have a ratio of

1 preference : 2 ordinary shares.

From (b) we have

1 preference : 1½ ordinary shares.
These give us a total of 2 : 3½ or 24 : 42.

From (c) above the proportion to be given to the ordinary shares must be reduced a little more. If we made the proportions 24 : 40 or ⅜ : ⅝ this would probably meet the case.

PROGRESS TEST 9

1. What do you understand by the term "a scheme of capital reduction"? (**1, 2**)

2. Why do companies undertake reconstructions? (**4**)

3. What is the essential criterion to justify a company reconstruction? (**5**)

4. What is meant by "preserving the equities" in relation to a reconstruction scheme? (**6**)

CHAPTER X

AMALGAMATIONS AND ABSORPTIONS

INTRODUCTION

An amalgamation of *two* companies consists of the *pooling* of their assets and liabilities. The object of an amalgamation is usually for the purpose of more economical working and the building of one strong unit in place of two weaker ones.

An absorption usually entails one strong unit swallowing a weaker one.

ABSORPTIONS

1. Method of absorption. An absorption is usually carried out by means of the following process:

> *By winding up one of the companies*, the assets and liabilities of which are taken over by an *existing* company.

No new company is formed. The absorbing company simply becomes a larger, and generally speaking, a stronger unit.

The recommended method by which problems should be solved is to use a technique similar to the one used in Chapter VIII for reconstructions. That is to say, a ledger account should be opened for *each item* appearing on the Balance Sheet of the company which is being wound up. If this is done no serious difficulty should arise over the mechanical aspect of the problem so long as it is remembered that *a double entry* must be made *for every adjustment*. This can normally only be done with safety when proper ledger accounts are opened. Students are terribly prone to do only *half* of each *double* entry (because they do not open ledger accounts) trusting that memory will see them through successfully. They are frequently mistaken.

2. Procedure in an absorption. The following examination problem illustrates the procedure followed in an absorption.

(C.A.)

On 25th March 1966, Alpha Ltd agreed to acquire the goodwill and assets, other than the balance at bank, of Beta Ltd as on 31st March 1966.

The Balance Sheet of Beta Ltd on 31st March 1966, was as follows.

Share capital in £1		Goodwill	£25,000
shares	£120,000	Buildings and plant	112,800
General reserve	16,000	Stock	21,200
Profit and Loss		Debtors	6,400
Account	8,000	Bank	10,600
6% debentures	30,000		
Creditors	2,000		
	£176,000		£176,000

The consideration payable by Alpha Ltd was agreed as follows:

(a) A cash payment equivalent to 2s. 6d. for every £1 share in Beta Ltd.

(b) The issue to Beta Ltd of 100,000 £1 shares, fully paid, in Alpha Ltd at an agreed value of 30s. per share.

(c) The issue of such an amount of fully paid 5% debentures of Alpha Ltd at a discount of 10% as is sufficient to discharge the 6% debentures of Beta Ltd at a premium of 5%.

The liabilities of Beta Ltd, other than debentures, were to be discharged by that company.

When computing the consideration, the directors of Alpha Ltd valued the buildings and plant at £150,000, the stock at £19,000, and the debtors at book value, subject to an allowance of 4% to cover doubtful debts.

You are required to draft the journal entries in the books of Alpha Ltd to record the acquisition.

SUGGESTED ANSWER

Even though the question asks for journal entries in the books of the *acquiring* company (Alpha Ltd) it is recommended that the student open an *account* for *each* asset and liability in the books of Beta Ltd so that its books may be closed and *a Realisation Account be built up*.

It will be necessary to open certain additional accounts but these will be introduced as we proceed.

Stage 1

Assuming that an account for each item on the Balance Sheet has been opened we will dispose of three of these forthwith by transferring the Share Capital, General Reserve and Profit and Loss Account balances to a Sundry Shareholders Account.

Sundry Shareholders Account

Balance c/d	£144,000	Transfer from:	
		Share Capital A/c	£120,000
		General Reserve A/c	16,000
		Profit and Loss A/c	8,000
	£144,000		£144,000
		Balance b/d	£144,000

Stage 2

As we are not given the purchase consideration this must next be ascertained. To do this we will open an account for *Alpha Ltd* and enter therein the various items by which the *purchase consideration* is to be satisfied.

Alpha Ltd Account

Realisation A/c	**£196,500**	Bank A/c (2s. 6d. per share on 120,000 shares)	£15,000
		Shares in Alpha Ltd A/c (100,000 shares at 30s. per share)	150,000
		Debentures in Alpha Ltd A/c (discharge of £30,000 debentures at a premium of 5%)	31,500
	£196,500		**£196,500**

We thus ascertain that the purchase consideration amounts to £196,500. This amount will now be credited to the *Realisation* Account.

Realisation Account

		Alpha Ltd A/c	**£196,500**

Stage 3

The next step is to debit Realisation Account with the *revised values of the assets* which are being taken over by Alpha Ltd. At this point we will deal with the Buildings and Plant, the Stock and the Debtors, leaving Goodwill until a later stage.

Buildings and Plant Account

Balance b/d	£112,800	Realisation A/c	£150,000
Sundry Shareholders A/c (Capital profit)	**£37,200**		
	£150,000		£150,000

Stock Account

Balance b/d	£21,200	Realisation A/c	£19,000
		Sundry Shareholders A/c	**£2,200**
	£21,200		£21,200

Debtors Account

Balance b/d	£6,400	Realisation A/c	£6,400

Realisation Account

Buildings and Plant A/c	£150,000	Alpha Ltd (per Stage 2)	£196,500
Stock A/c	19,000		
Debtors A/c	6,400		
Balance c/d	21,100		
	£196,500		£196,500
		Balance b/d	21,100

Sundry Shareholders Account

Stock A/c	**£2,200**	Balance (per	
Balance c/d	179,000	*Stage 1*)	£144,000
		Buildings and Plant	
		A/c	**37,200**
	£181,200		£181,200
		Balance b/d	£179,000

Stage 4

The question tells us that the *debtors were to be taken over at book value*. This has been done in *Stage 3*. There was, however, a proviso that the figure of £6400 was subject to an allowance of 4% to cover doubtful debts. This means, of course, that the shareholders of Beta Ltd have to be *charged* with this allowance amounting to £256 and we must, therefore, credit Realisation Account and debit the Sundry Shareholders Account with this sum.

Realisation Account

		Balance b/d (per	
		Stage 3)	£21,100
		Sundry Shareholders	
		A/c (Provision for	
		debtors)	**256**
			£21,356

Sundry Shareholders Account

Realisation A/c	**£256**	Balance b/d (per	
		Stage 3)	£179,000

Stage 5

The only item which remains to be entered in the Realisation Account is the value of the *goodwill*. As can be seen from *Stage 4* the balance on Realisation Account amounts to £21,356. This, then, *must* be the valuation placed upon Goodwill.

Realisation Account

		Balance b/d (per	
Goodwill A/c	**£21,356**	*Stage 4*)	£21,356

Goodwill Account

Balance b/d	£25,000	Realisation A/c Sundry Shareholders A/c (Goodwill	**£21,356**
		written off)	**3,644**
	£25,000		£25,000

Sundry Shareholders Account

Realisation A/c (per *Stage 4*)	256	Balance (per *Stage 3*)	£179,000
Goodwill A/c	**3,644**		
Balance c/d	175,100		
	£179,000		£179,000
		Balance b/d	£175,100

Stage 6

We need concern ourselves no further with the books of Beta Ltd. Our main purpose so far has been to build up the Realisation Account correctly so that we may use it as the *basis* for the entries in the books of Alpha Ltd. We will, however, show the Realisation Account in *full* for purposes of reference.

Realisation Account

Buildings and Plant	£150,000	Alpha A/c	£196,500
Stock A/c	19,000	Provision for	
Debtors A/c	6,400	Debtors A/c	256
Goodwill A/c	21,356		
	£196,756		£196,756

Stage 7

Turning to the books of Alpha Ltd we open the Business Purchase Account. This, of course, is simply a *reversal* of Beta Ltd's Realisation Account.

Business Purchase Account

Beta Ltd	£196,500	Building and Plant	
Provision for		A/c	£150,000
Doubtful Debts A/c	256	Stock A/c	19,000
		Debtors A/c	6,400
		Goodwill A/c	21,356
	£196,756		£196,756

Stage 8

The account for Beta Ltd is the most important one which concerns us now. The purchase consideration of £196,500 according to the details of the question is satisfied by those items shown below on the *debit* of the account of Beta Ltd.

Beta Ltd Account

Share Capital A/c	£100,000	Business Purchase	
Share Premium A/c	50,000	A/c	£196,500
5% Debentures A/c	31,500		
Cash A/c	15,000		
	£196,500		£196,500

To calculate the debenture consideration (note (*c*) on p. 157) start at the *end* of the instruction.

The 6% debentures amounting to £30,000 are to be discharged at a premium of 5%:

$$\frac{5}{100} \times £30,000 = £1,500$$

This will give the debenture holders a total entitlement of £31,500. They are to be issued with 5% debentures of Alpha Ltd *at a discount of* 10%. The figure of £31,500 represents 90% of the *nominal* value of the new debentures, which means, therefore, that the *discount* amounts to £3500.

The concluding entries will be:

5% Debentures Account

Balance c/d	£35,000	Beta Ltd	£31,500
		Debenture Discount	
		A/c	**3,500**
	£35,000		£35,000
		Balance b/d	£35,000

Debenture Discount Account

5% Debenture A/c	**£3,500**	

This question asked for the *Journal entries* in the books of Alpha Ltd to record the acquisition.

The journal entries which are required (and therefore, the ones which score the marks) are to be found from the entries in the Business Purchase Account and in the account of Beta Ltd. They are as follows:

		Dr.	*Cr.*
Sundries	Dr.		
Buildings and Plant A/c		£150,000	
Stock A/c		19,000	
Debtors A/c		6,400	
Goodwill A/c		21,356	
To Sundries			
Beta Ltd A/c			£196,500
Provision for Doubtful Debts A/c			256
		£196,756	£196,756

Being the purchase of Assets of Beta Ltd.

		Dr.	*Cr.*
Beta Ltd A/c	Dr.	£196,500	
To Sundries			
Share Capital A/c			£100,000
Share Premium A/c			50,000
5% Debentures A/c			31,500
Cash A/c			15,000
		£196,500	£196,500

Being discharge of the purchase consideration.

		Dr.	*Cr.*
Debenture Discount A/c	Dr.	£3,500	
To 5% Debentures A/c			£3,500

Being discount of 10% allowed on the issue of 5% debentures.

NOTE: It has not been considered necessary in working out the solution to show all the *closing* entries in the books of Beta Ltd as they are not strictly relevant to the question.

Until a student has had sufficient practice to enable him to feel that he has mastered this aspect of accountancy it is recommended that he does, in fact, *complete* all the entries. The reason for this suggestion is that it will give him a better *overall picture* of what is happening and help him to appreciate that nearly all problems in accountancy can be solved by the application of double entry to the *whole* of the problem.

Such a question as the one above is most revealing to an instructor. Frequently he finds that many students have a "hit-or-miss" approach and inevitably lose their way.

It is *vitally important*, therefore, that if, for example, a Balance Sheet is given in the question *all* of the items which appear therein should be converted into *Ledger Balances*. From this solid foundation *all* questions of this type can be readily solved.

AMALGAMATIONS

3. Difference between absorption and amalgamation. We have seen in the previous section that an *absorption* is, indeed, precisely what the word suggests. That is to say, *one business is absorbed* or swallowed up by *another*. Being thus absorbed it ceases to have a personality of its own. The absorbing company, on the other hand, *continues to exist* but in a bigger way than it did hitherto. Therefore, it is true to say that in *absorption* problems we will *always* find that there is *one winding up*.

Amalgamations differ from Absorptions in that the companies amalgamating (two or more) will *all be wound up* and *a new company formed* to take over these undertakings.

4. Procedure in amalgamations. The method of solving problems will, however, be very much the same as that used for absorptions and can best be seen from an example.

(C.A.)

The balance sheets, as on 31st March 1966, of two companies which were in liquidation for the purpose of amalgamation are as follows:

	Brass Ltd	Tacks Ltd		Brass Ltd	Tacks Ltd
Share Capital			*Fixed Assets*		
Authorised and Issued			Goodwill	£30,700	£5,000
£1 shares fully paid	£125,000	£100,000	Land and Build-		
General Reserve	15,000	7,500	ings	18,800	21,500
Profit and Loss A/c	5,450	4,700	Plant	25,000	32,000
	145,450	112,200		74,500	58,500
Current Liabilities			*Current Assets*		
Creditors	12,400	7,300	Stock	53,750	36,300
			Debtors	18,000	16,000
			Cash	11,600	8,700
	£157,850	£119,500		£157,850	£119,500

A new company, Brass Tacks Ltd, acquired the assets of both companies as on 1st April 1966 (with the exception of £500 retained in cash by the liquidator of each company to meet his expenses), and assumed their liabilities as on that date. It was agreed to make provision for doubtful debts at the rate of $2\frac{1}{2}\%$ of amounts outstanding and to write down the plant of Brass Ltd by 10% and that of Tacks Ltd by 15%. Apart from these the book values of the tangible assets were agreed to be correctly stated for all purposes.

It was decided that there was, in fact, no goodwill and that no item for this should appear in the books of Brass Tacks Ltd, but that nevertheless for the purpose of apportionment of the purchase consideration between the two liquidators, goodwill should be taken into account at the respective balance sheet figures.

The purchase consideration was by agreement duly satisfied on 1st May 1966, by the allotment at par to the respective liquidators of the necessary number of ordinary shares of 5s. each in Brass Tacks Ltd, credited as fully paid up.

You are required to draft journal entries recording the above transactions in the books of Brass Tacks Ltd showing the apportionment of the purchase consideration between the liquidators and indicating the number of shares allotted to each.

SUGGESTED ANSWER

As with the previous example it is suggested that an account be opened for *each* asset and liability appearing in the Balance Sheets of *both* companies. A separate sheet of paper should be used for the ledger of Brass Ltd and a separate one for Tacks Ltd.

This course is recommended to students as being sound practice more especially in the early stages of their study of this aspect of accounting since it enables them to see *exactly* what they are doing. As the student becomes more experienced in dealing with problems of this type it will be less important to open all accounts. If, however, as a result of taking short-cuts, a student finds that he fails to solve a problem he should revert to the recommended method. It takes a little longer, of course, but he should, by its use, find the correct solution with little difficulty.

In this example, for reasons of space, some of the accounts will not be shown, but those which have any important bearing on the solution will be set out in detail.

Stage 1

Open a Sundry Shareholders Account and dispose of the Share Capital, Reserves and Profit and Loss Account balances of Brass Ltd.

Sundry Shareholders of Brass Ltd Account

Balance c/d	£145,450	Share Capital A/c	£125,000
		Reserve A/c	15,000
		Profit and Loss A/c	5,450
	£145,450		£145,450
		Balance b/d	£145,450

Stage 2

The terms of this problem require slightly different treatment from that of the previous example and so we will proceed at once to the construction of the Realisation Account of Brass Ltd. The accounts for Land and Buildings, Stock and Debtors will be omitted as the transfers are straightforward. Plant and Cash Accounts are shown since these must be broken down.

Realisation Account (Brass Ltd)

Land and Buildings A/c	£18,800	Balance c/d	£124,150
Stock A/c	53,750		
Debtors A/c	18,000		
Plant A/c	22,500		
Cash A/c	11,100		
	£124,150		£124,150
Balance b/d	£124,150		

Plant Account

Balance b/d	£25,000	Realisation A/c Sundry Shareholders A/c (10% depreci- ation written off)	**£22,500** 2,500
	£25,000		£25,000

Cash Account

Balance b/d	£11,600	Liquidator's A/c Realisation A/c	**£500** 11,100
	£11,600		£11,600

Sundry Shareholders Account

Plant A/c Balance c/d	£2,500 142,950	Balance b/d (*Stage 1*)	£145,450
	£145,450		£145,450
		Balance b/d	£142,950

Liquidator's Account (Brass Ltd)

Cash A/c	**£500**		

Stage 3

We continue with the build-up of the Realisation Account dealing with the entries on the credit side.

Realisation Account (Brass Ltd)

Balance b/d (per *Stage 2*)	£124,150	Sundry Shareholders A/c (Provision for doubtful debts) Creditors A/c Balance c/d	**£450** **12,400** 111,300
	£124,150		£124,150
Balance b/d	£111,300		

Sundry Shareholders Account

Realisation A/c		Balance b/d (per	
(Provision)	**£450**	*Stage 2*)	£142,950
Balance c/d	142,500		
	£142,950		£142,950
		Balance b/d	£142,500

Creditors Account

Realisation A/c	**£12,400**	Balance b/d	**£12,400**

This completes the Realisation Account of Brass Ltd *with the exception of dealing with goodwill*. The question is framed in such a way that we must wait until we have produced the Realisation Account of Tacks Ltd before we can deal with the Goodwill Accounts of both companies.

Stage 4

In this stage we turn to the affairs of Tacks Ltd. The method will be exactly the same as that used for Brass Ltd and so we will only show the Realisation Account of Tacks Ltd at this point.

Realisation Account (Tacks Ltd)

Land and Buildings		Sundry Shareholders	
A/c	£21,500	A/c (Provision for	
Plant A/c (£32,000		doubtful debts)	**£400**
less 15%)	27,200	Creditors A/c	7,300
Stock A/c	36,300	Balance c/d	101,500
Debtors A/c	16,000		
Cash A/c (£8,700			
less £500)	8,200		
	£109,200		£109,200
Balance b/d	£101,500		

Stage 5

The question states that no amount for goodwill is to be brought into the books of the new company, Brass Tacks Ltd, but that for the purpose of apportioning the purchase consideration goodwill, as shown in the respective Balance Sheets, should be taken into account.

Realisation A/c	Brass Ltd	£111,300
Realisation A/c	Tacks Ltd	101,500
		212,800
Goodwill A/c	Brass Ltd	30,700
Goodwill A/c	Tacks Ltd	5,000
		£248,500

From the above table we can see that the *total of the purchase consideration*, *i.e.* the *net worth* of the *two companies combined*, amounts to £212,800.

Therefore, to obtain the apportionment we must make our calculations in the following manner:

	Brass Ltd	*Tacks Ltd*	*Total*
Net assets	£111,300	£101,500	£212,800
Goodwill	30,700	5,000	35,700
	£142,000	£106,500	£248,500

$$\text{Brass Ltd} \quad \frac{£142,000}{£248,500} \times 212,800 = £121,600$$

$$\text{Tacks Ltd} \quad \frac{£106,500}{£248,500} \times 212,800 = £91,200$$

Total purchase consideration £212,800

The shares are of 5s. denomination.

	5s. *shares*
Brass Ltd will be allotted 121,600 $\times$ 4	486,400
Tacks Ltd will be allotted 91,200 $\times$ 4	364,800
Total number of shares allotted	851,200

Stage 6

In this final stage we show the journal entries in the books of Brass Tacks Ltd.

		Dr.	Cr.
Sundries	Dr.		
Land and Buildings A/c		£18,800	
Plant A/c		22,500	
Stock A/c		53,750	
Debtors A/c		18,000	
Cash A/c		11,100	
To Sundries			
Provision for Doubtful Debts A/c			£450
Creditors A/c			12,400
Liquidator of Brass Ltd A/c			111,300
		£124,150	£124,150

Assets and liabilities taken over from the liquidator of Brass Ltd.

		Dr.	Cr.
Sundries	Dr.		
Land and Buildings A/c		£21,500	
Plant A/c		27,200	
Stock A/c		36,300	
Debtors A/c		16,000	
Cash A/c		8,200	
To Sundries			
Provision for Doubtful Debts A/c			£400
Creditors A/c			7,300
Liquidator of Tacks Ltd A/c			101,500
		£109,200	£109,200

Assets and liabilities taken over from Tacks Ltd.

		Dr.	Cr.
Liquidator of Brass Ltd A/c	Dr.	£121,600	
Liquidator of Tacks Ltd A/c		91,200	
To Ordinary Share Capital A/c			£212,800

Allotment of 851,200 ordinary shares of 5s. each per agreement.

PROGRESS TEST 10

1. What are the usual ways in which an amalgamation of companies may be effected? (1)
2. In what way does absorption differ from amalgamation? (3)

CHAPTER XI

SOURCES AND APPLICATIONS OF FUNDS

WORKING CAPITAL

1. The meaning of Working Capital. Looking back to our earliest studies in book-keeping we recall that we learned that every business requires *Capital* (in the form of *money*) to enable it to be set up and to be put in a *position to commence to trade*. This *capital, i.e. money*, is used to acquire a number of necessities. For example, every business requires premises, a certain amount of equipment such as fittings and furniture, and most important of all, a sufficient stock of goods to enable it to offer an attractive choice to its customers. Finally, it will need to have sufficient *cash* left over for the purpose of meeting its *immediate running expenses*.

The term "working capital" is used normally to indicate *the amount of surplus funds* a business has *available at any time* to enable it to meet demands requiring immediate settlement. Each week, for example, most businesses will need money for the *payment of wages*. Once in each month the firm will have to pay those creditors who have supplied it with goods on credit. Sufficient *money*, therefore, *must* be forthcoming for the settlement of liabilities such as these.

2. Current assets. The expression "current assets" is used to refer to those assets which are *continually on the move*. They are sometimes called the *circulating capital* of a business because they are constantly in motion.

Current assets fall under the following headings:

(*a*) Stock in trade.
(*b*) Debtors.
(*c*) Payments in advance (a form of debtors).
(*d*) Cash at bank.
(*e*) Cash in hand.

It requires very little thought to appreciate that the above assets are, by their very nature, subject to continual movement.

3. Current liabilities. The term "current liabilities" is given to those creditors which a business must satisfy *by a payment in cash in the very near future.*

(*a*) Trade creditors (for goods supplied).
(*b*) Accrued expenses (for services rendered).
(*c*) Income tax (payable within the current year).
(*d*) Dividends declared (payable almost immediately).
(*e*) Bank overdraft.

4. To calculate working capital. In order to ascertain the amount of working capital possessed by a firm we *subtract* the *total of the current liabilities* from the *total of the current assets.* The *difference* between these two totals is the *working capital.*

EXAMPLE 35

The Balance Sheet of XY Ltd as at 31st December 1964 was as under:

Share Capital		£20,000	*Fixed Assets*		
			Freehold Premises		£8,000
Profit and Loss			Fixtures and Fittings		1,280
Account		4,000			
		24,000			9,280
Current Liabilities			*Current Assets*		
Trade Creditors	£3,800		Stock	£5,600	
Accrued Expenses	450		Debtors	8,420	
		4,250	Prepayments	75	
			Cash at Bank	4,875	
					18,970
		£28,250			£28,250

Calculation of the working capital at 31st December 1964	
Current Assets	£18,970
Less: Current Liabilities	4,250
Working Capital	£14,720

5. Increasing the working capital. The working capital of a business may be *increased* in the following ways:

(*a*) By the *introduction* of more *cash* capital by the proprietor.
(*b*) By somebody *outside* the business *lending money* to it, *e.g.* in the case of a limited company by an issue of debentures.
(*c*) By the business making a *profit on its trading.*

(d) By the business *selling* some of its *fixed assets* thereby *increasing its cash resources*.

6. Decreasing the working capital. A *decrease* in the working capital will come about as a result of:

(a) *The owner* of a business *withdrawing cash* for his own use.
(b) *The declaration* of a dividend which has the effect of increasing current liabilities, *i.e.* by moving some of the Net Profit from the area of *fixed liabilities* into the area of *current liabilities*.
(c) *Making a loss on trading.*
(d) *The purchase of a fixed asset for cash, i.e.* by replacing *cash*, which is a *current asset* with a *fixed asset* such as machinery.

STATEMENTS OF SOURCES AND APPLICATIONS

7. Problems in examinations. Problems relating to working capital appear regularly in the professional examinations. They are generally referred to as "sources and application of funds" problems. The question usually requires the student to produce a reconciliation:

(a) Showing by how much the working capital has increased or decreased during a given period (usually of one year); and
(b) Preparing a statement setting out the *sources* from which *fresh* working capital *entered* the business *during* the period, and in what manner this was applied, *i.e. on what items it was spent*.

EXAMPLE 36

During the first week of January 1965, XY Ltd (*see* Example 35) made an issue of 10,000 £1 shares for cash and purchased machinery at a cost of £18,500. It sold part of its premises which had cost £1750 for the sum of £4250. During this week it was closed for trading and so the other assets and liabilities remained as they appeared in the Balance Sheet at 31st December 1964.

The above transactions would be recorded as follows:

Bank Account

1965			1965		
Jan. 1			Jan. 7		
Balance b/d		£4,875	Machinery A/c		£18,500
Jan. 7			Jan. 7		
Share Capital A/c		10,000	Balance c/d		625
Freehold Premises					
A/c		4,250			
		£19,125			£19,125
Jan. 7					
Balance b/d		£625			

Share Capital Account

			1965		
			Jan. 1		
			Balance b/d		£20,000
			Jan. 7		
			Bank		10,000
					£30,000

Freehold Premises Account

1965			1965		
Jan. 1			Jan. 7.		
Balance b/d		£8,000	Bank A/c		£4,250
Jan. 7			Balance c/d		6,250
Transfer to Capital					
Reserve (Profit					
on sale)		2,500			
		£10,500			£10,500
Balance b/d		£6,250			

Capital Reserve

			1965		
			Jan. 7		
			Freehold Premises		
			A/c		£2,500

Machinery Account

1965 Jan. 7 Bank Account	£18,500	

The Balance Sheet as at 7th January 1965 would then show the following position:

Fixed Liabilities		*Fixed Assets*		
Share Capital	£30,000	Freehold Premises		6,250
Capital Reserve	2,500	Machinery		18,500
Profit and Loss A/c	4,000	Fixtures and fittings		1,280
	36,500			26,030
Current Liabilities		*Current Assets*		
Trade		Stock	£5,600	
creditors £3,800		Debtors	8,420	
Accrued		Prepay-		
expenses 450		ments	75	
	4,250	Cash at		
		Bank	625	
				14,720
	£40,750			£40,750

Calculation of the working capital at 7th January 1965:

Current Assets	£14,720	
Less: Current Liabilities	4,250	
Working capital	£10,470	
Working capital at 31st December 1964	14,720	per Example 35
Working capital at 7th January 1965	10,470	per Example 36
Decrease	£4,250	

The working capital at 31st December 1964 was *increased* in the following ways:

Cash received on the *issue of shares*	£10,000
Cash received from the *sale of property*	4,250
	14,250
To this we add the working capital at 31st December 1964	14,720
	28,970
This total was *decreased* by the cash spent on the purchase of machinery	18,500
Working Capital at 7th January 1965	£10,470

8. The most general source of working capital. Although *working capital* may be introduced into a business by means of loans, fresh capital or even the sale of fixed assets, the most usual way for the working capital to be increased is by the business *making a profit on its trading.*

The truth of this statement can be verified very easily by means of a simple example.

EXAMPLE 37

A company, M Ltd, was formed with a share capital of £1000. Shares were of £1 each and all were fully paid up. Fixtures costing £100 were purchased before trading started. The Balance Sheet would have appeared as follows:

BALANCE SHEET *1st January*

Issued Share Capital	£1,000	Fixtures	100
		Bank	900
	£1,000		£1,000

The transactions for the first year of trading were as follows:

Cash purchases	£12,000
Cash sales	£15,000
Expenses (all paid for in cash)	£1,400

All takings were banked and all payments were made by cheque. There was no stock on hand at the end of the year.

CASH BOOK

Bank Account

Share Capital A/c	£1,000	Fixtures A/c	£100
Sales A/c	15,000	Purchase A/c	12,000
		Expenses A/c	1,400
		Balance	2,500
	£16,000		£16,000

Trading and Profit and Loss Account

Purchases	£12,000	Sales	£15,000
Gross Profit	3,000		
	£15,000		£15,000
Expenses	£1,400	Gross Profit	£3,000
Net Profit	1,600		
	£3,000		£3,000

BALANCE SHEET *31st December*

Issued Share Capital	£1,000	Fixtures	£100
Profit and Loss A/c	1,600	Bank	2,500
	£2,600		£2,600

After the purchase of the fixtures for £100 there was left the sum of £900 as *working capital* at the start.

All of the *profit* was *realised*, *i.e.* all transactions were on a *cash* basis, and so the net profit of £1600 can be seen to have been received by the company in *cash*. To the balance of £900 cash at bank on 1st January there has been *added* during the year the sum of £1600, *the profit realised in cash*, which gives a closing balance of £2500 cash at bank on 31st December. Thus the working capital amounts to £2500, since there are no current liabilities and the only current asset is the cash at bank. Thus the difference between the opening and closing working capital (£900–£2500) is £1600, which of course corresponds to the exact amount of *net profit* made during the year.

If the company had conducted its operations on a credit basis instead of for cash the same result would apply, since instead of collecting cash from the customers for goods sold a number of debtors would appear on the books. *Debtors* are, of course, *current* assets in the same way as is *cash*. Suppose, then, purely for the sake of illustrating the point, that all the sales in Example 35 had been on credit and that no cash had been received, the net profit would have been exactly the same, *i.e* £1600. If we assume that all the transactions, both buying and selling, were on credit the Balance Sheet would appear as under:

BALANCE SHEET 31st December

Issued Share Capital		£1,000	*Fixed Assets*		
Profit and Loss A/c		1,600	Fixtures		£100
Current Liabilities			*Current Assets*		
Creditors			Debtors	£15,000	
for			Bank	900	
goods	£12,000				15,900
Accrued Ex-					
penses	1,400				
		13,400			
		£16,000			£16,000

Subtracting *current liabilities* of £13,400 from *current assets* of £15,900 we are left with £2500 as the *working capitcl*, as before.

9. Measuring the increase or decrease of working capital over a period.
In order to measure the increase or decrease in the amount of working capital over a period of time it is necessary to have *two* Balance Sheets, *i.e.* one which sets out the position at the *start* of the period and the other which shows the state of affairs at the *end*. We calculate the amount of working capital as shown by each of the two Balance Sheets and compare one amount with the other. It thus at once becomes evident whether the working capital has increased or decreased by the end of the period.

10. Building up a "Sources and Applications" statement.
This can be quite a difficult problem and it will be necessary to explain in some detail how certain things must be dealt with in order to reconcile matters.

The following "pro forma" is suggested *as a basis:*

Working capital at the *start* of the period	£	—
Add: Sources from which *additional* working capital came, *i.e.* in detail		—
		—
Deduct: Items on which the additions set out above were *spent*, again in detail		—
Working capital at the *end* of the period	£	—

Before we look at the method of dealing with points on examination questions there is an important group of items which is, in practice, debited in the Profit and Loss Account but which needs to be adjusted in any reconciliation of the working capital.

11. The Revenue Account. It must, first of all, be clearly understood that the use of the term *Profit and Loss Account* in this section covers also the Manufacturing Account and the Trading Account. The term *Revenue Account* is frequently used as a convenient way of covering the three accounts referred to above without specifically mentioning one or other of them. This is particularly convenient when dealing with the charge for depreciation which could legitimately be debited in any one of them according to the terms of the question.

12. Special items debited. Certain items may be debited in the Profit and Loss Account of a business and these items require to be understood very clearly in relation to "Sources and Applications" statements. The most usual of these is depreciation.

(*a*) *Depreciation.* Where a business owns fixed assets it is the normal practice to write these off over their lifetime *by means of a depreciation charge* which is *debited in the Profit and Loss Account.* The corresponding credit will be made in the asset account concerned (or in a Depreciation Provision Account).

The important point to be appreciated here is that a double entry of this kind *does not involve any payment, i.e.* there is *no reduction* in the amount of cash held by the business. *It is simply a book-keeping entry.* All that happens is that the book value of a *fixed* asset is arbitrarily reduced and profits are reduced by the same amount. It follows, therefore, that the *working capital is not reduced* because *depreciation only affects fixed assets and not current assets.* Working capital is concerned only with *current* assets and *current* liabilities.

(*b*) *Preliminary expenses.* These are another example of an item which may be written off.

The entries involved would be a debit in the Profit and Loss Appropriation Account and a credit in the Preliminary Expenses Account.

Again, *current assets are not involved.* Therefore working capital is *unaffected.*

(*c*) *Goodwill.* A further example of these special items is where goodwill is being written off. Profit and Loss Appropriation Account is debited and Goodwill Account credited.

Yet again *current assets are not affected.* Goodwill is a *fixed* asset. The transaction, therefore, has *no* bearing on working capital.

The above examples are not to be regarded as being an exhaustive list of these special items. There are others such as the writing off of discount on debentures or discount on an issue of shares. It is, therefore, very important that the items debited in the Profit and Loss Account and Appropriation Account be carefully studied in order to ensure that any of these special items which may be included are properly dealt with in compiling the statement of sources and applications.

All of the *special items mentioned above must be added to the profit.* The *reason* for this is that:

(*a*) When fixed assets are purchased these are *paid for in money.*
(*b*) When a company is formed the preliminary expenses are *paid for in money.*
(*c*) When goodwill is acquired it has to be *paid for in money.*

13. Reduction in profits. With sources and applications problems we are always given an opening and a closing Balance Sheet. The opening Balance Sheet will contain a number of fixed assets such as those mentioned above. We may, therefore, say that these items *must* have been purchased in *earlier* years. That is to say, the *payment* of *money* was involved in each case *at the time the event happened.* When, therefore, these payments were made *the effect was felt on the working capital at those times.*

These payments were all regarded as items of capital expenditure at the time that each of these expenses was incurred, and, of course, they were *not* charged against the profits of the year in which they were made. Now that depreciation is being written off the amount so written off *is* charged against the profits of these *later* years. These profits, are, therefore, *reduced* accordingly.

14. Charging revenue expenditure. This reduction in the profits, however, does *not* have the same effect on the working capital as does the charging of *revenue* expenditure against it.

The charging of *revenue* expenditure means that *money* has already been *spent* during the year (or will be in the immediate future in paying off the accrued expenses). The effect of this spending is to *reduce* working capital.

15. Capital expenditure. The effect of *spending* money on items of *capital* expenditure means that working capital is *also* reduced.

Thus we see that *spending* is the operative word.

With regard to capital expenditure, then, the *effect* on the working capital is felt *immediately*, and what is more, *it is felt in full*. It therefore follows that if the *full effect has been felt* at the time the money was spent *it can have no further bearing on matters again*. Consequently, any debits for *depreciation* can have *no effect* on working capital.

Exactly the same principles apply to those other items of capital expenditure mentioned above as examples.

16. Reconciliations. As a result, when we are attempting to reconcile the sources and applications of working capital between two dates any debit for depreciation, etc. (*i.e.* charged against the profit), must be regarded as a *book-keeping* entry only and *not one which involves the movement of cash*. We must, therefore, *add back* such depreciation, etc., to the figure of *profit* when making our reconciliation.

(C.C.A.)

The following were the Balance Sheets of Ono Ltd as at 31st December 1964 and 31st December 1965:

	1964	1965
Ordinary Shares	£50,000	£50,000
Redeemable Preference Shares	20,000	15,000
Capital Redemption Reserve Fund	—	5,000
Profit and Loss Account	40,000	45,000
	£110,000	£115,000
Fixed Assets:		
Cost	120,000	97,000
Depreciation	40,000	24,000
	80,000	73,000
Net Current Assets	30,000	42,000
	£110,000	£115,000

During the year ended 31st December 1965:

(a) *Fixed assets were sold* for £10,000. (Cost £30,000. Depreciation accumulated £24,000.) The surplus has been credited to Profit and Loss Account.

(b) *The redeemable preference shares redeemed* were repaid to shareholders at a premium of 10% of par value.

Prepare a statement showing: (*i*) the sources, and (*ii*) the application of the working capital during 1965.

SUGGESTED ANSWER

The first thing to be done is to ascertain by how much the working capital has *increased or decreased*. In this particular problem the matter is very simple.

Net Current Assets at end	£42,000
Less: Net Current Assets at start	30,000
Increase in working capital	£12,000

Stage 1

In order to clarify the position regarding the fixed assets and depreciation we must *open* accounts for these items. By doing this we make it possible to draw certain conclusions.

Fixed Assets Account

1964		
Dec. 31		
Balance b/d	£120,000	

Depreciation Provision Account

	1964	
	Dec. 31	
	Balance b/d	£40,000

During the year 1965 some of the fixed assets which had originally cost £30,000 were sold for £10,000. Depreciation had been provided amounting to £24,000 on those assets which were sold.

The simplest way of dealing with this part of the question is to open a Fixed Assets Disposal Account. We therefore make the following entries:

Fixed Assets Account

1964		1965	
Dec. 31		Dec. 31	
Balance b/d	£120,000	Transfer to Fixed Assets Disposal A/c	**£30,000**

Depreciation Provision Account

1965		1964	
Dec. 31		Dec. 31	
Transfer to Fixed Assets Disposal A/c	**£24,000**	Balance b/d	£40,000

Fixed Assets Disposal Account

1965		1965	
Dec. 31		Dec. 31	
Fixed Assets A/c	**£30,000**	Depreciation Provision A/c	**£24,000**
Profit and Loss A/c	4,000	Bank A/c	10,000
	£34,000		**£34,000**

G

COMPANY ACCOUNTS

Profit and Loss Account

		1965
		Dec. 31
		  Fixed Assets
		    Disposal A/c
			£4,000

Bank Account

1965
Dec. 31
  Fixed Assets
    Disposal A/c
	£10,000		

Stage 2

We now complete the Fixed Assets Account, carrying down the balance of £97,000 shown in the Balance Sheet.

Fixed Assets Account

1964 Dec. 31		1965 Dec. 31	
Balance b/d	£120,000	Fixed Assets	
Bank A/c	7,000	Disposal A/c	£30,000
		Balance c/d	97,000
	£127,000		£127,000
Balance b/d	£97,000		

There is an obvious gap on the debit side which could only have been accounted for by the *purchase* of additional fixed assets amounting to £7000.

Bank Account

		1965 Dec. 31 Fixed Assets A/c	£7,000

Stage 3

The *closing* balance on the Depreciation Provision Account according to the Balance Sheet amounts to £24,000:

Depreciation Provision Account

1965			1964	
Dec. 31			Dec. 31	
Fixed Assets			Balance b/d	£40,000
Disposal A/c		£24,000	Profit and Loss A/c	**8,000**
Balance c/d		24,000		
		£48,000		£48,000
			Balance b/d	£24,000

Once again, there is an obvious deficiency in the above account. This time the shortage is on the credit side amounting to £8000. This must be inserted and debited to the Profit and Loss Account.

Profit and Loss Account

Depreciation Provision **£8,000**	

Stage 4

Turning now to the second note in the question we see that those preference shares which were redeemed during the year were repaid at a premium of 10% of their par value. The Balance Sheet tells us that £5000 of these shares were redeemed. 10% of £5000 is £500 which means that a sum of £5500 was paid out on the redemption.

Redeemable Preference Shares Account

1965		1964	
Dec. 31		Dec. 31	
Special Payment A/c	**£5,500**	Balance b/d	£20,000
Balance c/d	15,000	Premium on Re-	
		demption A/c	**500**
	£20,500		£20,500

Bank Account

		1965	
		Dec. 31	
		Fixed Assets A/c	£7,000
		Redeemable Pre-	
		ference Shares A/c	**5,500**

Premium on Redemption Account

1965
Dec. 31
  Redeemable Pre-
    ference Shares A/c **£500**	

Stage 5

As there is no sign of any premium on redemption in the Balance Sheet we must conclude that it has been written off to the Profit and Loss Account. *This, of course, is a mere book-keeping entry* and, as such, will have to be treated in our reconciliation in the same way as depreciation.

In exactly the same way we will debit the Profit and Loss Account with the £5000 transferred to the credit of Capital Redemption Reserve Fund. Again, this is *another book-keeping entry*, and nothing more.

The final balance on the Profit and Loss Account, £45,000, shows an increase of £5000 over the balance at the end of the previous year. That is to say, *after all of the above matters had been dealt with* there remained a balance of £5000 on the year's transaction and this was added to the £40,000 credit balance which had been brought forward.

We can now summarise those Profit and Loss Account items which have a bearing on our reconciliation, as follows:

Profit and Loss Account

Depreciation Provision	£8,000	Profit on sale of fixed	
Premium on Redemption	500	assets	**£4,000**
Capital Redemption			
Reserve Fund	5,000		
Balance of profit	5,000		

NOTE: The profit on sale of fixed assets is another mere book-keeping entry, but working in the opposite direction to depreciation, and must therefore be brought into our reconciliation statement.

We have now assembled all the relevant information and can proceed to prepare our statement of sources and applications of working capital.

Working capital at 31st December 1964		£30,000
Add: Net Profit	£5,000	
Depreciation	8,000	
Premium on Redemption	500	
Capital Redemption Reserve Fund	5,000	
Special Receipt: Cash from sale of fixed assets	10,000	
	———	28,500
		———
		58,500
Less: Special Payments: Purchase of fixed assets	7,000	
Redemption of Preference Shares	5,500	
Profit on sale of fixed assets	4,000	
	———	16,500
		———
		£42,000

An alternative presentation in summary could take the following form:

Additions to working capital	£28,500
Less: Deductions	16,500
	———
Increase in working capital	£12,000

SPECIMEN QUESTION 2

(C.A.)

The following are the summarised trial balances of Celerity Ltd as on 31st December 1966 and 1967:

	31st December 1966		31st December 1967	
Issued share capital		£200,000		£200,000
Capital reserve				47,600
5½% debentures				50,000
Debenture discount			£1,000	
Freeholds: at cost	£112,500			
at valuation			151,000	
Plant and machinery at cost	248,000		296,000	
Provision for depreciation of plant and machinery		114,200		125,350
Current assets	186,150		178,950	
Current liabilities		109,250		82,550
Balance on Profit and Loss Account from previous year		92,200		122,000
Net profit for the year		29,800		36,850
Dividend paid for the year 1966			20,000	
Provision for doubtful debts		1,200		1,350
Trade investment, at cost			18,750	
	———	———	———	———
	£546,650	£546,650	£665,700	£665,700

(1) The capital reserve on 31st December 1967 represented (*i*) the profit on the sale, for cash, of one freehold property, and (*ii*) the surplus arising on the revaluation of the remaining freeholds.

(2) During the year 1967 machinery costing £24,000 (accumulated depreciation £15,500) was sold for £10,300.

(3) On 1st July 1967, £50,000 debentures were issued for cash, at a discount of £1500.

(4) The net profit for the year 1967 is arrived at after crediting profit on the sale of machinery and after charging debenture interest and writing off debenture discount £500.

You are required to prepare statements showing:

(*a*) the net increase in working capital during the year 1967, and

(*b*) the sources and application of working capital during that year.

SUGGESTED ANSWER

CELERITY LTD

Statement showing the Net Increase in Working Capital during the year ended 31st December 1967

	31st December 1966	31st December 1967
Current assets	£186,150	£178,950
Less Bad debt provision	1,200	1,350
	184,950	177,600
Less Current liabilities	109,250	82,550
Working capital	£75,700	£95,050

Summary

Working capital at 31st December 1967	£95,050
Less working capital at 31st December 1966	75,700
Net *increase* in working capital	£19,350

Having calculated the working capital at the beginning and end of the period we will next consider the four footnotes to the question before preparing the statement of sources and applications.

(1) tells us *how* the *capital reserve* of £47,600, on 31st December 1967 was calculated. We will, therefore, debit the Freeholds Account and credit the Capital Reserve with this sum.

Freeholds Account

Balance b/d	£112,500	?	?
Capital Reserve:		Balance c/d	£151,000
profit on revaluation	47,600		
	£160,100		£

NOTE: The *difference* required to balance the two sides amounts to £9100 and the cash received from the sale is clearly *the source* of this entry. We must, therefore, include this sum of money as a *special receipt* in our statement of sources and applications.

(2) tells us that part of the plant which had cost £24,000 was sold for £10,300. This must be regarded as a *receipt of a special nature* as it has the effect of transferring an amount from the area of *fixed* assets to the area of *current* assets, thus *directly affecting the working capital*.

The best way of dealing with this part of the problem is, first of all, to transfer the *cost* price of the plant which was sold to a Plant Disposal Account. Then, turning to the Provision for Depreciation Account we transfer the *accumulated depreciation in respect of this part of the plant* to the *credit* side of the Plant Disposal Account which would then appear as follows:

Plant Disposal Account

Plant and Machinery		Provision for Depreci-	
A/c	£24,000	ation A/c	£15,500
?	?	Cash A/c	10,300
	£		£25,800

NOTE: The *difference* between the two sides can be seen to be £1800 and this, of course, represents the *profit* on the sale, which will be transferred to the credit side of the Profit and Loss Account, thereby swelling the net profit. Like depreciation, but working in the opposite direction, this is simply a book-keeping entry and, as such, will have to be *deducted* from the net profit when compiling the statement of sources and applications.

The Provision for Depreciation Account would have appeared in the books as shown below:

Provision for Depreciation Account

Plant Disposal A/c	£15,500	Balance b/d (1st Jan. 1967)	£114,200
Balance c/d	125,350	Profit and Loss A/c	?
	£140,850		£140,850
		Balance b/d	£125,350

The amount required to balance the two sides is £26,650, and this figure must have been *debited* to Profit and Loss Account, thus reducing the net profit. This sum will, therefore, have to be brought into the statement of sources and applications as *an addition* to the profit.

(3) contains information on two points:
(*a*) the *receipt* of money, £48,500, when debentures were issued; and
(*b*) a *book-keeping* entry of £1500.

$5\frac{1}{2}\%$ *Debentures Account*

	Cash A/c	£48,500
	Debenture Discount A/c	1,500
		£50,000

Debenture Discount Account

$5\frac{1}{2}\%$ Debenture A/c	£1,500	

We can see from the Trial Balance that the final balance on the Debenture Discount Account amounts to £1000 only, *i.e.* £500 has been written off, (and (4) confirms this).

(4) states that the profit for the year 1967, £36,850, has been arrived at:

(*a*) *after* charging debenture interest;
(*b*) *after* the profit on the sale of machinery has been credited; and
(*c*) *after* writing £500 off the debenture discount.

Therefore, the net profit on trading *before* these items were included would have been:

Net Profit per Trial Balance	£36,850
Less Profit on sale of machinery	1,800
	35,050
Add Debenture Discount written off	500
Adjusted Net Profit	£35,550

NOTE: Debenture Interest is a proper *charge involving the movement of cash* and is, therefore, ignored in the above calculation.

STATEMENT OF SOURCES AND APPLICATIONS OF WORKING CAPITAL

Working Capital at 1st January 1967		£75,700
Add Net Profit for the year	£35,550	
Depreciation	26,650	
Special receipts from:		
Sale of Freehold	9,100	
Sale of Plant	10,300	
Issue of Debentures	48,500	
		130,100
		205,800
Less Special Payments for:		
Dividend	£20,000	
Plant	72,000	
Trade Investments	18,750	
		110,750
Working Capital at 31st December 1967		£95,050

PROGRESS TEST 11

1. Define "working capital." **(1)**

2. How would you ascertain the working capital of a business? **(2–4)**

3. What are the principal ways in which working capital may be (*a*) increased; (*b*) decreased? **(5, 6)**

4. What is the most usual source from which a business obtains working capital? **(8)**

5. Set out a *pro-forma* statement for reconciling the working capital at the beginning of a trading period with that at the end. **(10)**

6. In what way is depreciation of special importance in dealing with "sources and application" problems? **(12)**

7. "Revenue expenditure reduces working capital whereas the charging of depreciation does not." Explain. **(13, 14)**

8. What effect does the purchase of fixed assets have upon the working capital of a business? **(15)**

CHAPTER XII

CONSOLIDATED BALANCE SHEETS: BASIC PRINCIPLES

THE CONTROLLING INTEREST

1. Shareholders' "rights." The capital of a limited company consists of a certain number of shares. These are of *two* main types: *ordinary* shares, and *preference* shares. Certain *rights* attach to each class of shares.

(*a*) *Ordinary shares* are sometimes referred to as the *risk* capital of a company. By this term we mean that *there are no safeguards* for the person who has invested money in such shares. So far as these shareholders are concerned it is "all or nothing." That is to say, in good years their reward will be great while in poor years they will receive little or nothing in the form of dividends. In addition, should the company be forced to go into liquidation the *ordinary shareholders will be the very last people to receive anything* on account of the money which they have invested in the company. In the great majority of liquidations they never receive a penny.

(*b*) *Preference* shares have the *right to priority of dividends*, and, very often, to priority of repayment of the capital in the event of liquidation. Even if the profits are not large in any particular year there may be sufficient to pay the preference shareholders their dividend. If, for any reason, no dividend is paid on the preference shares in any year the "missed" dividend *accumulates* (until such time as there are sufficient profits for a payment to be made) and the *arrears* of dividend *must* be paid to the preference shareholders before *any* dividend can be paid to the ordinary shareholders.

From this it can be seen that the term *risk capital* is a fair description of the ordinary shares.

2. Voting rights. Because of the risks taken by investing in *ordinary* shares a compensation is granted to the ordinary shareholders. This compensation takes the form of the *right to vote*. Preference shares do *not, as a rule*, have any voting rights.

Decisions of importance are taken by companies at their annual general meetings at which *all* shareholders are entitled to be present. Decisions are reached by means of votes; usually *one vote* to the holder of *one ordinary share*. By this *means* the *ordinary shareholders maintain control* of the decisions of the company while the preference shareholders have no say at all.

3. Controlling interest. From this it follows that if one company owns *more than fifty per cent of the ordinary shares of another company* it is in a position to *control the activities of that other company.* In such cases the company which has control is called a *holding* company and the one which is thus controlled is called a *subsidiary* company.

At the end of each financial year the *group, i.e.* the holding company and its subsidiary companies, will produce a Balance Sheet which is, in fact, an *amalgamation* of all the separate Balance Sheets of the companies which form the group.

This Balance Sheet is called a *Consolidated Balance Sheet.*

CONSOLIDATIONS: AT THE TIME OF MERGER

4. The Consolidated Balance Sheet. In this basic example the holding company is White Ltd. White Ltd has purchased (from the *individual shareholders* of Reddish Ltd) all of the shares in that company at a cost of £4000. White Ltd is called the holding company because it "holds" or owns the share capital of Reddish Ltd.

WHITE LTD BALANCE SHEET

Share Capital	£10,000	Plant	£3,000
Creditors	2,000	Stock	4,500
		Bank	500
		Investment:	
		Shares in Reddish	
		Ltd at cost	4,000
	£12,000		**£12,000**

REDDISH LTD BALANCE SHEET

Share Capital	£4,000	Motor Van	£600
		Debtors	3,350
		Cash	50
	£4,000		**£4,000**

To produce a *Consolidated* Balance Sheet of the two companies is a very simple matter. All that is necessary is that the item "Investment: Shares in Reddish Ltd—£4000" be *removed* from the Balance Sheet of *White Ltd* and *replaced by the actual assets* which appear in the Balance Sheet of *Reddish Ltd*.

CONSOLIDATED BALANCE SHEET

of White Ltd and its subsidiary Reddish Ltd

Share Capital	£10,000	Plant	£3,000
Creditors	2,000	Stock	4,500
		Bank	500
		Motor Van	600
		Debtors	3,350
		Cash	50
	£12,000		£12,000

5. What "consolidating" means. In order to consolidate, *i.e. amalgamate*, the Balance Sheets of two or more companies, where one of those companies owns *more than fifty per cent* of the *ordinary* shares in *each* of the others we must:

(a) *Eliminate* from the Balance Sheet of the *holding* company the asset entitled: "*Investment in subsidiary company.*"
(b) *Replace* the eliminated item with:

    (i) the *total* of all the *assets* of the *subsidiary* company;
    (ii) the *total* of all the liabilities of the *subsidiary* company; and
    (iii) *the amount paid by the holding company* for *goodwill.*

It must be clearly understood that we do *not* replace merely the amount of the investment. In the *Consolidated* Balance Sheet *we actually enter* the following items:

(a) *all the individual assets of the subsidiary company;*
(b) *all of its liabilities, and*
(c) *the cost of any goodwill included in the purchase price.*

The *net difference* between these two *totals equals the amount of the cost of the investment* which has to be eliminated.

6. Procedure. Therefore, in order to draw up a Consolidated Balance Sheet we must take the following steps:

(a) *enter all the assets* shown in the Balance Sheet of the holding company *except "Investment in subsidiary company"*;
(b) *enter all the liabilities* appearing in the holding company's Balance Sheet;
(c) *add the entire total of* the subsidiary company's assets to those of the holding company (as in (a) above);
(d) *enter the price paid* by the holding company for *goodwill*; and
(e) *add the entire total* of the subsidiary company's liabilities to those of the holding company (as in (b) above).

The result will be a *Consolidated* Balance Sheet.

The following Example illustrates a Consolidated Balance Sheet made as at the date of acquisition.

EXAMPLE 38

Kent Ltd buys *all* the shares in Bucks Ltd on 1st January, 1965. The Balance Sheets of the two companies on this date, immediately *after* the purchase, were as follows:

KENT LTD—BALANCE SHEET AS AT 1ST JANUARY 1965

Share Capital	£100,000	Assets	£110,000
General Reserve	12,000	Investment in Bucks	
Profit and Loss A/c	8,000	Ltd 20,000 shares	
		at cost	25,000
	120,000		
Creditors	15,000		
	£135,000		£135,000

BUCKS LTD—BALANCE SHEET AS AT 1ST JANUARY 1965

Share Capital		Assets	£29,000
20,000 £1 shares	£20,000		
General Reserve	3,000		
Profit and Loss A/c	2,000		
	25,000		
Creditors	4,000		
	£29,000		£29,000

We will first construct a "skeleton" consolidated Balance Sheet and enter in it the assets of the *subsidiary* company, Bucks Ltd, and also its liabilities, *i.e.* the amount owing to *outside* creditors.

"SKELETON" CONSOLIDATED BALANCE SHEET

	£			£
Share Capital		Assets:		
General Reserve		Kent Ltd £		
Profit and Loss A/c		Bucks Ltd 29,000		
Creditors:				
Kent Ltd £				
Bucks Ltd 4,000				
	£			£

From the skeleton set out above we can readily see how both the assets and liabilities of Bucks Ltd will appear in the Consolidated Balance Sheet.

All that now remains to be done is to *add to the above figures*:

(*a*) *all* the assets of Kent Ltd *except* the item "Investment in Bucks Ltd £25,000";
(*b*) *all* the amounts owing to *outsiders* (*i.e.* the creditors) which appear in the *holding* company's Balance Sheet; and
(*c*) *the holding company's* Share Capital, General Reserve and Profit and Loss Account balance.

CONSOLIDATED BALANCE SHEET

			Assets:		
Share Capital		£100,000	Kent		
General Reserve		12,000	Ltd	£110,000	
Profit and Loss A/c		8,000	Bucks		
		120,000	Ltd	29,000	
					£139,000
Creditors:					
Kent					
Ltd	£15,000				
Bucks					
Ltd	4,000				
		19,000			
		£139,000			£139,000

7. Certain items are omitted when consolidating. If we compare the items which make up the *Consolidated* Balance Sheet with the individual items which appear in the Balance Sheets *of the separate companies* we can see that certain items have been omitted when consolidating. As has already been noted the item "Investment in subsidiary company, £25,000" which is shown as an asset in the Balance Sheet of the *holding* company does *not* appear in the consolidation. One further point to note about the items from the *holding* company's Balance Sheet is that *every other item does appear* in the Consolidated Balance Sheet.

If we now turn to the *subsidiary* company's Balance Sheet we find that *three* of the items which appear in it have been *omitted* from the Consolidated Balance Sheet. These are:

(a) Share Capital;
(b) General Reserve; and
(c) Profit and Loss Account.

The rule when preparing a Consolidated Balance Sheet *as at the time of the merger* is:

Never include that part of the Share Capital and *undistributed* profit (*i.e.* General Reserve and Profit and Loss Account) of the subsidiary which belongs to the holding company.

The *aide memoire SCRAP ATOM* may be of assistance here:

S: Share
C: Capital
R: Reserves
A: And
P: Profit and Loss Account

of the *subsidiary* company,

A: At
T: Time
O: Of
M: Merger

must *never* appear in the *Consolidated* Balance Sheet.

8. Goodwill. We all know that when a business is bought as a "going concern" an element called *goodwill* enters into the calculation of the purchase price.

Stated briefly, *goodwill* (or the *cost of acquisition*) is the difference between the *net worth* of the business (as shown by its Balance Sheet) and the *price paid*. As has already been mentioned earlier in this chapter the price paid for any *goodwill must appear as a separate item* in the Consolidated Balance Sheet **(5)**.

EXAMPLE 39

Hunts Ltd buys *all* the shares in Beds Ltd on 1st February 1965. The Balance Sheets of the two companies on that date, *i.e.* immediately after the purchase, are as follows:

HUNTS LTD—BALANCE SHEET AS AT 1ST FEBRUARY 1965

Share Capital	£60,000	Assets	£48,000
General Reserve	7,000	Investment in Beds	
Profit and Loss A/c	3,000	Ltd 15,000 shares at	
	————	cost	27,000
	70,000		
Creditors	5,000		
	————		————
	£75,000		£75,000

BEDS LTD—BALANCE SHEET AS AT 1ST FEBRUARY 1965

Share Capital 15,000		Assets	£30,000
£1 shares	£15,000		
General Reserve	8,000		
Profit and Loss A/c	1,000		
	————		
	24,000		
Creditors	6,000		
	————		————
	£30,000		£30,000

Stage 1

In this example the first thing which has to be done is to calculate the *cost of the goodwill*. In order to do this we must open an account called Cost of Control Account in which we will make the following entries:

Cost of Control Account

Amount *paid* for		*Nominal value* of the	
15,000 shares	£27,000	shares *acquired*	£15,000
		Undistributed profits acquired:	
		General Reserve	8,000
		Profit and Loss A/c	1,000
			————
			24,000
		Excess = **Goodwill** c/d	**3,000**
	————		————
	£27,000		£27,000
Goodwill b/d	**£3,000**		

Stage 2

"SKELETON" CONSOLIDATED BALANCE SHEET

Share Capital	£	*Goodwill* (*i.e.* cost of	
General Reserve		Control)	£3,000
Profit and Loss A/c		Assets:	
	———	Hunts Ltd £	
Creditors:		Beds Ltd 30,000	
Hunts Ltd £			———
Beds Ltd 6,000			
	———		
			———
	═══		═══

Once again we can see quite clearly *which* of the assets and liabilities of the *subsidiary* company are to be included in the Consolidated Balance Sheet. Note particularly that the "*cost of control*," *i.e.* the goodwill, has been included as an asset in the skeleton Consolidated Balance Sheet.

Stage 3

To complete the consolidation all that is now needed is to *add to* the details shown in the "skeleton" above:

(a) *all* the assets of Hunts Ltd *except* the item headed "Investment in Beds Ltd £27,000."

(b) *all* the liabilities owing to outsiders which appear in the Balance Sheet of Hunts Ltd.

(c) The Share Capital, General Reserve and Profit and Loss Account balance of Hunts Ltd.

CONSOLIDATED BALANCE SHEET OF HUNTS LTD AND BEDS LTD AS AT 1ST FEBRUARY 1965

Share Capital	£60,000	Goodwill		£3,000
General Reserve	7,000	Assets:		
Profit and Loss A/c	3,000	Hunts Ltd £48,000		
	———	Beds Ltd 30,000		
	70,000		———	78,000
Creditors:				
Hunts Ltd £5,000				
Beds Ltd 6,000				
	———			
	11,000			
	———			———
	£81,000			£81,000
	═══			═══

9. Minority interests. Up till now we have dealt only with those cases in which a company acquires *all* the ordinary shares in the subsidiary company. At this point we must examine the position where the holding company acquires the ownership of *less than* 100 *per cent* of the shares in the subsidiary.

Where these circumstances arise a new factor is introduced which is known as the *minority interest*. This term is used when referring to those shareholders of the subsidiary company whose *shares have not been acquired by the holding company* and who, therefore, remain *outside the group*.

In the Consolidated Balance Sheet the minority interest will be treated in much the same way as will the *outside creditors*. That is to say:

The proportion of *"scrap atom"* (*see* **7**) belonging to the minority interest (*i.e.* the shareholders outside the group) must *always* appear in the *Consolidated Balance Sheet*.

EXAMPLE 40

Yorks Ltd acquires 75,000 ordinary shares in Lancs Ltd on 1st March 1965. The Balance Sheets of the companies immediately *after* the merger were:

YORKS LTD—BALANCE SHEET AS AT 1ST MARCH 1965

Share Capital		Investment in Lancs	
50,000 £1 pre-		Ltd	
ference shares	£50,000	75,000 £1 ordinary	
200,000 £1		shares at cost	£90,000
ordinary shares	200,000		
General Reserve	15,000		
Profit and Loss A/c	2,000		
		Other Assets	190,000
	267,000		
Creditors	13,000		
	£280,000		£280,000

LANCS LTD—BALANCE SHEET AS AT 1ST MARCH 1965

Share Capital		Assets	£158,000
40,000 £1 pre-			
ference shares	40,000		
80,000 £1			
ordinary shares	80,000		
General Reserve	12,000		
Profit and Loss A/c	8,000		
	140,000		
Creditors	18,000		
	£158,000		£158,000

NOTE: The preference shares of Lancs Ltd have no voting rights and must, therefore, be treated as part of the minority interest, *i.e.* shares held *outside* the group.

Stage 1

The first step to be taken is to ascertain the cost of control. Proceeding as before we build up the following account:

Cost of Control Account

Amount **paid** for		**Nominal** value of	
75,000 shares	£90,000	shares acquired:	
Capital Reserve c/d	3,750	*i.e.* **15/16** of 80,000	75,000
		General Reserve:	
		i.e. **15/16** of £12,000	11,250
		Profit and Loss A/c:	
		i.e. **15/16** of £8,000	7,500
	£93,750		£93,750
		Capital Reserve b/d	£3,750

NOTE: Here the *holding* company did *not* have to pay anything for goodwill. On the contrary, it paid less than the net worth of the proportion of the assets which it acquired, *i.e. it made a profit on the deal*. This profit is transferred to *capital reserve*.

Stage 2

We must now introduce a new step, that of *re-drafting* the Balance Sheet of Lancs Ltd in order to prepare it for consolidation, for we have a fresh element to consider, *i.e.* the *minority interest*.

RE-DRAFTED BALANCE SHEET OF LANCS LTD
PRIOR TO CONSOLIDATION

Interest of those share-holders who are *outside* the group			Assets	£158,000
(a) Preference Shares		£40,000		
(b) Ordinary Shares:				
1/16 of £80,000	£5,000			
(c) General Reserve:				
1/16 of £12,000	750			
(d) Profit and Loss A/c:				
1/16 of £8,000	500			
		6,250		
Minority interest		£46,250		
Creditors		18,000		
Capital Reserve		3,750		
Interest of Yorks Ltd		90,000		
		£158,000		£158,000

A point of special importance which must be noted is the manner in which the item "Interest of Yorks Ltd, £90,000" is dealt with on consolidation.

If reference is made to the Balance Sheet of Yorks Ltd it will be seen that there is an item headed "Investment in Lancs Ltd £90,000."

These two items of £90,000 are clearly *equal* but *opposite* and so *cancel out*.

Both of these items should, therefore, be omitted from the Consolidated Balance Sheet since no point would be served by including them.

Stage 3

"SKELETON" CONSOLIDATED BALANCE SHEET

	£			£
Share Capital			Assets	
Preference shares	£		Yorks Ltd	
Ordinary shares			Lancs Ltd	158,000
General Reserve				
Profit and Loss A/c				
Capital Reserve		3,750		
Creditors				
Yorks Ltd				
Lancs Ltd	18,000			
Minority Interest		46,250		

Stage 4

CONSOLIDATED BALANCE SHEET OF YORKS LTD AND LANCS LTD AS AT 1ST MARCH 1965

Share Capital				Assets		
Preference shares	£50,000			Yorks Ltd	£190,000	
Ordinary shares	200,000			Lancs Ltd	158,000	
		£250,000				£348,000
General Reserve		15,000				
Profit and Loss A/c		2,000				
		267,000				
Capital Reserve		3,750				
Creditors						
Yorks Ltd	13,000					
Lancs Ltd	18,000					
		31,000				
Minority Interest		46,250				
		£348,000				£348,000

CONSOLIDATIONS: AT A LATER DATE

10. Constructing a Consolidated Balance Sheet at a date after acquisition. So far we have only considered consolidating *at the time of merger (atom)* and have not considered the matter at any *later* date.

Quite obviously, in practice, most Consolidated Balance Sheets will be prepared as at dates *after* the merger since, normally, one will be prepared for the group *every year*. This being so we must ask ourselves, "What, if anything, is different when consolidating at one of these later dates?"

As we have already seen when preparing a Consolidated Balance Sheet at the time of the merger we *exclude* the balances standing to the credit of the *subsidiary company's* Share Capital, General Reserve and Profit and Loss Account *("scrap") except* such part of those balances which belong to those shareholders *outside the group, i.e.* the *minority interest.*

At a later date, however, matters are not so simple.

In the years which follow the merger the subsidiary company will be engaged in trading and will make either a profit or a loss.

The proportion of any such profit (or loss) earned by the *subsidiary* company *since the date of acquisition* which belongs to the *holding* company, must *always* appear in the Consolidated Balance Sheet.

It is, therefore, of the *utmost* importance that we *analyse* very carefully the details of the subsidiary company's Profit and Loss Account *and* its General Reserve.

11. Undistributed profits. The term "undistributed profits" is used normally to embrace any balances which may be standing to the credit of:

(*a*) General Reserve; and
(*b*) Profit and Loss Account.

When building up a Consolidated Balance Sheet we must observe the following rule:

When consolidating *at any date after the merger* the balances on the *General Reserve* and the *Profit and Loss Account* of the *subsidiary* company must be analysed into:

(*a*) *Pre*-acquisition profits; and
(*b*) *Post*-acquisition profits.

The term *pre-acquisition profits* means those *undistributed* profits which stand on the subsidiary company's General Reserve and Profit and Loss Account at the time of the merger (*atom*).

Post-acquisition profits mean those profits earned *since* the merger and which still remain undistributed at the date of any later consolidation.

EXAMPLE 41

Lothian Ltd acquired 15,000 ordinary shares in Nairn Ltd on 1st June 1965. The Balance Sheets of the two companies *on 31st May 1966*, were:

LOTHIAN LTD—BALANCE SHEET AS AT 31ST MAY 1966

Share Capital		Fixed Assets	
150,000 £1 shares	£150,000	Land and Buildings	£100,000
General Reserve	18,000	Plant	14,000
Profit and Loss A/c	3,600		
			114,000
	171,600	Current Assets	61,000
Creditors	28,400	Investment	
		15,000 Shares	
		in Nairn Ltd	
		at cost	25,000
	£200,000		£200,000

NAIRN LTD—BALANCE SHEET AS AT 31ST MAY 1966

Share Capital			Fixed Assets	
20,000 £1 shares		£20,000	Plant, etc.	£14,000
Profit and Loss A/c			Current Assets	18,000
Balance at				
1st June				
1965	£400			
Add Net				
Profit for				
year	3,600			
		4,000		
Creditors		8,000		
		£32,000		£32,000

NOTE: Your attention is drawn particularly to:

  (*i*) *the date of acquisition, i.e.* 1st June *1965;* and
  (*ii*) *the date of consolidation, i.e.* 31st May *1966.*

Stage 1

The first step is, as usual, to find the cost of control, *i.e. at the date on which the shares were acquired.*

Cost of Control Account

Amount **paid** for			**Nominal** value of		
15,000 shares	£25,000		shares acquired:		
			Three-quarters of		
			£20,000		£15,000
			Profit and Loss A/c:		
			Three-quarters of		
			£400		300
					15,300
			Goodwill c/d		9,700
	£25,000				£25,000
Goodwill b/d	£9,700				

Stage 2

Before redrafting the Balance Sheet of Nairn Ltd we will calculate the amounts due to the minority interest shareholders and to the holding company respectively.

MINORITY INTEREST:

At the date at which the consolidation is to be made, *i.e.* on 31st May 1966 (*one year after the date of acquisition*), the minority shareholders will be entitled to the following:

(a) *The nominal amount* of their holding of the £1 ordinary shares, *i.e.* one-quarter of 20,000 shares of £1 each	£5,000
(b) *One quarter* of all of the *undistributed profits* as at 31st May 1966, *i.e.* one-quarter of £4000	1,000
Minority interest	£6,000

NOTE: The £1000 of *undistributed profit* is made up of:

(*i*) *One-quarter* of the balance of £400 standing to the credit of Profit and Loss Account at 1st June 1965	£100
(*ii*) *One-quarter of the profit earned* during the year ended 31st May 1966 (which was £3600)	900
	£1,000

THE HOLDING COMPANY'S INTEREST:

(a) The amount *paid* for 15,000 shares of £1 each	£25,000
(b) *Three-quarters* of the *profit earned* during the year ended 31st May 1966 (which was £3600)	2,700
	£27,700

Stage 3

Having ascertained the respective interests of the minority shareholders and the holding company we can now redraft the Balance Sheet of Nairn Ltd, as follows:

REDRAFTED BALANCE SHEET OF NAIRN LTD
READY FOR CONSOLIDATION

Minority interest			Fixed Assets		
Ordinary shares, ¼ of £20,000		£5,000	Per original Balance Sheet		£14,000
Profit and Loss A/c, ¼ of £4,000		1,000	Goodwill		9,700
		6,000			23,700
Creditors		8,000	Current Assets		18,000
Interest of Lothian Ltd					
Cost of 15,000 shares	£25,000				
Profit and Loss A/c, ¾ of £3,600	2,700				
		27,700			
		£41,700			£41,700

If so desired a skeleton Consolidated Balance Sheet may now be prepared along the lines laid down earlier in this chapter.

"SKELETON" CONSOLIDATED BALANCE SHEET

Share capital			Fixed Assets		
General Reserve			Lothian Ltd		
Profit & Loss A/c			Nairn Ltd	£14,000	
Lothian Ltd					
Nairn Ltd		£2,700	Goodwill		£9,700
Creditors			Current Assets		
Lothian Ltd			Lothian Ltd		
Nairn Ltd		8,000	Nairn Ltd	18,000	
Minority Interest		£6,000			

NOTE: Lothian Ltd's share of the profit earned **since** acquisition, *i.e.* £2700, has to be included in the "skeleton" consolidated balance sheet.

Stage 4

CONSOLIDATED BALANCE SHEET OF LOTHIAN LTD
AND NAIRN LTD AS AT 31ST MAY 1966

Share Capital			Fixed Assets		
150,000 £1 shares		£150,000	Lothian Ltd	£114,000	
General Reserve		18,000	Nairn Ltd	14,000	
					£128,000
Profit and Loss A/c			Goodwill		9,700
Lothian Ltd	£3,600		Current Assets		
Nairn Ltd	2,700		Lothian Ltd	61,000	
		6,300	Nairn Ltd	18,000	
Creditors					79,000
Lothian Ltd	28,400				
Nairn Ltd	8,000				
		36,400			
Minority interest		6,000			
		£216,700			£216,700

PROGRESS TEST 12

1. What do you understand by the term "controlling interest"? **(3)**

2. When preparing a Consolidated Balance Sheet certain items which appear in the Balance Sheet of (*a*) the holding company, and, (*b*) the subsidiary companies, must *never* be shown in the consolidation. What are these items? **(7)**

3. What is the purpose of the Cost of Control Account? Which items must be brought into this account? **(8)**

4. The term "minority interest" appears in almost every Consolidated Balance Sheet. What do you understand by this term? Which items would you expect to find making up this item? (**9**)

5. When consolidating at any date *after* acquisition it is necessary to analyse the undistributed profits. What are undistributed profits? Why is it necessary to analyse them? (**10, 11**)

CHAPTER XIII

CONSOLIDATED BALANCE SHEETS: ADVANCED MATTERS

INTRODUCTION

1. Consolidating with two (or more) subsidiaries. When there are two or more subsidiary companies to be dealt with in consolidating the problem naturally becomes more complex since more preparatory work is necessary.

(*a*) In the Balance Sheet of the *Holding* company under the heading "Investment in Subsidiary Companies" will appear brief details giving the name of *each* subsidiary and the amount which was paid for the respective shares.

(*b*) The first step in consolidation will be the usual one of *ascertaining the cost of control*. Where two or more subsidiaries are involved, however, it will be necessary to open a "Cost of Control Account" for *each* of the subsidiary companies. Thus, if there are three subsidiaries we must open *three* separate Cost of Control Accounts in order to find out the *individual* goodwills or capital reserves as the case may be.

2. Introduction of double entry. In the next chapter a suggested method of dealing with examination problems is set out. This differs in technique from what has been shown previously. What has gone before was designed to show the student *the general principles* underlying the process of consolidation. If he so wishes he may, of course, continue to adopt that method, but it is felt that he will probably find the method set out in the next chapter superior in that he will be able to *employ double entry throughout the entire problem* and so find his way through the more puzzling aspects quite easily.

Before we pass on to that, however, there are some other important matters to be dealt with.

DIVIDEND PAYMENTS

3. Dividends. When dividends are paid by *subsidiary* companies these must be examined with some care.

First of all, we have to bear in mind that *dividends are paid out of profits*. Dividends are paid to the *shareholders* who may be either:

(*a*) Members of the group; or
(*b*) Outsiders, *i.e.* the *minority interest*.

Furthermore, dividends depend upon the class of share held, either preference or ordinary.

It is the general practice to regard *preference* shares as being held by the minority interest because in all but exceptional cases the *preference shares do not carry any voting rights*: and, as a consequence, the holders of non-voting shares have no say in the control of the company. It follows, therefore, that any preference dividends will normally be considered as *belonging exclusively to the minority interest*.

4. Dividends payable from current profits. There are three main points to be considered.

(*a*) *Preference dividends.* Should a question contain a *provision* for a dividend in respect of preference shares, *i.e.* shown as a debit in the Profit and Loss Account of a subsidiary company, such provision should be treated as belonging to the minority interest.
(*b*) *Ordinary Dividends.* Where dividends are *proposed* for the *ordinary* shareholders a distinction will need to be drawn between:

(*i*) the amount due to the *holding* company; and
(*ii*) the amount due to the *minority interest*,

and suitable *apportionments* made.

NOTE: It must be appreciated that if dividends have only been provided for (but have *not yet been paid*) they must automatically be treated as being part of the *undistributed profit* at the date of consolidation.

(*c*) *Preference dividends not provided for.* It is most important to remember that the dividends on *preference* shares are *cumulative* unless the shares are stated quite positively to be *non-cumulative*.

A point which sometimes occurs in an examination problem is for the question to make no reference to a provision for preference dividends in its Profit and Loss Account. We must be on the look-out for such points and remember to provide for any such dividend which *automatically* will have accrued provided that the profits are sufficient to cover it.

5. Dividends payable out of pre-acquisition profits. Sometimes a subsidiary company, which has recently come under the control of a holding company, *pays a dividend out of profits which were made* **before** *it became a subsidiary.*

When such a thing happens it simply means that the *price paid* for the shares was an inflated price, *i.e.* the share price was based on a *cum div.* valuation.

The dividend is duly paid at a slightly later date, *i.e.* at a time when the *holding* company is the owner of the shares. When, therefore, the dividend is received by the holding company it should be credited, *not* to the Profit and Loss Account (of the holding company) as *income*, but to the Cost of Control Account so that it will serve as **a reduction in the purchase price** and, consequently, reduce the price paid for the goodwill.

NOTE: For a fuller explanation of this matter the student is referred to Chapter XV dealing with Consolidated Profit and Loss Accounts.

EXAMPLE 42

On 1st January 1966 Q Ltd acquired 60% of the ordinary shares of R Ltd at a cost of £26,000. The issued capital of R Ltd was £30,000 in £1 ordinary shares. On 8th February 1966 R Ltd paid a dividend of 15% *out of profits which had been made before the date of acquisition, i.e.* for the year ended 31st December 1965.

The Profit and Loss Account of R Ltd as at 31st December 1965, was as follows:

Proposed dividend		Balance at 31st Decem-	
(net)	£4,500	ber 1964	£2,150
Balance	3,570	Net Profit for 1965	
		after taxation	5,920
	£8,070		£8,070

Goodwill would have been ascertained in the usual manner, *viz*:

Cost of Control Account

Amount paid for 18,000 shares ($\frac{6}{10}$ of £30,000)	£26,000	Nominal value of shares acquired	£18,000
		Profit and Loss A/c ($\frac{6}{10}$ of £3,570)	2,142
		Transfer to Goodwill A/c	5,858
	£26,000		£26,000

Goodwill Account

Cost of Control A/c	£5,858

Normally, when a company receives a dividend from a subsidiary this income will be credited to the Profit and Loss Account.

However, in the *exceptional* case of a holding company receiving a dividend from a subsidiary *out of the profits which the subsidiary company made before it was taken over*, such dividend must *never* be credited to the Profit and Loss Account of the holding company. *Instead*, the dividend must be used to *reduce the amount paid for goodwill*.

The following further entries would then be made in the Goodwill Account:

Goodwill Account

Cost of Control A/c	£5,858	Transfer from Dividend A/c ($\frac{6}{10}$ of £4,500)	£2,700
		Balance c/d	3,158
	£5,858		£5,858
Balance b/d	£3,158		

NOTE: The dividend was at the rate of 15%. The capital of R Ltd was £30,000. 15% of £30,000 = £4500, of which 60% was paid to Q Ltd, *i.e.* £2700.

TRANSACTIONS WITHIN A GROUP

6. Bills of exchange. Sometimes we find that bills of exchange appear in the Balance Sheets of companies within a group as the result of some form of *inter-company transactions*.

EXAMPLE 43

Let us suppose that A Ltd, the holding company, sold goods to B Ltd for £1000 and it was arranged that B Ltd would pay for them by means of four separate bills of exchange of £250 each, payable respectively two months, three months, four months and five months after acceptance.

B Ltd, being the acceptor of the bill, will *debit the personal account of A Ltd* in the Bought Ledger and *credit Bills Payable Account*.

A Ltd, on the other hand, will hold these bills as an asset, crediting the personal account of B Ltd in the Sales Ledger, *debiting Bills Receivable Account*.

In the *Consolidated* Balance Sheet, therefore, we would have an asset under the heading of "Bills Receivable, £1000," and at the same time a liability entitled "Bills Payable £1000." Since these two items are both *equal and opposite* representing inter-company indebtedness they will cancel out in the Consolidated Balance Sheet.

7. When bills of exchange are discounted. Transactions may take place through the bank or through a discounting house.

(*a*) *Bills receivable*. It may happen that the company which holds the bills of exchange, *i.e. as bills receivable*, may wish to convert some of them into cash, and for this purpose pays them into the bank. In such a case the entries would be:

Debit   Bank Account.
Credit   Bills Receivable Account.

(*b*) *Contingent liability*. The usual practice in such a case is to enter a note at the foot of the Balance Sheet of the company which has discounted the bills calling the attention of members to the fact that there is a *contingent liability* in respect of the bills receivable which have been discounted.

The *contingency* arises from the possibility that the company which has *accepted* the liability of *paying* these bills when they mature may not be able to do so owing to lack of funds. Should this happen the bank which *discounted* the bill (or bills) will require *compensation* (to the full extent of the bill which it discounted) from the company which discounted it.

(c) *Accounting procedure.* When we are consolidating the Balance Sheets of companies which have had transactions of this nature *between themselves* the procedure is straightforward. We simply *offset* the bills receivable held by one company (*i.e.* the drawer of the bills) against the bills payable owing by the other company (*i.e.* the *acceptor*). Thus, if *none* of the bills receivable have been discounted the asset and the liability cancel out on consolidation. If, on the other hand, *some* of the bills have been discounted and the date of maturity has not been reached then *those bills which have been discounted* must appear *as an* **actual liability** *in the Consolidated Balance Sheet.*

EXAMPLE 44

Sub Ltd accepted five bills for £200 each, drawn by P. A. Ltd, the holding company. P. A. Ltd discounted two of these bills immediately. At the year end (which was the same for both companies) the date for presentation of the bills had not been reached. The ledger entries at the end of the year would appear as shown below.

In the ledger of Sub Ltd:

Bills Payable Account

	P.A. Ltd A/c (5 bills of £200 each) £1,000

In the ledger of P. A. Ltd:

Bills Receivable Account

Sub. Ltd A/c (5 bills of £200 each)	£1,000	Bank A/c (2 bills, each for £200, discounted) Balance c/d	£400 600
	£1,000		£1,000
Balance b/d	£600		

The Consolidated Balance Sheet would show these in the following manner:

Liabilities

Bills Payable	£1,000	
Less Held by		
P. A. Ltd	600	
	———	£400

H

8. Inter-company trading. It is to be expected that a certain amount of business will be transacted *between members of a group* of companies. When trading takes place in these circumstances it will be carried on in the normal way and no distinction will be made in the entries in the books of the companies concerned from any other transactions which they enter into with outside concerns. That is to say, the selling company will sell its goods at its *normal* selling price and make its *normal profit* on such sales regardless of whether the customer is a member of the group or not.

A problem does arise, however, in consolidation where the goods are sold to a company *within the group* if the goods, or any part of them, remain unsold at the end of the group's financial year.

EXAMPLE 45

H Ltd, the holding company, *owns all the shares* of Sub Ltd. On the last day of the financial year H Ltd sells goods (which cost it £750) to Sub Ltd for £1000. Sub Ltd received the goods on the same day but was unable to sell any of them. Sub Ltd had no other stock and these goods were, therefore, *the closing stock of Sub Ltd*. H Ltd, of course, treated the transaction as a normal sale and the profit of £250 appeared in its accounts for the year which ended on the same day. The closing stock of H Ltd was £6400.

When the accounts of the two companies are consolidated they are, as we know, amalgamated. In other words, when consolidated, the final results appear as if they were those of one business. In this example Sub Ltd is a 100% subsidiary and no question of any minority interest enters into the matter.

If no adjustments were made the closing stock of Sub Ltd would appear at £1000. In the Consolidated Balance Sheet this would be added to the stock of H Ltd, *i.e.* £6400. Thus the total stock on consolidation would appear as £6400 *plus* £1000 = £7400. Consider what the position would have been had H Ltd not sold those goods. Its stock would have amounted, *at cost*, to £7150, *i.e.* £6400 *plus* £750. Thus we can see that for the consolidation the closing stock of Sub Ltd must be *reduced* by £250, *to bring it down to cost*. At the same time the Profit and Loss Account balance of H Ltd must also be reduced by this same sum of £250 *when consolidating* since, from the point of view of the group, this simply is not true profit.

Let us look at the entries in the books, simplified to bring out the point of the example.

Stage 1

H LTD
Trading Account

Purchases	£6,400	Sales (of the £750 item)	£1,000
Purchases	750	Stock A/c	6,400
Gross Profit	250		
	£7,400		£7,400

Profit and Loss Account

		Gross Profit	£250

Stock Account

Trading A/c	£6,400		

SUB LTD
Trading Account

Purchases (from H Ltd)	£1,000	Stock A/c	£1,000

Stock Account

Trading A/c	£1,000		

Stage 2

On consolidation, the adjustments in respect of the unrealised profit would be:

H LTD
Profit and Loss Account

Stock A/c, Sub Ltd	£250	Gross Profit (per *Stage 1*)	£250

SUB LTD
Stock Account

Trading A/c (per *Stage 1*)	£1,000	Profit and Loss A/c, H Ltd		£250
		Balance c/d		750
	£1,000			£1,000
Balance b/d	£750			

Thus, in the Consolidated Balance Sheet the profit would be eliminated and the Stock would appear as under:

Stock

H Ltd	£6,400	
Sub Ltd	750	
		£7,150

EXAMPLE 46

Major Ltd *owns 75% of the shares* in Minor Ltd. On the last day of the financial year Minor Ltd sold goods to Major Ltd for £400. Minor Ltd had purchased them for £300. Major Ltd was unable to sell any of them before the close of the financial year and accordingly included them in the closing stock at the price it had paid, *i.e.* £400.

When the accounts of the two companies are consolidated an adjustment for the unrealised profit will have to be made and the stock reduced to cost. In this case, however, there is a significant difference in the treatment to that shown in the previous example. The reason for this is that Minor Ltd is *not* a 100% subsidiary. *One-quarter* of the share capital of Minor Ltd *is not owned by Major Ltd* and, therefore, from the viewpoint of these *minority* shareholders the sale of the goods to Major Ltd is one which shows a *profit* of £100 of which £25 belongs to them.

The entries required to make the adjustment would be as follows:

Section 1

MINOR LTD
Trading Account

Purchases	£300	Sales (to Major Ltd)	£400
Gross Profit	100		
	£400		£400

Profit and Loss Account

	Gross Profit	£100

MAJOR LTD
Trading Account

Purchases	£400	Stock A/c	£400

Stock Account

Trading A/c	£400		

Section 2

MINOR LTD
Profit and Loss Account

Stock A/c, Major Ltd	£75	Gross Profit	£100
Minority Interest A/c	25		
	£100		£100

Minority Interest Account

	Profit and Loss A/c	£25

MAJOR LTD
Stock Account

Trading A/c	£400	Profit and Loss A/c, Minor Ltd	£75
		Balance c/d	325
	£400		£400
Balance b/d	£325		

EXAMPLE 47

Great Ltd *owns 80% of the share capital* of Small Ltd. On the last day of the financial year it sold goods to Small Ltd for £800. The goods had cost Great Ltd £550. Small Ltd had not sold any of these goods and, therefore, included them in the closing stock at cost, *i.e.* £800.

Once again, an adjustment will have to be made for the *unrealised* profit. This time, however, Great Ltd the *holding* company, made the sale. As it owns four-fifths of the capital of Small Ltd, only four-fifths of the profit will have to be eliminated, *the remaining one-fifth having been earned* at the expense of the minority shareholders of Small Ltd, who must be regarded as outsiders.

The simplified entries would be as follows:

Section 1

GREAT LTD

Trading Account

Purchases	£550	Sales (to Small Ltd)	£800
Gross Profit	**250**		
	£800		£800

Profit and Loss Account

	Gross Profit **£250**

SMALL LTD

Trading Account

Purchases	£800	Stock A/c	**£800**

Stock Account

Trading A/c	**£800**	

Section 2

SMALL LTD

Stock Account

Trading A/c	£800	Profit and Loss A/c,	
		Great Ltd	**£200**
		Balance c/d	600
	£800		£800
Balance b/d	£600		

GREAT LTD

Profit and Loss Account

Stock A/c, Small Ltd	£200	Gross Profit	£250
Balance c/d	50		
	£250		£250
		Balance b/d	£50

9. Sub-subsidiary companies. It is by no means uncommon to find two companies in a group both holding shares in a third company.

Holding companies may control their subsidiaries either *directly* or *indirectly*. *Indirect control* is exercised where a *direct subsidiary* of the holding company itself controls yet another company by owning more than 50% of the voting shares of that company.

EXAMPLE 48

> H Ltd owns three-fifths of the shares of X Ltd and three-quarters of the shares of B Ltd.

Here we have an example of *direct control* by the holding company of both subsidiaries.

EXAMPLE 49

> H Ltd owns three-quarters of the shares of X Ltd.
> X Ltd owns four-fifths of the shares of B Ltd.

This is an example of H Ltd having no *direct* control of B Ltd. It is only by virtue of its holding in X Ltd that it controls B Ltd.

In this case H Ltd's financial interest in B Ltd amounts to $\frac{3}{4} \times \frac{4}{5}$ of B Ltd's capital, *i.e.* an interest of three-fifths, or 60%.

EXAMPLE 50

> H Ltd owns three-fifths of the shares of B Ltd and two-thirds of the shares of X Ltd.
> X Ltd owns one-fifth of the shares of B Ltd.

Although B Ltd is not a subsidiary of X Ltd the fact that X Ltd owns one-fifth of its shares means that the control exercised by H Ltd *directly* on B Ltd (60%) will be increased by a further two-thirds of one-fifth, *i.e.* two-fifteenths or 13·33%, thus giving H Ltd a *total controlling interest* of 73·33%.

EXAMPLE 51

> H Ltd owns three-quarters of the shares of A Ltd.
> A Ltd owns two-thirds of the shares of B Ltd.
> B Ltd owns four-fifths of the shares of C Ltd.

Here we have a *chain of ownership*, each company being a *direct* subsidiary of the one above it. H Ltd's interest in C Ltd amounts to only 40%, *i.e.* $\frac{3}{4} \times \frac{2}{3} \times \frac{4}{5} = \frac{2}{5}$, or 40%.

Since each company is a subsidiary of the one immediately above it then the *Companies Act* states that, in such circumstances, *each is deemed to be a subsidiary of the holding company*.

10. The accounting problem. Where sub-subsidiaries are involved the accounting aspect of consolidation becomes a trifle complicated. Should a Consolidated Balance Sheet *at the date of acquisition* be required the matter is straightforward. The real problem arises when consolidation is required at some date *after* acquisition. Fortunately, the problem only really concerns *the amount of profit made by the subsidiaries since the date of acquisition*.

To be sure that this is dealt with correctly we must always start with the subsidiary *most remote* from the holding company. By operating in this manner we can liken our progress to that of *climbing a ladder*. The reason for proceeding thus is that it is *vital* that the company occupying the next rung up the ladder *must* be *credited* with the proper amount of profit to which it is entitled before it can, in its turn, pass on the proper amount of profit to which its own immediate superior is entitled, and so on in progression.

Until the senior company knows how much profit it is entitled to from its own subsidiary it cannot pass on the amount of profit due *from itself* to the company on the next rung above.

So long as this point is remembered and acted upon no trouble should be experienced when consolidating with sub-subsidiaries.

SAMPLE QUESTION

Prepare a Consolidated Balance Sheet of X Ltd and its two subsidiaries, Y Ltd and Z Ltd, from the Balance Sheets and information set out below.

	X	Y	Z		X	Y	Z
Capital	£5,000	£4,000	£3,000	Assets	£8,000	£5,000	£5,500
Profit and				Investments:			
Loss A/c	4,000	2,000	1,800	4,000 shares			
Creditors	3,000	1,000	700	in Y	4,000		
				2,000 shares			
				in Z		2,000	
	£12,000	£7,000	£5,500		£12,000	£7,000	£5,500

The shares in Y Ltd were acquired one year ago by X Ltd. The balance of £2000 standing on Profit and Loss Account was all earned since acquisition.

Similarly, in the case of Y Ltd. It acquired the shares in Z Ltd one year ago. All the profit of Z Ltd was earned since acquisition.

SUGGESTED ANSWER

If we consolidated the Balance Sheets of X Ltd and Y Ltd *first*, *i.e.* without dealing with Z Ltd, the result would appear as follows:

CONSOLIDATED BALANCE SHEET OF X LTD AND Y LTD

Share Capital		£5,000	Assets		
Profit and Loss A/c			X Ltd	£8,000	
X Ltd	£4,000		Y Ltd	5,000	
Y Ltd	2,000				£13,000
		6,000			
Creditors			**Shares in Z Ltd**		**2,000**
X Ltd	3,000				
Y Ltd	1,000				
		4,000			
		£15,000			£15,000

We would thus be left with Z Ltd "floating," so to speak, and the only thing to do would be to integrate it with the above consolidation of X Ltd and Y Ltd. Therefore, the obviously sensible thing to do is to *start* with Z Ltd and "*pre*-consolidate" with Y Ltd and then incorporate the results into X Ltd's Balance Sheet and thus obtain a proper Consolidated Balance Sheet.

Pre-consolidating Z Ltd with Y Ltd

There is *no goodwill* to be worked out in this problem since Y Ltd paid £2000 for 2000 £1 shares in Z Ltd. We are left, therefore, with only the minority interest of Z Ltd to ascertain.

The minority interest in this case consists of:

(*a*) 1000 £1 shares	£1,000
(*b*) One-third share of the profit for the year	600
Minority interest of Z Ltd	£1,600

This leaves £1200 of undistributed profit to be *credited* to the Profit and Loss Account of Y Ltd.

The Balance Sheets of Y Ltd and Z Ltd can now be "*pre-consolidated*" with the following result:

BALANCE SHEETS OF Y LTD AND Z LTD PRE-CONSOLIDATED

Share Capital (Y Ltd)		£4,000	Assets		
Profit and Loss A/c			Y Ltd	£5,000	
Y Ltd	£2,000		Z Ltd	5,500	
Z Ltd	1,200				£10,500
		3,200			
Creditors					
Y Ltd	1,000				
Z Ltd	700				
		1,700			
Minority interest		1,600			
		£10,500			£10,500

NOTE: The above "pre-consolidated" Balance Sheet is not unlike the "skeleton" Consolidated Balance Sheets shown in Chapter XII. In this case all the *totals*, with the exception of the Share Capital, have been included in the final consolidation. These have been shown in italics for ease of reference.

The final consolidation

Having completed the "pre-consolidation" we may now incorporate the results with the Balance Sheet of X Ltd and so obtain the Consolidated Balance Sheet of the group.

CONSOLIDATED BALANCE SHEET OF X LTD, Y LTD AND Z LTD

Share Capital		£5,000	Assets		
Profit and Loss A/c			X Ltd	£8,000	
X Ltd	£4,000		*Y Ltd*	*10,500*	
Y Ltd	*3,200*				£18,500
		7,200			
Creditors					
X Ltd	3,000				
Y Ltd	*1,700*				
		4,700			
Minority Interest		*1,600*			
		£18,500			£18,500

The purpose of this example, which is very simple, is to demonstrate the advisability of starting from the most *remote* subsidiary and then working *upwards* towards the holding company. In such an example as this complications have been kept to a minimum so that the student may more easily appreciate the commonsense of *starting from* the subsidiary which is farthest from the holding company.

In the next chapter a suggested method of dealing with any Consolidated Balance Sheet problem is set out. This method applies to "sub-subsidiaries" as well as to ordinary subsidiaries and does not require pre-consolidation. There is, however, no reason why the pre-consolidation method should not be employed if so desired.

PROGRESS TEST 13

1. What are the three main points to be considered when dealing with dividends payable out of current profits? **(4)**

2. An important principle is involved when dividends are paid out of pre-acquisition profits. What is this principle? To which account must such pre-acquisition dividends be credited when received? **(5)**

3. How should bills of exchange be dealt with when consolidating? **(7)**

4. Where goods which have been sold to another company *within the group* remain unsold (in whole or in part) at the end of the accounting year how should these be treated when consolidating? **(8)**

5. What do you understand by the terms, (*a*) direct control; and (*b*) indirect control? **(9)**

6. When a consolidation problem involves both subsidiary and sub-subsidiary companies what procedure must be adopted? What is the reason for this? **(10)**

CHAPTER XIV

CONSOLIDATED BALANCE SHEETS: DEALING WITH EXAMINATION PROBLEMS

In the previous chapters on Consolidated Balance Sheets we applied ourselves to the theory underlying their compilation and tried to show precisely *what* happens, and, equally important, the reason *why*.

It is now proposed to show a simple and straightforward method of dealing with examination problems.

DOUBLE ENTRY BOOK-KEEPING

1. Unnecessary procedures. In the first place *it is not necessary*, unless we so wish, to open either:

(a) a *re-drafted* Balance Sheet of the subsidiary company; or
(b) a "*skeleton*" Consolidated Balance Sheet.

These two expedients were resorted to in order to show just what was happening when we consolidated.

2. Recommended method. Secondly, it is suggested that the student will be well advised when dealing with consolidations to concentrate on his *basic* stock in trade, *i.e.* his knowledge of *double entry book-keeping*. This knowledge, correctly applied, places the solution of *any* Consolidated Balance Sheet problem *easily* within his grasp.

The most important feature of this method is to treat *all* the companies involved as if they are part of one and the *same firm*.

That is to say, for the purposes of consolidation we must *ignore* the fact that there are two or more different companies, and make all the adjustments which may be necessary as though we were dealing with only *one set of books*.

CONSOLIDATION AT THE TIME OF MERGER

RULES FOR PROCEDURE

3. Rule A. *Open Ledger Accounts* (*holding company*)

On a *separate sheet* of paper, open a *ledger* account for *every* balance which appears in the Balance Sheet of the *holding company*.

4. Rule B. *Open Ledger Accounts* (*subsidiary companies*)

On a *separate sheet* of paper, open a *ledger* account for *every* balance which appears in the Balance Sheet of *each subsidiary* company, *i.e.* a separate sheet should be used for each subsidiary company.

5. Rule C.

(*a*) *Open Cost of Control Accounts*

Open a *separate account* called "Cost of Control Account" for *each* subsidiary company *on its own sheet*. Thus, if there are three subsidiary companies you must have *three* separate Cost of Control Accounts.

(*b*) *Dispose of* "*Shares in subsidiary company*"

Turn to the *holding* company's ledger sheet and *close off* the asset account headed "Shares in subsidiary company" by *crediting* this account. The corresponding debit will be made in the Cost of Control Account of the subsidiary company. *Repeat* the process for any other subsidiary companies. In this way we dispose of the asset "Shares in subsidiary company" so far as the *holding* company is concerned.

Since there is now no balance on this account in the holding company's ledger we fulfil the first part of the precept which requires that balances showing investments *in* subsidiary companies are *replaced* by the actual assets and liabilities of those subsidiary companies, *i.e.* the investment is eliminated from the holding company's Balance Sheet.

6. Rule D. *Transfer nominal value of shares*

Taking each subsidiary company *in turn* we transfer *from* the Share Capital Account the *nominal value* of the shares which have been acquired and *credit the cost of control Account* with this amount; *i.e.*:

Debit   Share Capital Account of the subsidiary company.

Credit   Cost of Control Account which has been raised in that subsidiary company's books.

7. Rule E. *Open Minority Interest Account*

The next step is to open an account for the shareholders of the subsidiary company who are outside the group. The heading is "Minority Interest Account."

Close off the Share Capital Account of the subsidiary company by debiting it with whatever amount is required for this purpose, *i.e.* the balance remaining on the account, and enter the corresponding credit in the minority Interest Account.

Thus we fulfil the rule that *none* of the subsidiary company's *share capital* may appear (as such) in the Consolidated Balance Sheet.

8. Rule F. *Transfer undistributed profits*

Transfer the holding company's *proportion of undistributed profits* (*i.e.* on General Reserve Account and Profit and Loss Account) *at the time of merger* (*atom*) to the credit of Cost of Control Account; *i.e.*:

Debit   General Reserve Account and Profit and Loss Account of the subsidiary company.

Credit Cost of Control Account.

9. Rule G. *Credit Minority Interest Account*

Close off General Reserve Account and Profit and Loss Account by transferring the balance remaining on each account to the credit of Minority Interest Account.

10. Rule H. *Close Cost of Control Account*

Close off Cost of Control Account and transfer the balance to the debit of Goodwill Account (or to the credit of Capital Reserve) in the ledger sheet of the subsidiary company.

EXAMPLE 52

Holding Ltd acquired 15,000 £1 shares in Held Ltd at the close of business on 31st December 1965. The Balance Sheets of the two companies at the time of acquisition were as follows:

Holding Ltd at 31st December 1965

Share Capital		Sundry Assets	£34,000
50,000 £1 shares	£50,000		
Profit and Loss A/c	6,000	Shares in Held Ltd	
		15,000 £1 shares at	
		cost	22,000
	£56,000		£56,000

Held Ltd at 31st December 1965

Share Capital		Sundry Assets	£30,000
20,000 £1 shares	£20,000		
General Reserve	6,000		
Profit and Loss A/c	4,000		
	£30,000		£30,000

Stage 1

Following the rules laid down the first thing to be done is to open ledger accounts for all the balances appearing in the respective Balance Sheets.

HOLDING LTD (the parent company)
Share Capital Account

		Balance	£50,000

Sundry Assets Account

Balance	£34,000		

Profit and Loss Account

		Balance	£6,000

Investment Account—(shares in Held Ltd)

Balance	£22,000		

HELD LTD (75% subsidiary company)
Share Capital Account

		Balance	£20,000

Sundry Assets Account

Balance	£30,000		

General Reserve Account

	Balance	£6,000

Profit and Loss Account

	Balance	£4,000

The important point to bear in mind is that from this point on we pay *no* attention to the fact that the balances set out above are taken from the books of *two different companies*.

They must be considered as belonging to *one and the same firm*.

Stage 2

HOLDING LTD

Investment Account—(shares in Held Ltd)

Balance	£22,000	Cost of Control A/c (Held Ltd)	**£22,000**
	£22,000		**£22,000**

HELD LTD

Cost of Control Account

Shares in Held Ltd A/c (Holding Ltd)	**£22,000**	

As can be seen *no notice* is taken of the fact that the two above accounts are in the books of different companies. We treat them as though they appear in the **same** ledger.

Stage 3

We continue to build up the Cost of Control Account.

HELD LTD

Share Capital Account

Cost of Control A/c	**£15,000**	Balance	£20,000
Balance c/d	5,000		
	£20,000		**£20,000**
		Balance b/d	£5000

Cost of Control Account

Shares in Held Ltd A/c (per *Stage 2*)	£22,000	Share Capital A/c	**£15,000**
		Balance c/d	7,000
	£22,000		£22,000
Balance b/d	£7,000		

Stage 4

The Cost of Control Account is completed as shown below. *Note especially* how double entry book-keeping is being employed exclusively.

HELD LTD

General Reserve Account

Cost of Control A/c (¾ share)	**£4,500**	Balance (per *Stage 1*)	£6,000
Balance c/d	1,500		
	£6,000		£6,000
		Balance b/d	1,500

Profit and Loss Account

Cost of Control A/c (¾ share)	**£3,000**	Balance (per *Stage 1*)	£4,000
Balance c/d	1,000		
	£4,000		£4,000
		Balance b/d	£1,000

Cost of Control Account

Balance b/d (from *Stage 3*)	£7,000	General Reserve A/c	**£4,500**
Capital Reserve	**500**	Profit and Loss A/c	**3,000**
	£7,500		£7,500

Capital Reserve Account

	Cost of Control A/c	**£500**

Stage 5

The concluding entries will be concerned with building up Minority Interest Account.

HELD LTD
Share Capital Account

Minority Interest A/c	**£5,000**	Balance b/d (from *Stage 3*)	£5,000

General Reserve Account

Minority Interest A/c	**£1,500**	Balance b/d (from *Stage 4*)	£1,500

Profit and Loss Account

Minority Interest A/c	**£1,000**	Balance b/d (from *Stage 4*)	£1,000

Minority Interest Account

	Share Capital A/c	**£5,000**
	General Reserve A/c	**1,500**
	Profit and Loss A/c	**1,000**
		£7,500

Once again, the student's attention is drawn to the fact that *double entry book-keeping* is used exclusively, throughout.

Furthermore, the use of double entry book-keeping emphasises those earlier rules:

(a) that the asset in the holding company's Balance Sheet entitled "Investment in subsidiary company"; and

(b) that the Share Capital, Reserves and Profit and Loss Account balances of the subsidiary company at the time of merger,

must *never appear* in the Consolidated Balance Sheet. *No balances remain on those accounts.*

CONSOLIDATED BALANCE SHEET OF HOLDING LTD AND HELD LTD

Share Capital		Sundry Assets		
50,000 £1 shares	£50,000	Holding		
Profit and Loss A/c	6,000	Ltd	£34,000	
Capital Reserve	500	Held Ltd	30,000	
Minority Interest	7,500		———	£64,000
	———			———
	£64,000			£64,000

The first eight rules (A–H) together with Example 52 show how a Consolidated Balance Sheet *at the time of merger* may be constructed (**3–10**).

We will now deal with the rules to be followed when preparing a Consolidated Balance Sheet *at some later date*.

CONSOLIDATION AT A LATER DATE

RULES FOR PROCEDURE

11. Rule I. *Dividends paid out of* **pre**-*acquisition profits*

Assuming that a dividend has been paid out of *pre-acquisition* profits of the subsidiary company and that it has been credited to the Profit and Loss Account of the holding company at some date after the merger (which is a most likely point the examiner will include in the question) we must:

Debit The Profit and Loss Account of the holding company (in the Ledger Account in the holding company's section).

Credit Cost of Control Account (in the Ledger Account in the subsidiary company's section).

12. Rule J. *Dividends from* **post**-*acquisition profits*

If a proposed dividend has been debited to the Profit and Loss Account of the subsidiary company against the current year's profit (*i.e.* although it has been proposed it has not yet been paid and therefore remains, for the moment, undistributed) this must be dealt with when consolidating.

In the subsidiary company's ledger a Dividend Account will have been opened already, and the balance on this account will appear as a liability on the company's Balance Sheet. The corresponding debit will have been made in the Profit and Loss Account.

In the ledger section (opened for consolidation) *this Dividend Account must now be closed*:

Debit   Dividend Account.

Credit   (a) Minority Interest Account

           (i) with any proposed preference dividend; and

           (ii) with the appropriate proportion of any proposed ordinary dividend.

       (b) Profit and Loss Account of the subsidiary company with the holding company's proportion of the ordinary dividend (*i.e.* this amount must be written back into the Profit and Loss Account).

13. Rule K. *Inter-company transactions*

(a) *Goods sold* **by** *the holding company* to the subsidiary *still unsold* by the subsidiary.

The holding company's proportion of unrealised profit must be excluded from the holding company's profit.

     Debit   Profit and Loss Account of holding company (in holding company's ledger).

     Credit   Stock Account (or Current Assets Account) (in the subsidiary's ledger).

(b) *Goods sold to the holding company by the subsidiary* and still unsold by the holding company.

     Credit   Stock Account (or Current Assets) (in the holding company's ledger).

     Debit   Profit and Loss Account of the subsidiary company (in the subsidiary's ledger).

(c) *Where the holding company has purchased debentures* in the subsidiary company and debenture interest payable by the subsidiary has been provided (on the entire issue, of course), the proportion which belongs to the holding company must be eliminated.

     Debit   Debenture Interest Receivable Account (in the holding company's ledger).

     Credit   Debenture Interest Payable Account (in the subsidiary's ledger).

14. Rule L. *Inter-company debts*

(a) *Where the holding company has purchased debentures* in the subsidiary these must be cancelled, *i.e.* the debentures appear as an investment in the holding company's Balance Sheet.

Debit Debentures Account (in subsidiary's ledger) with the holding company's proportion.

Credit Debentures in Subsidiary Company Account (in holding company's ledger), *i.e.* the entire investment must be eliminated.

(b) *Where there are bills of exchange outstanding* between holding company and subsidiary:

Debit Bills Payable Account (in whichever company they appear as a liability).

Credit Bills Receivable Account (in the other company's ledger).

SPECIMEN QUESTION 1

(C.I.S. FINAL (adapted))

The summarised Balance Sheets of Hill Ltd and its subsidiary company Dale Ltd, as on 31st December 1964, were as follows:

HILL LTD

Issued Share Capital			Fixed Assets	£120,000
(150,000 shares of £1 each)		£150,000	Investment:	
Profit and Loss A/c			20,000 shares in Dale Ltd	34,000
Balance at 31st			Current Assets	48,000
December 1963	£11,000			
Net Profit 1964	14,000			
Dividend from				
Dale Ltd	2,000			
		27,000		
Creditors		25,000		
		£202,000		£202,000

DALE LTD

Issued Share Capital			Fixed Assets	£31,000
(25,000 shares of £1 each)		£25,000	Current Assets	19,500
Profit and Loss A/c				
Balance at 31st				
December 1963	£8,000			
Net Profit 1964	5,000			
		13,000		
Creditors		12,500		
		£50,500		£50,500

Hill Ltd acquired the shares in Dale Ltd on 31st December 1963.

The Profit and Loss Account of Dale Ltd for the year 1963 was debited with a proposed dividend of £2500 for the year 1963, and this dividend was paid in March 1964.

No dividends are proposed in respect of the year 1964.

Prepare a Consolidated Balance Sheet as on 31st December 1964.

SUGGESTED ANSWER

NOTE: All adjustments which are necessary for consolidation have been shown in italics.

HILL LTD (holding company)

Share Capital Account

		Balance	£150,000

Profit and Loss Account

Cost of Control A/c	*£2,000*	Balance 31st December	
(dividend received out of		1963	£11,000
pre-acquisition profits)		Net Profit 1964	14,000
Balance c/d	*25,000*	Dividend from Dale	
		Ltd	2,000
	£27,000		£27,000
		Balance b/d	*£25,000*

Creditors Account

		Balance	£25,000

Fixed Assets Account

Balance	£120,000		

20,000 shares in Dale Ltd Account

Balance	£34,000	*Cost of Control A/c*	£34,000

Current Assets Account

Balance	£48,000		

DALE LTD (subsidiary company)

Share Capital Account

Cost of Control A/c	£20,000	Balance	£25,000
Minority Interest A/c	*5,000*		
	£25,000		£25,000

Profit and Loss Account

Cost of Control A/c	£6,400	Balance 31st December 1963	£8,000
Minority Interest A/c	*1,600*		
	£8,000		£8,000
Minority Interest A/c	*1,000*	Net profit 1964	5,000
Balance c/d	*4,000*		
	£5,000		£5,000
		Balance b/d	£4,000

Creditors Account

		Balance	£12,500

DALE LTD (subsidiary company) (continued)

Fixed Assets Account

Balance	£31,000		

Current Assets Account

Balance	£19,500		

Cost of Control Account

Shares in Dale Ltd	£34,000	Share Capital A/c	£20,000
		Profit and Loss A/c	6,400
		Balance c/d	7,600
	£34,000		£34,000
Balance b/d	£7,600	Profit and Loss A/c	
		Hill Ltd.	2,000
		Goodwill A/c	5,600
	£7,600		£7,600

Minority Interest Account

		Share Capital A/c	£5,000
		Profit and Loss A/c	
		1963	1,600
			6,600
		Profit and Loss A/c	
		1964	1,000
			£7,600

Goodwill Account

Cost of Control A/c	£5,600		

CONSOLIDATED BALANCE SHEET OF HILL LTD AND DALE LTD
AS AT 31ST DECEMBER 1964

Issued Share Capital		Fixed Assets	
(150,000 shares of		Hill Ltd £120,000	
£1 each)	£150,000	Dale Ltd 31,000	
Profit and Loss A/c		————	151,000
Hill Ltd £25,000			
Dale Ltd 4,000		Goodwill	5,600
————	29,000		
Creditors		Current Assets	
Hill Ltd 25,000		Hill Ltd 48,000	
Dale Ltd 12,500		Dale Ltd 19,500	
————	37,500	————	67,500
Minority Interest	7,600		
	£224,100		£224,100

SPECIMEN QUESTION 2

(C.C.S. FINAL (adapted))

The summarised Balance Sheets of W Ltd, S Ltd, and T Ltd, as at 31st March 1964 were as follows:

	W Ltd £000	S Ltd £000	T Ltd £000		W Ltd £000	S Ltd £000	T Ltd £000
Share Capital (£1				Sundry Assets	347	64	42
ordinary shares)	300	30	16	30,000 shares in S			
Profit and Loss A/c				Ltd at cost	60	—	—
Balance at 31st				12,000 shares in			
March 1962	76	18	8	T Ltd at cost	13	—	—
Net Profit 31st							
March 1963	21	7	4				
Net Profit to 31st							
March 1964	23	9	4				
6% Debentures	—	—	10				
	£420	£64	£42		£420	£64	£42

W Ltd acquired its shares:

in S Ltd on 31st March 1962
in T Ltd on 31st March 1963.

Included in the item "Sundry Assets" of S Ltd is £16,000 of stock bought from T Ltd on 29th March 1964. T Ltd makes all sales at $33\frac{1}{3}\%$ above cost.

No dividends have been paid or proposed by any of the companies.

Required: Consolidated Balance Sheet for the group at 31st March 1964.

SUGGESTED ANSWER

NOTE: All adjustments which are necessary for consolidation have been shown in italics.

W. LTD
Share Capital Account

		Balance	£300

Profit and Loss Account

		Balance 31st March 1962	£76
		Net Profit to 31st March 1963	21
		Net Profit to 31st March 1964	23
			£120

Sundry Assets Account

Balance	£347		

30,000 shares in S Ltd Account

Balance	£60	*Cost of Control A/c*	*£60*

12,000 shares in T Ltd Account

Balance	£13	*Cost of Control A/c*	*£13*

CONSOLIDATED BALANCE SHEET OF W LTD, S LTD AND T LTD AS AT 31ST MARCH 1964

Share Capital		£300,000	Sundry Assets	
			W Ltd	£347,000
			S Ltd	61,000
			T Ltd	42,000
Profit and Loss A/c				£450,000
W Ltd	£120,000			
S Ltd	16,000			
		136,000	Goodwill	
			S Ltd	12,000
			Less Capital	
			Reserve, T Ltd	8,000
6% Debentures		10,000		4,000
Minority Interest		8,000		
		£454,000		£454,000

NOTE: The goods sold by T Ltd to S Ltd on 29th March 1964 had cost £12,000. The profit was, therefore, £4000. Of this sum 75% (£3000) must be considered as not having been realised, since profit made *within* the group cannot be considered as having been earned until the goods are *finally sold* by S Ltd. The only profit to count for purposes of consolidation is 25% of £4000 (*i.e.* £1000) in respect of the *minority* shareholders.

S LTD
Share Capital Account

Cost of Control A/c £30	Balance		£30

Profit and Loss Account

Cost of Control A/c £18	Balance 31st March 1962		£18
	Net Profit 31st March 1963		7
Balance c/d	16	Net Profit 31st March 1964	9
	£16		£16
		Balance b/d	£16

Sundry Assets Account

Balance	£64	T Ltd Profit and Loss A/c	£3
		Balance c/d	61
	£64		£64
Balance b/d	£61		

Cost of Control Account

Shares A/c (W. Ltd)	£60	Share Capital A/c (S Ltd)	£30
		Profit and Loss A/c (31st March 1962)	18
		Goodwill A/c	12
	£60		£60

Goodwill Account

Cost of Control A/c £12	

NOTE: All of the above figures represent thousands and so three zeros should be added to each.

T LTD
Share Capital Account

Cost of Control A/c	£12	Balance	£16
Minority Interest A/c	4		
	£16		£16

Profit and Loss Account

Cost of Control A/c	£9	Balance 31st March 1962	£8
Minority Interest A/c	3	Net Profit 31st March 1963	4
	£12		£12
S Ltd—Stock A/c	3	Net Profit 31st March 1964	4
Minority Interest A/c	1		
	£4		£4

6% Debentures Account

	Balance	£10

Cost of Control Account

Shares A/c (W. Ltd)	£13	Share Capital A/c (T Ltd)	£12
Capital Reserve	8	Profit and Loss A/c (31st March 1962 and 31st March 1963)	9
	£21		£21

Capital Reserve Account

	Cost of Control A/c	£8

Sundry Assets Account

Balance	£42

Minority Interest Account

		Share Capital A/c	£4
		Profit and Loss A/c	3
			7
		Profit and Loss A/c (at 31st March 1964)	1
			£8

The Balance Sheets of Allen Ltd, Bray Ltd and Carden Ltd, at 31st December 1966 are as follows:

ALLEN LTD

Share Capital		Fixed Assets	£46,000
100,000 ordinary		Investments	
shares of £1 each	100,000	in Bray Ltd	
Profit and Loss A/c	20,000	40,000 £1 shares	
Creditors	25,000	at cost	50,000
		in Carden Ltd	
		20,000 £1 shares	
		at cost	24,000
		Current Assets	25,000
	£145,000		£145,000

BRAY LTD

Share Capital		Fixed Assets	£26,000
50,000 ordinary		Investments	
shares of £1 each	£50,000	in Carden Ltd	
Profit and Loss A/c	5,000	5,000 £1 shares	
Creditors	17,500	at cost	6,000
		Current Assets	40,500
	£72,500		£72,500

CARDEN LTD

Share Capital		Fixed Assets	£15,300
30,000 ordinary		Current Assets	22,300
shares of £1 each	£30,000		
Profit and Loss A/c	3,000		
Creditors	4,600		
	£37,600		£37,600

Allen Ltd and Bray Ltd acquired their holdings in Carden Ltd on 1st January 1966, and Allen Ltd purchased its holding in Bray Ltd on the same date. The profits of Bray Ltd and Carden Ltd for the year ended 31st December 1966 are £4500 and £2000 respectively, and no dividends have been declared.

You are required to prepare a Consolidated Balance Sheet for the group as at 31st December 1966.

SUGGESTED ANSWER

Allen Ltd, Bray Ltd and Carden Ltd

Taking the Balance Sheet for each company we open an account for *each* balance, both assets and liabilities, and enter therein the appropriate amount.

We must, first of all, deal with the books of Carden Ltd and complete all the *pre-consolidation* entries.

Stage 1. Entries in the books of Carden Ltd (1st part)

Share Capital Account

Cost of Control A/c		Balance b/d	£30,000
Bray Ltd ($\frac{1}{6}$)	£5,000		
Cost of Control A/c			
Allen Ltd ($\frac{4}{6}$)	20,000		
Minority Interest A/c	5,000		
	£30,000		£30,000

Profit and Loss Account

Cost of Control A/c		1966	
Bray Ltd ($\frac{1}{6}$)	£167	Jan. 1	
Cost of Control A/c		Balance b/d	£1,000
Allen Ltd ($\frac{4}{6}$)	667		
Minority Interest ($\frac{1}{6}$)	166		
	£1,000		£1,000

NOTE: The credit balance of £1000 represents the *pre-acquisition* profit only.

Fixed Assets Account

Balance b/d	£15,300	

Current Assets Account

Balance b/d	£22,300	

Cost of Control Account—(BRAY LTD)

Bray Ltd			Share Capital A/c	£5,000
Investment A/c	£6,000		Profit and Loss A/c	167
			Goodwill A/c	833
	£6,000			£6,000

Cost of Control Account—(ALLEN LTD)

Allen Ltd			Share Capital A/c	£20,000
Investment A/c	£24,000		Profit and Loss A/c	667
			Goodwill A/c	3,333
	£24,000			£24,000

Goodwill Account

Cost of Control A/c:			
Bray Ltd	£833		
Allen Ltd	3,333		
	£4,166		

CARDEN LTD—Minority Interest Account

		Share Capital A/c	£5,000
		Profit and Loss A/c	166
			£5,166

Creditors Account

		Balance b/d	£4,600

Stage 2. Entries in the books of Carden Ltd (2nd part)

In this stage the only matter we have to deal with is the profit made *during* 1966. We will, however, include all accounts which have to be incorporated in the Consolidated Balance Sheet so that by reference to this stage (*i.e. Stage 2*) the student will the more easily see all the balances which must be included therein.

Profit and Loss Account

Minority Interest A/c ($\frac{1}{6}$)	£334	1966 Dec. 31	
Profit and Loss A/c (Bray Ltd $\frac{1}{6}$)	333	Net Profit for the year to 31st December 1966	£2,000
Balance c/d	1,333		
	£2,000		£2,000
NOTE: The credit balance of £2,000 represents the *post*-acquisition profit only.		Balance b/d	£1,333

CARDEN LTD—*Minority Interest Account*

	Balance b/d (from *Stage 1*)	£5,166
	Profit and Loss A/c	334
		£5,500

Goodwill Account

Balance b/d (per *Stage 1*)	£4,166

Fixed Assets Account

Balance b/d (per *Stage 1*)	£15,300

Current Assets Account

Balance b/d (per *Stage 1*)	£22,300

Creditors Account

		Balance b/d (per *Stage 1*)	£4,600

This completes the workings as far as Carden Ltd is concerned and each of the balances set out above in *Stage 2* can now be taken directly to the Consolidated Balance Sheet.

Stage 3. Entries in the books of Bray Ltd

Share Capital Account

Cost of Control A/c (Allen Ltd ⅘)	£40,000	Balance b/d	£50,000
Minority Interest A/c	10,000		
	£50,000		£50,000

Profit and Loss Account

Cost of Control A/c (Allen Ltd ⅘)	£400	1966 Jan. 1	
Minority Interest A/c (⅕)	100	Balance b/d (*pre*-acquisition profit)	£500
	£500		£500
Minority Interest A/c (⅕)	967	1966 Dec. 31	
Balance c/d	3,866	Net Profit for year	4,500
		Profit and Loss A/c (Carden Ltd)	333
	£4,833		£4,833
		Balance b/d	£3,866

Creditors Account

		Balance b/d	£17,500

Fixed Assets Account

Balance b/d	£26,000		

Investment in Carden Ltd

Balance b/d	£6,000	Bray Ltd. Cost of Control A/c	£6,000
	£6,000		£6,000

Current Assets Account

Balance b/d	£40,500		

Cost of Control Account

Allen Ltd. Investment A/c	£50,000	Share Capital A/c	£40,000
		Profit and Loss A/c	400
		Goodwill A/c	9,600
	£50,000		£50,000

Goodwill Account

Cost of Control A/c	£9,600		

BRAY LTD—*Minority Interest Account*

		Share Capital A/c	£10,000
		Profit and Loss A/c (pre-acquisition)	100
		Profit and Loss A/c (post-acquisition)	967
			£11,067

This completes the entries needed and we now proceed to the construction of the Consolidated Balance Sheet. Note that in this example it has not been considered necessary to show the ledger accounts in the books of Allen Ltd, the holding company.

I

Stage 4

CONSOLIDATED BALANCE SHEET OF ALLEN LTD, BRAY LTD AND
CARDEN LTD AS AT 31ST DECEMBER 1966

Share Capital		£100,000	Fixed Assets		
Profit and Loss A/c			Allen Ltd	£46,000	
Allen Ltd	£20,000		Bray Ltd	26,000	
Bray Ltd	3,866		Carden		
Carden Ltd	1,333		Ltd	15,300	
		25,199			£87,300
			Goodwill		
			Bray Ltd	9,600	
Minority Interest			Carden		
Bray Ltd	11,067		Ltd	4,166	
Carden Ltd	5,500				13,766
		16,567			
			Current Assets		
Creditors			Allen Ltd	25,000	
Allen Ltd	25,000		Bray Ltd	40,500	
Bray Ltd	17,500		Carden		
Carden Ltd	4,600		Ltd	22,300	
		47,100			87,800
		£188,866			£188,866

PROGRESS TEST 14

1. What is the most important feature of the recommended method for the preparation of a Consolidated Balance Sheet? (2)

2. What is the basic idea underlying this recommended method? (2)

3. If you were consolidating the Balance Sheets of a holding company and its three subsidiaries how many Cost of Control Accounts would you deem it necessary to open? (5)

4. How would you eliminate the Shares in Subsidiary Company Account which appears in the Balance Sheet of the holding company? (5)

5. None of the share capital of the subsidiary companies should appear in the Consolidated Balance Sheet. Explain how you would deal with this problem and name the accounts concerned. (6, 7)

6. How would you dispose of the balances of undistributed profit, *i.e.* the balances on the Profit and Loss Account and General

Reserve Account standing in the Balance Sheet of a subsidiary company? (**8, 9**)

7. In what way should pre-acquisition profits of subsidiary companies be dealt with? (**11**)

8. What are the rules for dealing with inter-company transactions when consolidating? (**13**)

9. How should Bills of Exchange be dealt with in consolidations? (**14**)

CHAPTER XV

THE CONSOLIDATED PROFIT AND LOSS ACCOUNT (I)

INTRODUCTION

Where a group of companies is under the control of a holding company it is the practice for the group to produce a *consolidated Profit and Loss Account* as well as a Consolidated Balance Sheet.

1. Contents of the consolidated Profit and Loss Account. The *consolidated* Profit and Loss Account consists of:

(a) *An amalgamation of the profits made during the* **past year** *by all* the companies *in the group* (including the holding company); and

(b) *A similar amalgamation of any balances of undistributed profit brought forward* from **previous years** of all the companies within the group, *i.e.* this will include any profit which has been transferred to General Reserve.

2. Deductions. From the *combination* of the above figures there must be *deducted* a number of items.

The items which must be deducted from this amalgamation of the profits as set out above may be more easily remembered by the help of the *aide-memoire DUMPS*:

D: *Dividends payable* by one company in the group to another *within the group, i.e. inter-company* dividends.

U: *Unrealised profit* on goods sold by one company in the group to another within the group.

M: *Minority interest, i.e.* any part of the profits of a subsidiary which belong to shareholders outside the group.

P: *Pre-acquisition profits* of a

S: *Subsidiary company, i.e.* profits which had been *earned by the subsidiary before* the date of acquisition by the holding company.

3. Procedure to follow. When preparing a consolidated Profit and Loss Account it is suggested that the following plan of construction be adopted:

(a) *Net profit on trading for the* **past** *year.* The net profit for the year, *i.e.* the balance which has been brought down from the main part of the Profit and Loss Account (the trading section) should always appear as *the first item* on the *credit* side of the consolidated Profit and Loss Account.

Therefore, under this *main heading* place:

(i) the *net profit for the year* of the *holding company*, followed by

(ii) the *net profit* of *each subsidiary* company separately.

Consolidated Profit and Loss Account—Credit side

Net Profit on trading for the year	
Rainbow Ltd (holding co.)	£10,000
Red Ltd (subsidiary co.)	3,000
Yellow Ltd (subsidiary co.)	4,800
Orange Ltd (subsidiary co.)	2,950
	£20,750

(b) *Profit of other years* **since** *acquisition.* Any profits of *earlier years* earned by a subsidiary company since the date of acquisition but which still remain *undistributed* must be next entered on the *credit side* of the consolidated Profit and Loss Account in the same manner as those in (a) above.

(c) **Pre**-*acquisition profits.* *None* of the profits which were earned *before* the holding company acquired shares in the subsidiary *should be credited* in the consolidated Profit and Loss Account.

MINORITY INTEREST AND PRE-ACQUISITION PROFITS

4. Cost of Control Account. Before proceeding to an example it is important to call to mind that when studying *consolidated Balance Sheets* we became familiar with an account which we called "Cost of Control Account."

In this account, it will be remembered, we credited that *part of pre-acquisition profit* which became the property of the holding company. The *remainder* of the pre-acquisition profit was credited to the *Minority Interest Account*. Thus all of the pre-acquisition profits would have been transferred from the Profit and Loss Account of the subsidiary company when constructing a *consolidated* Balance Sheet, and the account would be left closed off showing *no* balance. Quite obviously the same position would hold good when preparing a *consolidated* Profit and Loss Account.

5. Consolidation illustrated. The student is advised to study the following examples and exercises in consolidating with great thoroughness, in this and subsequent paragraphs.

EXAMPLE 53

Rainbow Ltd acquired 75% of the ordinary share capital of Orange Ltd on 31st December 1966. There was a balance of £8000 standing to the credit of the Profit and Loss Account of Orange Ltd at the date of acquisition.

For the purposes of *consolidation* the following would be the position:

ORANGE LTD—*Profit and Loss Account*

1966			1966		
Dec. 31			Dec. 31		
Cost of Control A/c		£6,000	Balance b/d		£8,000
Minority Interest					
A/c		2,000			
		£8,000			£8,000

Cost of Control Account

			1966		
			31st Dec.		
			Profit and Loss A/c		
			(75% of £8,000)		£6,000

Minority Interest Account

			1966		
			31st Dec.		
			Profit and Loss A/c		
			(25% of £8,000)		£2,000

From the example it is clear that the balance of £8000 *pre-acquisition profit* has now been accounted for, and that, purely from the consolidation viewpoint, there is *no balance on the Profit and Loss Account* of Orange Ltd *at the time of merger* (ATOM). It follows, therefore, that *no* part of the *pre*-acquisition profits will appear in the Consolidated Profit and Loss Account, since no profit remains on the account to be dealt with.

SAMPLE QUESTION

Rain Ltd held two-thirds of the ordinary share capital of Shower Ltd which it acquired on 31st December 1961. The balances standing to the credit of the Profit and Loss Accounts of the respective companies on 31st December 1963, *i.e. two* years afterwards, were made up in the following manner:

	Holding Co. *Rain Ltd*	*Subsidiary Co.* *Shower Ltd*
Net Profit for 1963	£1,860	£2,760
Balance brought forward from the previous year	4,500	3,330
	£6,360	£6,090

On 31st December 1961, the date of acquisition, the Profit and Loss Account of Shower Ltd showed a credit balance of £1200.

Prepare a Consolidated Profit and Loss Account for the year ended 31st December 1963.

ANSWER

Minority Interest: *Outside shareholders in Shower Ltd*			*Net Profit for 1963:*		
1. Current year's profits, one-third of	£2,760		Rain Ltd	£1,860	
	= £920		Shower Ltd	2,760	
2. Previous profits undistributed	3,330				£4,620
Less: Pre-acquisition profits	1,200		*Profits of earlier years not yet distributed i.e.* Balances brought forward from previous years		
one-third of	£2,130		Rain Ltd		4,500
	= 710		Shower Ltd	3,330	
		£1,630	*Less: Pre*-acquisition profit	1,200	
Balance c/d		9,620			2,130
		£11,250			£11,250
			Balance b/d		£9,620

6. Alternative method of presentation. The Consolidated Profit and Loss Account may be presented in the form of a table, if so desired. Using the figures from the preceding example:

		Rain Ltd £6,360	Shower Ltd £6,090	Total £12,450
Final balance on Profit and Loss Account		£6,360	£6,090	£12,450
Less Minority Interest:				
1963 profit, Shower Ltd = one-third of	£2,760		−920	−920
		6,360	5,170	11,530
1962 balance, Shower Ltd	£3,330			
Deduct Pre-acquisition profit	1,200			
Net profit for 1962	£2,130			
one-third of	£2,130		−710	−710
		6,360	4,460	10,820
Less Pre-acquisition profit			−1,200	−1,200
		£6,360	£3,260	£9,620

NOTE: In the two years where profit has arisen since acquisition, *i.e.* in the years ended 31st December 1962 and 31st December 1963, only that part of the profit of Shower Ltd (the subsidiary company) which belongs to Rain Ltd will, in effect, be credited to the Consolidated Profit and Loss Account.

The amount of profit which is now due to the minority interest can be shown as follows:

Minority Interest Account

1. Proportion of 1963 profit (one-third of £2,760)	£920
2. Profit of other years since date of acquisition (one-third of £2,130)	710
3. Pre-acquisition profit (one-third of £1,200)	400
	£2,030

7. Six graduated exercises in consolidating. Before we proceed further it is vitally important that the following exercises are worked in order to ensure that you really understand what has been dealt with up to this point.

EXERCISE 1

Fields Ltd acquired 60% of the ordinary share capital of Meadows Ltd on 31st March 1961.

The Profit and Loss Accounts of the two companies at 31st March 1962 were:

	Fields Ltd	*Meadows Ltd*
Net Profit, year to 31st March 1962	£6,000	£3,000
Balance b/f from previous year	7,520	2,650
	£13,520	£5,650

Prepare a consolidated Profit and Loss Account for the year ended 31st March 1962.

EXERCISE 2

Rhodes Ltd acquired 75% of the ordinary share capital of Close Ltd at 31st December 1960, and 80% of the ordinary shares of Crescent Ltd on the same date.

The Profit and Loss Accounts of the companies at 31st December 1961 were as follows:

	Rhodes Ltd	*Close Ltd*	*Crescent Ltd*
Net profit, year to 31st December 1961	£10,000	£4,000	£6,600
Balance b/f from previous year	3,800	940	1,250
	£13,800	£4,940	£7,850

Prepare a consolidated Profit and Loss Account for the year ended 31st December 1961.

EXERCISE 3

Wagon Ltd acquired 90% of the ordinary share capital of Cart Ltd on 30th June 1961, and 60% of the ordinary shares of Dray Ltd on the same date.

The Profit and Loss Accounts of the companies at 30th June 1962 were as follows:

	Wagon Ltd	Cart Ltd	Dray Ltd
Net profit, year to 30th June 1962	£14,000	£1,000	£4,200
Balance b/f from previous year	3,150	1,584	2,475
	£17,150	£2,584	£6,675

Prepare a consolidated Profit and Loss Account for the year ended 30th June 1962.

EXERCISE 4

Butcher Ltd acquired 75% of the ordinary share capital in Baker Ltd on 31st May 1960.

The Profit and Loss Accounts of the companies at 31st May 1962 were as follows:

	Butcher Ltd	Baker Ltd
Net profit, year to 31st May 1962	£6,780	£4,832
Balance b/f from previous year	2,925	788
	£9,705	£5,620

On 31st May 1960, the date of acquisition, the credit balance on the Profit and Loss Account of Baker Ltd was £200.

Prepare a consolidated Profit and Loss Account for the year ended 31st May 1962.

EXERCISE 5

Bricks Ltd acquired 80% of the ordinary share capital of Mortar Ltd on 31st December 1959. It also acquired 75% of the ordinary shares of Trowell Ltd on 31st December 1960.

The Profit and Loss Accounts of the respective companies at 31st December 1961 were as follows:

	Bricks Ltd	Mortar Ltd	Trowell Ltd
Net profit, year to 31st December 1961	£7,500	£4,000	£3,240
Balance b/f from previous year	1,800	1,550	1,880
	£9,300	£5,550	£5,120

On 31st December 1959, the date on which the shares in Mortar Ltd were acquired, the balance standing to the credit of the Profit and Loss Account of Mortar Ltd was £500.

Prepare a consolidated Profit and Loss Account for the year ended 31st December 1961.

EXERCISE 6

Sword Ltd acquired 90% of the ordinary share capital of Lance Ltd on 30th June 1960. On 30th June 1961 it acquired two-thirds of the ordinary shares of Dagger Ltd.

The Profit and Loss Accounts of the three companies at 30th June 1962 were as follows:

	Sword Ltd	Lance Ltd	Dagger Ltd
Net profit, year to 30th June 1962	£7,000	810	£1,344 Loss
Balance b/f from previous year	4,380	1,570	285
	£11,380	£2,380	£1,059 Dr.

At 30th June 1960 the credit balance on the Profit and Loss account of Lance Ltd was £1,700.

Prepare a consolidated Profit and Loss Account for the year ended 30th June 1962.

8. Solutions to exercises

EXERCISE 1

Consolidated Profit and Loss Account

Minority Interest Meadows Ltd, four-tenths of £3,000	£1,200	Net Profit, year to 31st March 1962		
Balance	15,320	Fields Ltd	£6,000	
		Meadows Ltd	3,000	
				9,000
		Profit of earlier years		
		Fields Ltd		7,520
	£16,520			£16,520

EXERCISE 2
Consolidated Profit and Loss Account

	Net profit, year to 31st December 1961		
	Rhodes Ltd	£10,000	
	Close Ltd (three-quarters of £4,000)	3,000	
	Crescent Ltd (four-fifths of £6,600	5,280	
			18,280
	Profit of earlier years		
	Rhodes Ltd		3,800
			£22,080

EXERCISE 3
Consolidated Profit and Loss Account

	Net profit, year to 30th June 1962		
	Wagon Ltd	£14,000	
	Cart Ltd (nine-tenths of £1,000)	900	
	Dray Ltd (six-tenths of £4,200)	2,520	
			£17,420
	Profit of earlier years		
	Wagon Ltd		3,150
			£20,570

EXERCISE 4

Consolidated Profit and Loss Account

Net profit, year to 31st May 1962			
Butcher Ltd		£6,780	
Baker Ltd (three-			
quarters of £4,832)		3,624	
		———	£10,404
Profit of earlier years			
Butcher Ltd		£2,925	
Baker Ltd	£788		
Less: Pre-acquisi-			
tion profit	200		
	———		
	£588		
Three-quarters of £588	=	441	
		———	3,366
			£13,770

EXERCISE 5

Consolidated Profit and Loss Account

Net profit, year to 31st December 1961			
Bricks Ltd		£7,500	
Mortar Ltd (four-fifths			
of £4,000)		3,200	
Trowell Ltd (three-			
quarters of £3,240)		2,430	
		———	£13,130
Profit of earlier years			
Bricks Ltd		£1,800	
Mortar Ltd	£1,550		
Less: Pre-acquisi-			
tion profit	500		
	———		
	£1,050		
Four-fifths of £1,050	=	840	
		———	2,640
			£15,770

EXERCISE 6

Consolidated Profit and Loss Account

Net profit, year to 30th June 1962			
Sword Ltd		£7,000	
Lance Ltd (nine-tenths of £810)		729	
		7,729	
Less : Dagger Ltd (two-thirds of £1,344 *loss*)		896	
			£6,833
Profits of earlier years			
Sword Ltd		£4,380	
Lance Ltd	£1,570		
Less : Pre-acquisition	1,700		
Loss of	£130		
Nine-tenths of £130 Loss =		−117	
			4,263
			£11,096

PROGRESS TEST 15

1. Make a list of those items which must be eliminated when preparing a consolidated Profit and Loss Account. (2)

2. How must pre-acquisition profits be dealt with when consolidating? (3(c), 4)

CHAPTER XVI

THE CONSOLIDATED PROFIT AND LOSS ACCOUNT (II)

Having worked the six graduated consolidating exercises at the end of the last chapter the student should by now feel that he has a sound grasp of the main features of the construction of a consolidated Profit and Loss Account.

DIVIDENDS AND UNREALISED PROFIT

We have concentrated so far on minority interests (*M*) and pre-acquisition profits of a subsidiary company (*PS*) which cover the last three letters of the *aide-memoire*, *DUMPS*. Now we must turn to the first two letters, *i.e.* *D* for dividends and *U* for unrealised profit.

1. Dividends (inter-company). Assuming that the holding company has no investments outside the group it can be said at once that the only item to appear in a consolidated Profit and Loss Account under the heading "Dividends" is any dividend *paid* by the *holding* company (or proposed to be paid by it).

Note well the word *paid*.

Dividends *received* by the holding company will be received by virtue of the shares it holds in the subsidiary companies, *i.e.* in the form of income from investments. These dividends will therefore appear as *credit* entries in the holding company's ordinary Profit and Loss Account.

In the respective Profit and Loss Accounts of the *subsidiary* companies the above dividends would, of course, appear as *debit* entries. It is evident that when *all* the individual Profit and Loss Accounts are consolidated these dividends must cancel each other out and thus will not appear in the consolidated Profit and Loss Account.

EXAMPLE 54

AB Ltd own all the shares in CD Ltd. These shares were acquired ten years ago. The net profits of the respective companies for the year just ended are as follows:

| AB Ltd | £7,200 | (before crediting any dividends receivable) |
| CD Ltd | £6,500 | (before debiting any dividends on the Profit and Loss Account) |

£13,700

CD Ltd now proposes to pay a dividend of £4750 out of its profits.

The Profit and Loss Accounts of the companies would appear respectively:

Profit and Loss Account of AB Ltd

Balance c/d	£11,950	Net profit for the year	£7,200
		Dividend receivable from CD Ltd	4,750
	£11,950		£11,950
		Balance b/d	£11,950

Profit and Loss Account of CD Ltd

Proposed dividend	£4,750	Net profit for the year	£6,500
Balance c/f	1,750		
	£6,500		£6,500
		Balance b/f	£1,750

If the two Profit and Loss Accounts are consolidated as they stand we would have the following position:

Consolidated Profit and Loss Account of AB Ltd and CD Ltd

Dividend **payable**	£4,750	Net profit for the year	
		AB Ltd	£7,200
Balance c/f	13,700	CD Ltd	6,500
			£13,700
		Dividend **receivable**	4,750
	£18,450		£18,450
		Balance b/f	£13,700

NOTE: The total of the two balances was made up as follows:

Before *consolidation*

AB Ltd	£11,950
CD Ltd	1,750
	£13,700

From this consolidation it is very clear that no effective purpose is served by including the dividend because such entries are *self-cancelling*. The position would be as follows if the dividend were ignored both as a receipt and as a payment.

Consolidated Profit and Loss Account of A B Ltd and C D Ltd

	Net profit for the year:	
	AB Ltd	£7,200
	CD Ltd	6,500
		£13,700
		£13,700

In the above example we have considered the case of a 100% subsidiary. What would be the position if CD Ltd were, say, only a 90% subsidiary?

The minority shareholders would be entitled to 10% of the profit of £6,500, *i.e.* £650. This figure would, of course, *include* the dividend of £475, being one-tenth of the total dividend of £4,750.

Consolidated Profit and Loss Account of AB Ltd and CD Ltd

Minority Interest:			Net profit for the year:		
One-tenth of			AB Ltd	£7,200	
£6,500, *i.e.*			CD Ltd	6,500	
£650					13,700
Dividend	475				
Undistributed					
profit	175				
		£650			
Balance c/f		£13,050			
		£13,700			£13,700
			Balance b/f		£13,050

2. Dividends paid out of pre-acquisition profits. It frequently happens that shortly after a holding company has acquired shares in a subsidiary company the subsidiary *pays* a dividend out of the profits which it had made *before* it was taken over, *i.e.* out of the *pre*-acquisition profits.

By the time that the date has arrived for the dividend to be *paid* (usually a short time after the declaration) the holding company has become the registered owner of the shares. It is thus entitled to receive in cash such part of the total dividend payment as is proportionate to the number of shares it holds.

EXAMPLE 55

Subco Ltd has an issued capital of £12,000 in ordinary shares of £1 each. Parco Ltd buys all the shares in Subco Ltd for £20,000.

BALANCE SHEET OF SUBCO LTD AT DATE OF ACQUISITION

Share Capital			Sundry Assets	£13,740
12,000 ordinary shares		£12,000	Cash at Bank	2,260
Profit and Loss A/c		2,000		
Creditors				
Trade	£500			
Proposed dividend	1,500			
		2,000		
		£16,000		£16,000

The Cost of Control Account would appear as under:

Cost of Control Account

Amount paid for shares	£20,000	Nominal value	£12,000
		Undistributed balance (Profit and Loss A/c)	2,000
		Goodwill c/d	6,000
	£20,000		£20,000
Goodwill b/d	£6,000		

From the above account we see that at the date of acquisition the cost of goodwill was £6000.

Shortly afterwards, however, Subco Ltd paid a dividend of £1500 out of the *pre-acquisition profits*. Since Parco Ltd owned all the shares *at the date of payment* obviously the whole amount paid by Subco Ltd will be received by Parco Ltd. Thus Parco Ltd, although it had to pay £20,000 in cash to acquire the shares, now receives a payment in cash of £1500 in respect of profits made *before* it (Parco Ltd) became the owner. In other words the *true cost* of the shares to Parco Ltd was £18,500. Assuming that no other transactions had taken place between the date of acquisition and the payment of the dividend the Balance Sheet of Subco Ltd *after* payment would be as follows:

BALANCE SHEET—SUBCO LTD

Share Capital		Sundry Assets		£13,740
12,000 ordinary		Cash at Bank £2,260		
shares	£12,000	*Less* dividend		
Profit and Loss A/c	2,000	paid	1,500	
Creditors				760
Trade	500			
	£14,500			£14,500

The books of Parco Ltd would show the following entries:

Bank Account

Subco Ltd Dividend	£1,500	

Cost of Control Account

Goodwill b/d	£6,000	Bank A/c: Dividend received from Subco Ltd out of its pre-acquisition profits	£1,500
		Balance c/d: *Revised* cost of goodwill	4,500
	£6,000		£6,000
Goodwill b/d	£4,500		

3. Examination problems. If the matter of a dividend being paid out of pre-acquisition profits is introduced into an examination question it will almost certainly be shown in the same way as any other dividend would be shown, *i.e.* as a credit entry *in* the Profit and Loss Account of the holding company. This represents a great *error of principle* and the adjusting entries in such a case would be:

Debit Profit and Loss Account of the **holding** company.
Credit Cost of Control Account.

EXAMPLE 56

JK Ltd acquired *all* the ordinary shares of LM Ltd on 1st January 1966.

The Profit and Loss Accounts of the two companies at 31st December 1966, *i.e.* one year later, were:

JK Ltd Profit and Loss Account for the year ended 31st December 1966

	Net profit *for year 1966* £8,000
	Dividend received from LM Ltd *in respect of 1965 profits* 750
	£8,750

LM Ltd Profit and Loss Account for the year ended 31st December 1966

Dividend paid in respect of 1965 profits	£750	Net profit *for year 1966*	£3,600
Balance c/d	2,850		
	£3,600		£3,600
		Balance b/d	£2,850

If we consolidated the accounts we would obtain the following results:

Consolidated Profit and Loss Account of JK Ltd and LM Ltd for year to 31st December 1966

Cost of Control A/c (Dividend paid by LM Ltd to JK Ltd)	£750	Net profit for the year JK Ltd	£8,000		
Balance c/f	11,600	LM Ltd	3,600		£11,600
		Dividend received (from LM Ltd in respect of *pre-aquisition profits*)			750
	£12,350				£12,350
		Balance b/f			£11,600

NOTE: If, in addition, we were preparing a Consolidated Balance Sheet, the corresponding credit of the £750 dividend debited above would be made in the Cost of Control Account *thus reducing the goodwill.*

The above example shows a dividend paid out of pre-acquisition profits in the case of a fully-owned subsidiary. To ensure that the matter is properly understood let us take an example involving an 80% subsidiary.

EXAMPLE 57

On 1st January 1963 DE Ltd acquired 8000 ordinary shares in GH Ltd whose total issued capital was 10,000 £1 ordinary shares. GH Ltd paid a dividend of 10% in respect of its 1962 profits on 4th April 1963. The Profit and Loss Accounts of the two companies at 31st December 1963, *i.e.* one year later, read as follows:

DE Ltd Profit and Loss Account for year ended 31st December 1963

Net profit for year 1963	£7,250
Dividend received from GH Ltd in respect of 1962 profits (*i.e.* pre-acquisition profits)	800
	£8,050

GH Ltd Profit and Loss Account for year ended 31st December 1963

Dividend paid in April, 1963 in respect of 1962 profit (10% of £10,000 *i.e.* the Issued Capital)	£1,000	Net profit for year 1963 £5,740 Balance b/f from 1962 (*i.e.* pre-acquisition profit *after* providing for dividend of £1,000) 2,500	

Let us first of all consider the position immediately before the shares were acquired by DE Ltd.

GH Ltd had a credit balance on Profit and Loss Account of £2500.

When dealing with the acquisition we would have therefore had the following:

GH Ltd Profit and Loss Account year to 31st December 1962

Cost of Control A/c	£2,000	Net profit	£2,500
Minority Interest A/c	500		
	£2,500		£2,500

Cost of Control Account

Profit and Loss A/c (GH Ltd, four-fifths of £2,500)	£2,000

Minority Interest Account

Profit and Loss A/c (GH Ltd, one-fifth of £2,500)	£500

Thus, it can be seen that there is no balance left on the Profit and Loss Account so far as consolidation is concerned.

(It must be clearly understood that the above entries would not be made in the ledger accounts of GH Ltd; they are purely of a memorandum character and used only for the purposes of consolidation.)

Turning now to the Profit and Loss Account of DE Ltd, the holding company, we see that 80% of the total dividend, *i.e.* the correct proportion to which it is entitled, has been credited therein. As has already been pointed out this is an error of principle and must be corrected. We will, therefore, debit the Profit and Loss Account of DE Ltd with £800 and credit the Cost of Control Account of GH Ltd. The effect of this is to reduce the price paid for the goodwill.

4. Unrealised profits (inter-company). If PQ Ltd, which owns all the shares in RS Ltd, sells goods to RS Ltd no profit can be made by the companies *as a group* as an immediate result of this transaction. The matter has to go a stage further, *i.e.* the goods need to be *sold by* RS Ltd to outside customers, before the profit can truly be counted as made.

Consequently, if the goods are still held in stock by RS Ltd on the date as at which a Consolidated Profit and Loss Account is being prepared, an adjustment would have to be made. PQ took credit for the profit when the goods were sold to RS Ltd. We must therefore eliminate this profit by debiting it in the Consolidated Profit and Loss Account. The Stock Account of RS Ltd would accept the corresponding credit and so in the Consolidated Balance Sheet the stock figure would be reduced by this amount.

EXAMPLE 58

CD Ltd owns all the shares in EF Ltd. On 31st May 1962, the last day of the accounting year of both companies, CD Ltd sold goods to EF Ltd. These goods had cost CD Ltd £240, and they were sold to EF Ltd for £300.

When the group accounts are being prepared the profit of £60 which is, in fact, not a truly realised profit (and therefore in the circumstances not a profit at all) must be debited to the Consolidated Profit and Loss Account thus:

Consolidated Profit and Loss Account of CD Ltd and EF Ltd

Unrealised profit on goods sold to EF Ltd £60	

The corresponding credit would be made in the Stock Account of EF Ltd so that in the Consolidated Balance Sheet the *total* figure shown for stock would be reduced by £60.

EXAMPLE 59

In the above example CD Ltd owned *all* the shares in EF Ltd. We will now suppose that CD Ltd owns only 75% of the capital of EF Ltd. Taking the details to be the same, *i.e.* that goods which cost CD Ltd £240 were sold to EF Ltd for £300, we will have to adjust the figures as follows:

(a) The profit of £60 is no longer to be considered as being entirely unrealised because there is now a minority interest element to be considered.

We will rightly conclude that the proportion of the goods sold to the minority shareholders represents goods sold to outsiders. It follows, therefore, that CD Ltd (from the point of view of the group) will properly consider that the proportion of profit contained in the sale to the minority interest must be counted as part of the profit of the group.

(b) The debit entry in the Consolidated Profit and Loss Account will, in this case, appear as follows:

Profit on goods sold to EF Ltd	£60	
Less Amount attributable to minority interest, *i.e.* a quarter of £60	15	
	——	£45

SAMPLE QUESTION

The final sections of the Profit and Loss Accounts of Gorse Ltd, Heather Ltd and Broom Ltd, for the year to 31st December 1963, are as follows:

GORSE LTD

Proposed dividend	£20,000	Net profit for 1963	£24,600
Balance c/f	14,000	Balance at 31st December 1962	9,400
	£34,000		£34,000

HEATHER LTD

Balance c/f	£10,000	Net profit for 1963	£8,000
		Balance at 31st December 1962	2,000
	£10,000		£10,000

BROOM LTD

Net loss for 1963	£1,400	Balance at 31st	
Balance c/f	300	December 1962	£1,700
	£1,700		£1,700

Gorse Ltd acquired the whole share capital of Broom Ltd on 31st December 1962, and three-quarters of the share capital of Heather Ltd on 31st December 1961.

The balance of £2000 on the Profit and Loss Account of Heather Ltd at 31st December 1962 represents a credit balance of £1200 brought forward from 1961, and a net profit of £800 in 1962.

No dividend has been paid by either Heather Ltd or Broom Ltd since the holding company acquired the shares.

You are required to prepare the final section of the Consolidated Profit and Loss Account for the year to 31st December 1963.

ANSWER

Consolidated Profit and Loss Account of Gorse, Heather and Broom Ltd for the year ended 31st December 1963

Minority interest:		Net profit for 1963:		
Heather Ltd	£2,200	Gorse Ltd	£24,600	
		Heather Ltd	8,000	
			32,600	
Proposed dividend (by		*Less*		
holding company)	20,000	Loss:		
Balance c/d	19,200	Broom Ltd	1,400	
				31,200
		Undistributed profit of earlier years:		
		Gorse Ltd	9,400	
		Heather Ltd	2,000	
			11,400	
		Less		
		Pre-acqui-sition profit	1,200	
				10,200
	£41,400			£41,400

Note that in the Consolidated Profit and Loss Account the *entire* pre-acquisition profit of £1200 is deducted from the *total* undistributed profit of *earlier years* in arriving at the final consolidation. The detailed breakdown of Heather Ltd's Profit and Loss Account is shown below.

Heather Ltd, Profit and Loss Account

31st Dec. 1961			31st Dec. 1961	
Cost of Control ($\frac{3}{4}$)	900		Balance b/f	£1,200
Minority Interest ($\frac{1}{4}$)	300			
	£1,200			£1,200
31st Dec. 1963			31st Dec. 1962	
Minority Interest ($\frac{1}{4}$)	2,200		Net Profit	800
Balance c/d	6,600		31st Dec. 1963	
			Net Profit	8,000
	£8,800			£8,800
			Balance b/d	£6,600

SPECIMEN QUESTION
(C.I.S.)

You are required to prepare the Consolidated Profit and Loss Account of A Ltd, a holding company, and its three subsidiary companies B Ltd, C Ltd and D Ltd, for the year ended 31st December 1963.

The separate Profit and Loss Accounts for the year 1963 are as follows:

COMPANY A LTD

Dividend for year 1963	£8,000		Net Profit for 1963	£14,150
Balance c/f	18,550		Balance b/f 1962	8,000
			Dividends received	4,400
	£26,550			£26,550

COMPANY B LTD

Preference dividend (for 1963)	£150		Net Profit for 1963	£250
Balance c/f	100		Balance b/f from 1962	—
	£250			£250

COMPANY C LTD

Interim dividend for 1963	£4,000	Net Profit for 1963	£6,000
Balance c/f	8,500	Balance b/f from 1962	6,500
	£12,500		£12,500

COMPANY D LTD

Net loss for 1963	£1,650	Balance b/f from 1962	£1,800
Final dividend for 1962	1,400	Balance c/f	1,250
	£3,050		£3,050

The issued share capital of the subsidiary companies is as follows:

	B Ltd	*C Ltd*	*D Ltd*
Ordinary shares:			
Total	£20,000	£40,000	£30,000
Held by A Ltd	16,000	30,000	30,000
6% Preference shares:			
Total	10,000	—	—
Held by A Ltd	*nil*	—	—

A Ltd acquired the shares in B Ltd and D Ltd on 31st December 1962. The shares in C Ltd were acquired on 31st December 1961, when the credit balance on the Profit and Loss Account of C Ltd was £2000. C Ltd paid no dividend in 1962.

In December 1963 A Ltd sold goods to D Ltd for £1875, and these goods were still held by D Ltd on 31st December 1963. The cost of these goods to A Ltd was £1500.

SUGGESTED ANSWER

(a) The first thing to be done is to prepare a *detailed Profit and Loss Account* of C Ltd (the company in which a controlling interest was acquired *more than* one year ago), and break it down, as shown below, into the *separate* years concerned.

C Ltd, Profit and Loss Account

31st Dec. 1961			31st Dec. 1961	
Cost of Control			Balance b/f	£2,000
A/c (¾)	£1,500			
Minority interest (¼)	500			
	£2,000			£2,000
31st Dec. 1963			31st Dec. 1962	
Minority interest			Net Profit for year	4,500
one-quarter of			31st Dec. 1963	
£10,500	2,625		Net Profit for year	6,000
Balance c/d three-				
quarters of				
£10,500	7,875			
	£10,500			£10,500
			Balance b/d	£7,875

(b) *Inter-company dividends.* The total sum credited to the holding company's Profit and Loss Account amounts to £4400. This sum consists of:

(i)	from C Ltd, three-quarters of £4000	£3,000	
(ii)	from D Ltd, the full sum of £1400	£1,400	
			£4,400

NOTE: The *only dividends* which must appear in the *Consolidated* Profit and Loss Account are those *paid* (or proposed) *by the holding company, i.e.* £8000, as shown in the Profit and Loss Account of A Ltd.

(c) *Unrealised (inter-company) profits.* Goods which had cost A Ltd £1500 had been sold to D Ltd (a 100% subsidiary) in December 1963, for £1875. These goods were still held by D Ltd at 31st December 1963.

The profit of £375 must, therefore, be eliminated when consolidating.

Consolidated Profit and Loss Account

Dividends			Net Profit for 1963				
A Ltd		£8,000	A Ltd	£14,150			
Unrealised			B Ltd	250			
profit			C Ltd	6,000			
on goods sold by				———			
A Ltd to D Ltd		375		20,400			
Minority interest			*Less:* D Ltd				
B Ltd			Net Loss	1,650			
Preference				———			£18,750
dividend	£150		Undistributed profit of				
One-fifth			earlier years:				
share of			A Ltd		£8,000		
net profit	20		B Ltd		*nil*		
C Ltd			C Ltd	6,500			
(per (*a*)			*Less:* Pre-				
above)	2,625		acqui-				
	———	2,795	sition				
Balance c/f		20,080	profit	2,000			
				———	4,500		
			D Ltd	1,800			
			Less: Pre-				
			acqui-				
			sition				
			profit	1,800	—		
					———	£12,500	
		£31,250				£31,250	

PROGRESS TEST 16

1. What book-keeping entries must be made when a subsidiary company pays a dividend out of pre-acquisition profits? (**2, 3**)

2. What adjustments are necessary when accounting for unrealised profits in a consolidated Profit and Loss Account? (**4**)

CHAPTER XVII

CORPORATION TAX

INTRODUCTION

1. Introduction of Corporation Tax. Until 1965 the profits of
limited companies were taxed according to the provisions of
the *Income Tax Act*, 1952, as amended by the annual *Finance
Acts*.

Tax was levied under two headings:

(*a*) Income tax, (Case I of Schedule D); and
(*b*) Profits tax.

The Corporation Tax has now replaced these two taxes in so
far as the **trading** profit of *limited companies* are concerned.
Income tax remains as the tax levied on *individuals*. There
can also be a charge to income tax under a new schedule known
as Schedule F in respect of what are termed "distributions."

2. Scope of the tax. A limited company is liable to pay
Corporation Tax upon "its income and gains." These two
elements are together referred to as the "profits." In addition,
and *as a completely separate matter*, it must account to the
Inland Revenue for *income tax* on the following:

(*a*) *dividends* paid out of profits;
(*b*) other *distributions* made out of profits; and
(*c*) *interest* payments and annual charges.

Corporation Tax is not charged on dividends *received* by a
company.

BASIS OF ASSESSMENT

3. Financial years. Corporation Tax is to be assessed, *i.e.*
measured or calculated, for each *Financial Year* which ends
on 31st March. This financial year is *the year of the Inland
Revenue* which, for the purposes of Corporation Tax, commences on 1st April in one year and ends on 31st March in the

following year. Each financial year will be referred to as "financial year 19—," and the specific year will be that particular year **in which 1st April falls**. Thus the Corporation Tax year which begins on 1st April 1967, will be called "financial year 1967."

4. Accounting Periods. It is the normal practice for a company to make up its accounts once each year, *e.g.* year ending 30th September 1967. For the purpose of Corporation Tax this "business year" will be known as the *Accounting Period*. An accounting period must not exceed twelve months. Assessments will be made on a *current year* basis, *i.e.* on the profits arising *in* the accounting period.

5. Computation of income. The *basic rule* for the calculation of income is that it must be computed in accordance with income tax principles. This means that income which arises from various sources will be added together to provide the *total profits* on which a *single assessment* to Corporation Tax will be made.

6. Apportionments. The profits of an *accounting period* will be *apportioned* between the two *financial years* in which the twelve months of the accounting period fall (unless, of course, the company's accounting period corresponds with the Inland Revenue's financial year, *i.e.* ending on 31st March).

EXAMPLE 60

The profits of Q Ltd for the year ended 30th June 1967 are £2400.

Let us suppose that the rates of Corporation Tax covering these *accounting periods* are:

Financial year 1966 = 40%
Financial year 1967 = 35%

The assessment will be as follows:

Q Ltd's *Accounting Period to 30th June 1967*

Financial year *1966*:

(a) 1st July 1966 to 31st March 1967,
nine-twelfths of £2400 = £1800.

$$\textit{Corporation Tax at 40\% on £1800} \qquad = £720$$

Financial year *1967*:

(*b*) 1st April 1967 to 30th June 1967,
three-twelfths of £2400 = £600.

$$\textit{Corporation Tax at 35\% on £600} \qquad = £210$$

Total Corporation Tax for the accounting period = £930.

7. Distributions. A company must account to the Inland Revenue for *income tax* in respect of dividends which it has paid and other distributions it has made. The major item classed as "distributions" will be dividends paid by a company. Other items falling under this heading are:

(*a*) the issue of bonus shares where there has been a repayment of preference share capital; and
(*b*) if share capital is repaid at a *premium*, the premium will be treated as a distribution.

8. Annual payments. A company must account to the Inland Revenue for income tax in respect of the following payments:

(*a*) *Yearly* interest;
(*b*) Annuities;
(*c*) Other annual payments;

since such payments are allowed to be *charged* against a company's profits for Corporation Tax purposes.

EXAMPLE 61

W Ltd had issued £40,000 5% debentures. The annual interest, £2000, was paid net (£1175) but the gross amount was debited in the company's Profit and Loss Account.

The entries would be as follows:

Bank Account

	Debenture Interest A/c £1,175

Debenture Interest Account

Bank A/c	£1,175	

When the interest has been paid the following entries will be necessary:

Debenture Interest Account

Bank A/c	£1,175	
Income Tax A/c (tax at 8s. 3d.)	825	
	£2,000	

Income Tax Account (Annual Payments)

	Debenture Interest A/c £825

Debenture Interest Account will be closed by transferring £2000 to the debit of Profit and Loss Account.

Profit and Loss Account

Debenture Interest A/c	£2,000	

9. Capital gains. The basic rule for the computation of capital gains for the purposes of Corporation Tax is that they must be computed in accordance with the principles applying for the Capital Gains Tax. The amount to be included for assessment to Corporation Tax is the amount of the chargeable gains of the *accounting period*.

10. Relief for losses. If a company incurs a loss on its trading in an accounting period it may carry such loss forward and set it against *profits* from its trading made in any *subsequent* accounting period. Alternatively, if a company has incurred a trading loss in a particular accounting period it may claim to set off the loss for Corporation Tax against *any profits of any other kind* made in the *same* accounting period.

11. Capital allowances. The ordinary capital allowances, *e.g.* on plant and machinery, are given as deductions from the profits in computing Corporation Tax. Balancing charges are to be treated as receipts from trading.

K

TAXATION OF PROFITS

12. The taxation of profits before Corporation Tax was introduced. Companies used to be liable to two separate forms of taxation on their profits:

(a) *Income tax* chargeable at the standard rate; and
(b) *Profits tax* chargeable at an appointed percentage of the profits.

For some years before the introduction of the Corporation Tax the standard rate of income tax stood at 7s. 9d. in the £, while profits tax remained steady at 15%. The following example illustrates the position.

EXAMPLE 62

Z Ltd had profits of £20,000 as adjusted for taxation. The assessment to tax would have been as follows:

Income Tax £20,000 at 7s. 9d.		£7,750
Profits Tax 15% of £20,000		3,000
	Total taxation liability	£10,750

Thus, there remained £9250 available to be distributed as dividend to the shareholders. If we suppose that this entire amount was paid to them the total profit of £20,000 would have been disposed of in the following way:

Paid to the Inland Revenue (as above)	£10,750
Paid to the shareholders	9,250
	£20,000

The shareholders would receive warrants which, in total, would have shown the following information:

Gross dividend at $x\%$	£15,102
Less Income tax at 7s. 9d. in £	5,852
Net dividend	£9,250

The income tax of £5852 shown as a deduction from the gross dividend forms a part of the total income tax, £7750, charged on the company's profits. When the company paid its tax of £7750 *the lesser sum of £5852 was deemed to be included* in the payment.

To explain the matter in another way we could say that on the total profit of £20,000 a taxation liability (for income tax *and* profits tax) amounting to £10,750 became due. There thus remained £9250 as profit *which had suffered tax in full* and which, therefore, could be distributed in its entirety (if the company so chose) *without there being any further liability to tax whatsoever.*

This state of affairs has changed with the introduction of Corporation Tax as will be seen in the following paragraphs (**13–20**).

13. The taxation of profits after the introduction of Corporation Tax. The position as set out in the previous paragraph has been altered with the introduction of Corporation Tax. A company is still liable to *two* separate forms of taxation:

(*a*) *Corporation Tax* chargeable at an appointed percentage on its profits; and
(*b*) *Income tax* chargeable at the standard rate *on the dividends it pays.*

When a company pays a dividend (or makes any other distribution) it is authorised to *deduct* out of the distribution an amount equal to *income tax at the standard rate.* Whatever sum of money is actually *paid* will be regarded by the Inland Revenue as being the *net* amount of the distribution. Thus an actual payment *in cash* of £1000 as a dividend would be treated by the Inland Revenue as a *gross* dividend of £1633 13*s.* 1*d.* (when the standard rate of income tax is 7*s.* 9*d.*).

This means that the paying company will have to account to the Inland Revenue for £633 13*s.* 1*d.* That is to say, the company would be liable to pay income tax amounting to £633 13*s.* 1*d.* assessed under Schedule F *in addition* to £1000 to the shareholders, unless it can claim some degree of "set-off" as explained below (*see* **21**).

EXAMPLE 63

The adjusted profits of Y Ltd amounted to £20,000. The company pays a dividend of £9250 in cash. Corporation Tax is levied at 40% and, *for the purposes of this example*, income tax is chargeable at 7*s.* 9*d.*

The assessment to tax would have been:

Corporation Tax at 40% on £20,000	£8,000
Income Tax £15,102 at 7s. 9d. (on a *net* dividend of £9,250)	5,852
Total taxation liability	£13,852

The liability to *income tax* is arrived at in the following manner:

Net dividend paid to shareholders	9,250
Add Income tax at 7s. 9d. (*i.e.* in order to *gross-up* the dividend)	5,852
Gross dividend	£15,102

We can see that there is a considerable increase in the taxation liability where the Corporation Tax method is employed as against the earlier method described in 12 above. A comparison of the two methods shows:

Corporation Tax method		
Corporation Tax	£8,000	
Income Tax	5,852	
		£13,852
Old method (shown in Example 62)		10,750
Increase in tax liability		£3,102

NOTE: With the introduction of Corporation Tax in the 1965 *Finance Act*, the standard rate of income tax was raised to 8s. 3d.

14. Penalising distributions. If we take another look at Example 63 we see that the Corporation Tax payable amounts to £8000. If the company had *not* paid any dividend there would have been a saving in tax of £5852. Suppose the dividend had been cut by half, *i.e.* dividend £4625 instead of £9250. In this case the total tax to be paid would have been £8000 plus £2926, a total of £10,926. From this it can be seen that the *total* amount of tax payable is *directly governed* by the amount paid out in dividends.

The following table may help. We will assume that the dividend to be *paid* is £8750 in each case.

Income Tax and Profits Tax Method		*Corporation Tax and Income Tax on Dividends Method*	
PROFIT	£20,000	PROFIT	£20,000
Income Tax at 8s. 3d.	£8,250	Corporation Tax at 40%	£8,000
Profits Tax at 15%	3,000	Income Tax on grossed-up dividend of £8750 at 8s. 3d.	6,144
Total tax payable	£11,250	Total tax payable	£14,144
Dividend *paid*	8,750	Dividend *paid*	8,750
			£22,894
		Total amount of dividends and taxation payable in *excess of* profits earned	2,894
TOTAL PROFITS	£20,000	TOTAL PROFITS	£20,000

It is clear from the table that the payment of the same dividend when Corporation Tax is in operation means that the company must find nearly £3000 *more* than the profit earned to satisfy the joint requirements of the Inland Revenue and the shareholders. This obviously is an unsatisfactory state of affairs and means that the company would be living beyond its means.

If the dividend is reduced by half the position is as shown in the table at the top of page 284.

In this second table we can see that the total amount of *tax* payable in each case is nearly the same. The striking difference in the amount of the dividends paid shown in the first table (£8750) and the second table (£4375) emphasises how *the Corporation Tax rules penalise the company which pays out the larger dividend.*

Income Tax and Profits Tax Method		Corporation Tax and Income Tax on Dividends Method	
PROFIT	£20,000	PROFIT	£20,000
Income Tax at 8s. 3d.	£8,250	Corporation Tax at 40%	£8,000
Profits Tax at 15%	3,000	Income Tax on grossed-up dividend of £4375, *i.e.* only *half* the amount of the previous dividend	3,072
Total tax payable	£11,250	Total tax payable	£11,072
Dividend *paid*	8,750	Dividend *paid*	4,375
			15,447
		Balance c/f	4,553
TOTAL PROFIT	£20,000	TOTAL PROFIT	£20,000

15. Income from investments. Two broad classes of investment income feature in the Corporation Tax provisions. These are:

(a) Franked investment income; and
(b) Unfranked investment income.

16. Franked investment income. This is the term given to dividends *received* from other United Kingdom *companies*. The Concise Oxford Dictionary defines the word "frank" as meaning in this context "exempt from future payment." Applying this meaning to dividends *received from another company* we must understand that the company's *profits* will already have *suffered Corporation Tax.* The principle is that Corporation Tax on any profits shall only be charged *once.* Therefore, as the profits of the paying company have already been charged to Corporation Tax, when those profits are distributed as dividends at some later date, they shall not bear any further *Corporation Tax* charge. Hence the expression "*franked* investment income," *i.e.* exempt from future payment (of Corporation Tax). We have already seen that dividends *paid* by a company now incur a liability to *income tax, i.e.* they must be treated as *net* payments after tax has been deducted. In the hands of the receiving company these are effectively *net* dividends, *i.e.* dividends received *after* income tax has been deducted.

17. Suggested accounting entries. When a company *receives* dividends from its investments the standard accounting practice is to credit the Profit and Loss Account with the *gross* amount of the dividend even though only the *net* amount is actually received. The Bank Account would be debited with the net amount of the dividend and Dividend Account credited. The dividend received must now be grossed-up by the company which receives it and the income tax so calculated credited to Dividend Account, the Income Tax (Schedule F) Account being debited. As a result the Inland Revenue would then appear as a *debtor* in the books of the recipient.

EXAMPLE 64

X Ltd receives a dividend of £470 in cash from Z Ltd, the entries would be:

Bank Account

Dividends Receivable A/c	£470	

Dividends Receivable Account

	Bank A/c	£470

The amount received, £470, should now be "grossed-up" to appear in the Profit and Loss Account as a gross figure of £800. Income tax at 8*s.* 3*d.* in £ on £800 amounts to £330 thus giving £470 as the *net* amount of the dividend.

The entries to be made are:

Dividends Receivable Account

	Bank A/c	£470
	Income Tax (Schedule F) A/c	330
		———
		£800

Income Tax (Schedule F) Account

Dividends Receivable A/c £330	

Thus we show the Inland Revenue as a *debtor* of X Ltd.
The entry in the Profit and Loss Account will be as follows:

Profit and Loss Account

	Dividends Received £800

NOTE: You are reminded that *dividends received* are not liable to Corporation Tax since they are not regarded as forming part of the "profits" of a company.

18. Unfranked investment income. This term is used to describe any form of investment income *other than* dividends received. This covers interest on loans or debentures, interest on Government and local authority stocks, bonds, etc. Income from royalty rights are also included under this heading.

Normally, unfranked investment income will be received *after* tax has been deducted at the standard rate in exactly the same way as dividends are received from companies, *i.e.* net. (There are one or two exceptions to the rule about deduction of tax at the source, *e.g.* 3% Defence Bonds and $3\frac{1}{2}$% War Loans are paid *gross*.)

19. Origins of unfranked investment income. Suppose a company holds an investment of £2000 in a 4% Government Stock. It will be entitled to receive interest of £80 per annum (gross). Suppose that the same company also holds 800 £1 shares in a company which pays a dividend of 10% gross. This means that another £80 of investment income (gross) will come into the hands of the investing company. Setting these two investments out in the form of a chart we can observe their similarities:

Unfranked Investment Income 4% Government Stock		*Franked Investment Income £1 shares in company*	
At Cost	£2,000	At Cost	£800
Interest for one year (gross)	£80	Dividend of 10% for one year (gross)	£80
Less Income Tax at 8s. 3d.	33	*Less* Income Tax at 8s. 3d.	33
Cash received	£47	*Cash received*	£47

Why is one of the above called "unfranked" investment income and the other "franked" investment income? To find the answer we have to consider from what *source* the paying agent obtained the funds.

(a) *The franked investment income* came from the *profits* of the company; profits which were liable to Corporation Tax. The rule, we must remember, is that Corporation Tax must be borne only once. The paying company's profits will have already been so charged. Hence, in the hands of the receiving company this is "*franked* investment income."

(b) *Unfranked investment income.* Now what of the interest from the holding in 4% Government Stock? Where did the funds come from? They came, not from profits but *from taxation.* Interest paid on Government or Local Authority Stocks comes from central and local taxes levied upon business and private individuals. This is income in the hands of the authority but it is *not* profit from trading and is not subject to Corporation Tax.

Thus when the interest is received by the investing company (less *income tax*) it has to be treated as part of that company's profits which are to be charged to Corporation Tax. It will be grossed up by adding back the income tax deducted and Corporation Tax will be payable on the gross amount, *i.e.* £80.

(c) *Book-keeping entries.* These will be on the same lines for "Unfranked Investment Income" as those for "Franked Investment Income." It is suggested, however, that a *separate* taxation account headed "Tax on Annual Payments" be employed here in order to keep the two types of income apart. The reason for making this suggestion is that it will simplify the "final adjustment" with the Inland Revenue at the end of the year. This matter is dealt with more fully under the general heading "Set-off" which follows shortly and in the two worked examples at the end of this chapter.

20. Payment of dividends out of profits. We have seen how dividends *received* by a company will have already had income tax deducted with the *net* amount only coming into the hands of the recipient company. This principle of deducting tax before the payment of a dividend applies to all UK companies and so we may very easily have the case of a company both *receiving* dividends from its investments and *paying* dividends to its shareholders. This is two-way traffic. When a dividend *is paid* by a company it must treat the amount paid as if it were the net dividend. This so-called *net* figure must then be grossed-up by income tax at the standard rate. The amount of tax thus added on must be paid over to the Inland Revenue under Schedule F.

The accounting entries required would be:

> *Debit:*   Profit and Loss Appropriation Account with the *gross* amount of the dividend (the income tax may be shown inset).
> *Credit:* Dividend Payable Account.

When payment is made it is the *net* amount which has to be recorded:

> *Debit:*   Dividend Payable Account.
> *Credit:* Bank Account.

There will thus be more on the credit than on the debit side of the Dividend Account, *i.e.* the income tax for which the company is liable under Schedule F will need to be inserted in order to balance off the account. Thus, the entries will be:

> *Debit:*   Dividend Account.
> *Credit:* Income Tax (Schedule F) Account.

In this way we will show the Inland Revenue to be a creditor for the amount of Schedule F income tax owing by the company.

SET-OFF

21. Franked investment income. A company can obtain tax relief on dividends which it has *received net* (income tax having been deducted by the paying company) by means of what is called "set-off" against the income tax *on the dividends it pays* out of its own profits.

22. Other income received. Income which is referred to technically as "annual payments," received by a company together with other income received *net* is charged to Corporation Tax since it is deemed to form part of the profits. It must be remembered that these receipts are *grossed-up* before being credited to the Profit and Loss Account. The income tax which is included in this credit, however, may be "set-off" *against the Corporation Tax liability* of the company for the accounting period in which the payment is made. Alternatively, if the company *makes* annual payments, etc., it may "set-off" any liability in this respect against *the income tax* which it has had to include in its profits, *i.e.* in the form of "annual payments" received.

23. Interim set-off. The rules for "set-off" operate only in respect of tax on *the same category of income*. This means that tax suffered on franked investment income *received* may only be set-off against the income tax on dividends which it *pays* (and, of course, other distributions it makes). In the same way, income tax borne in respect of unfranked income received *less* tax may be "set-off" only against its own payments made, from which it has itself deducted tax.

24. The machinery of accounting for tax. A company which *pays* dividends or which makes annual payments must make a *monthly return* to the Collector of Taxes, *paying* whatever sum of income tax is *due*. If, on the other hand, it *receives* dividends or other income from which income tax has been deducted, the company may take credit for the tax suffered. Thus, if the company has suffered more tax than it has already paid it will receive reimbursement of such payment from the Collector of Taxes. This process will go on month by month *the categories* referred to in the previous section *being disregarded*. It is only **at the end of the year** that a final adjustment will be made setting out the tax receivable and payable into the two separate categories. As a result, a further payment may become due to the Inland Revenue.

25. Final adjustment. On the final adjustment it may be that the company has suffered more tax in respect of franked investment income than it has been able to reclaim in respect of its own distributions. In such a case this surplus of franked investment income may be carried forward against *future* dividends payable. It may *not* be used against tax on annual payments. Any surplus of tax suffered on annual payments *received* may be set against any liability to Corporation Tax.

EXAMPLE 65

PQR Ltd makes up its accounts to 31st December annually.

During the year ended 31st December 1967 the company paid debenture interest of £1500 (net) on 30th June. It received franked investment income on 31st October amounting to £2550 (net).

Income tax at 8*s*. in the £.

The income tax (at 8*s*.) retained by the company on the debenture interest amounted to £1000. This has to be paid over to the Collector of Taxes on the monthly settlement immediately following the interest payment.

The income tax suffered on the dividend received (franked investment income) amounted to £1700 and claim for a refund (which is limited to the amount of tax already paid over to the Inland Revenue, £1000) will be made in the monthly settlement following 31st October.

Stage 1

Debenture Interest Account

1967		
30th June	Bank A/c	£1,500
30th June	Tax on Annual Payments A/c	1,000
		£2,500

Tax on Annual Payments Account

		1967		
		30th June	Debenture Interest A/c	£1,000

Stage 2

The debenture interest was paid in the tax month ending on 5th July 1967. A cheque for the tax due, £1000, must be paid by 19th July 1967.

Tax on Annual Payments Account

1967			1967		
19th July	Bank A/c	£1,000	30th June	Debenture Interest A/c	£1,000

Stage 3

When the dividend is received the following entries would be made:

Dividend Received Account

	1967		
	31st Oct.	Bank A/c	£2,550
	31st Oct.	Income Tax (Sch. F) A/c	1,700
			£4,250

Income Tax (Schedule F) Account

1967		
31st Oct.	Dividend Received A/c	£1,700

Stage 4

In the return to the Collector of Taxes for tax month ending on 5th November 1967, a claim will be made for relief (so far as is permitted) on the tax suffered on the franked investment income.

Repayment will be limited to the amount of tax already paid over to the Inland Revenue earlier in the year, *i.e.* £1000. This would be recorded as follows if we suppose that the refund is made on 1st December:

Income Tax (Schedule F) Account

1967			1967		
31st Oct.	Dividend Received A/c	£1,700	1st Dec.	Bank A/c	£1,000
			31st Dec.	Balance c/d	700
1968		£1,700			£1,700
1st Jan.	Balance b/d	£700			

When the "final adjustment" is made with the Inland Revenue any "interim set-off" made which disregarded the *categories* of income must now be corrected. This will mean that a payment of £1000 will have to be made to the Collector of Taxes in respect of the debenture interest which was paid "net," *i.e.* less tax.

The tax suffered when the dividend was received amounted to £1700. This sum will now be carried forward and will be available for relief against any tax due by the company in respect of any *future* distributions which it may make.

The *Memorandum* accounts dealing with the "categories" will then read as follows:

Memorandum   *Tax on Annual Payments Account*

Bank A/c	£1,000	Debenture Interest A/c	£1,000

Memorandum   *Income Tax (Schedule F) Account*

Dividend Received A/c	£1,700

EXAMPLE 66

DEF Ltd makes up its accounts to 31st March annually.

During the year ended 31st March 1968 the following transactions took place:

1967		£
26th May	Dividend paid (net)	3,000
23rd July	Royalty received (net)	1,200
11th Aug.	Debenture interest paid (net)	600
1968		
8th Jan.	Dividend received (net)	2,700

Income tax at 8s. in the £.

Stage 1

Dividend Paid Account

1967				
26th May	Bank A/c	£3,000		
26th May	Income Tax (Sch. F) A/c	2,000		
		£5,000		

Income Tax (Schedule F) Account

		1967		
		26th May	Dividend Paid A/c	£2,000

Stage 2

Payment of the tax must be made by 19th June 1967.

Income Tax (Schedule F) Account

1967			*1967*		
19th June	Bank A/c	£2,000	26th May	Dividend Paid A/c	£2,000

Stage 3

Royalty Received Account

	1967		
	23rd July	Bank A/c	£1,200
	23rd July	Tax on Annual Payments A/c	800
			£2,000

Tax on Annual Payments Account

1967		
23rd July	Royalty Received A/c	£800

Stage 4

In the monthly settlement for 5th August, claim will be made for the £800 to be repaid by the Inland Revenue. Since the company has already paid £2000 in tax the entire amount of £800 will be repayable.

Note particularly that at this point no notice is taken of the category into which the payment or refund falls.

Tax on Annual Payments Account

1967			1967		
23rd July	Royalty Received A/c	£800	9th Sept.	Bank A/c	£800

Stage 5

Debenture Interest Account

1967		
11th Aug.	Bank A/c	£600
11th Aug.	Tax on Annual Payments A/c	400
		£1,000

Tax on Annual Payments Account

	1967		
	11th Aug.	Debenture Interest A/c	£400

Stage 6

The tax must be paid by 19th September.

Tax on Annual Payments Account

1967 19th Sept.	Bank A/c	£400	1967 11th Aug.	Debenture Interest A/c	£400

Stage 7

Dividend Received Account

			1968 8th Jan. 8th Jan.	Bank A/c Income Tax (Schedule F) A/c	£2,700 1,800
					£4,500

Income Tax (Schedule F) Account

1968 8th Jan.	Dividend Received A/c	£1,800			

Stage 8

The position now is that the company has paid to the Inland Revenue a net total of £1600, *i.e.*:

Tax on dividend paid	£2,000
Tax on debenture interest paid	400
	2,400
Less Repaid on royalty received	800
	£1,600

As the company has suffered tax on the dividend received amounting to £1800 the full sum of £1600 must be repaid.

Income Tax (Schedule F) Account

1968 8th Jan.	Dividend Received A/c	£1,800	1968 7th Mar. 7th Mar.	Bank A/c Balance b/d	£1,600 200
		£1,800			£1,800
7th Mar.	Balance b/d	£200			

Stage 9

We now come to the "final adjustment" at the end of the income tax year of assessment 1967–68 wherein the "categories" have to be sorted out.

Dealing first with the Schedule F tax we have the following position:

Memorandum   *Income Tax (Schedule F) Account*

1968 8th Jan. 5th April	Dividend Received A/c Balance c/d	£1,800 200	1967 26th May	Dividend Paid A/c	£2,000
		£2,000			£2,000
			1968 6th April	Balance b/d	200

This balance of £200 owing to the Inland Revenue must now be paid by the company.

The Annual Payments position is:

Memorandum   *Tax on Annual Payments Account*

1967 23rd July	Royalties Received A/c	£800	1967 11th Aug. 1968 5th April	Debenture Interest A/c Balance c/d	£400 400
		£800			£800
1968 6th April	Balance b/d	400			

The debit balance of £400 may now be set against any liability of the company to Corporation Tax. If there is no such liability it may be carried forward to future years.

PROGRESS TEST 17

1. In relation to Corporation Tax define:

    (*a*) Financial Year, (*b*) Accounting Period. (**3, 4**)

2. Compare the taxation position of a company, (*a*) before, and (*b*) after, the introduction of Corporation Tax. (**12, 13**)

3. Define franked investment income. (**16**)

4. What is unfranked investment income and how does it differ from franked investment income? (**18, 19**)

5. State the principle of "set-off." (**21, 22, 23**)

6. How must a company account for tax on distributions and annual payments? (**24, 25**)

EXAMINATION TECHNIQUE

Preparation

The only road to certain success in accountancy examinations is for the student to have acquired a *thoroughly sound knowledge* of double entry book-keeping. Unless this knowledge is soundly based he will forever find himself in a twilight world where some things are understood dimly and where a great deal is completely incomprehensible. Many students, most unfortunately, fall into this category and, as a result, fail miserably in their efforts to master the subject of accountancy.

It must be pointed out that to have a thoroughly sound knowledge of the principles of book-keeping the student must know first of all, *why* things are done. It may be claimed with some justification that book-keeping is a logical science. This is manifest to anyone who really understands book-keeping. If it is accepted that book-keeping *is* logical it follows that *reasoning* can be applied to its problems. This is the key. There is, indeed, a basic reason for everything that is done in book-keeping, and since the principles of book-keeping are applied one hundred per cent to accountancy problems it follows that without a thorough knowledge of the fundamentals, examination success will be very hard to attain.

There is a second ingredient which is required for success in accountancy examinations. This is *practice* in the working of problems. Furthermore, this practice must be a continuous discipline. In the months of preparation before the examination a very great deal of the student's time must be devoted to the working of problems. Accountancy is not a subject which can be mastered by reading only. It is an intensely practical subject and practical subjects can only be mastered by *constant practice*. Ideally, at least two hours per day for five days a week should be spent on working practical problems in accountancy during the months of preparation for your examination. For this you should acquire as many past examination papers *with worked solutions* as you can. It does not matter which examining body's papers you obtain; they will all afford you the opportunity for plentiful and varied practice. (Quite a number of organisations specialise in supplying past examination papers and they usually advertise in the professional journals.)

In addition, you should obtain *several* books on accountancy.

Do not rely on just one book. One finds that some books deal with specific aspects of accountancy better than others. Again the approach of one author may appeal to one student but not to another. Hence, a little variety in your textbooks may prove to be of great value.

At the examination

In these hints on examination technique two assumptions have been made. These are:

(a) that the student has covered the syllabus; and
(b) that he has a reasonable grasp of the principles of the subject.

To these a third could well be added, *i.e.* that no student can reasonably hope to achieve one hundred per cent of the available marks, neither is it necessary for him to do so to pass the examination. This is not only a comforting thought but it is also common sense and should be borne in mind when in the examination hall. It is better to answer some of the questions *really well* and gain sufficient marks in that way than to answer all inadequately and probably fail.

Most of the professional bodies require the candidate to answer five questions in accountancy examinations. It is only very occasionally that the answers to six questions are called for. Some bodies give a choice, *e.g.* seven questions are set with five to be answered.

(a) *Choice.* Where a choice of questions is offered the student should be very careful to answer *only one of the alternatives*.

It is by no means uncommon to find students disregarding this point. Whether they do this in error or because they find that they can answer both, it must be pointed out most emphatically that they will only be credited with the marks attaching to *one* of their answers. Which one will depend upon the view taken by the examiner. He may adopt the view that the first one dealt with by the candidate is the one which is to count. On the other hand, he may be more charitable and take the trouble to mark both answers, crediting the candidate with the higher scoring answer. Both questions would, of course, carry the same possible maximum mark.

(b) *Allocation of marks.* In accountancy examinations marks are allocated to certain parts of the answers. It is most important for the student to realise this. A simple illustration will make this easier to appreciate.

Suppose a question set out the trial balance of a company and beneath it a number of adjustments which had to be incorporated in the final accounts and Balance Sheet. The total marks for the question might be 25.

Three marks might be awarded for dealing correctly with the

provision for doubtful debts, one mark for deducting a pre-payment from the Profit and Loss Account charge for insurance and a fifth mark for entering the balance under current assets in the Balance Sheet. Two marks might be given to the correct treatment of goods on sale or return in the Trading Account and yet another mark for the inclusion of the item in the closing stock in the Balance Sheet. This pattern will be continued throughout the remainder of the question. Finally, an award of, say, three marks might be given for presentation.

Many students seem to think that because they have managed to balance both sides of the Balance Sheet they will score full marks. This is far from reality. Conversely, many feel that because they have not balanced they will score no marks. This again is far from true.

This leads automatically to the next point.

(c) *Time wasted.* If the student has prepared himself reasonably well for the examination he will expect to find some questions, at least, of a type that he recognises and which he can make a fair attempt at answering. Often, however, having worked through a question, he finds that he must have gone wrong at some point since his final answer is clearly incorrect.

There is a great danger here that he will spend an inordinate amount of time trying to locate his mistake. At this stage he should do no more than quickly run over his answer, making a pencil cross against any points of doubt unless, of course, he can see the cause of his error at once. In this latter case the necessary adjusting entries should be made. It is more likely, however, that his error will not be immediately apparent and, in that case, his best plan is to leave matters as they stand and *not waste any time at all* at this stage.

Examinations have been failed by many students because they have wasted a vast amount of time in a fruitless effort to discover an error. In so many cases its discovery would have made only a very small difference to the number of marks earned.

If the mistake is not immediately apparent, *move to the next question at once.*

(d) *Allocating time to questions.* If you have a watch, *place it on the desk in front of you.*

The normal maximum marks for an accountancy paper is one hundred. The normal time allowance for an accountancy paper is three hours. This allows nearly two minutes per mark. Nearly every professional examination shows the number of marks allocated to each question so you can make a rough calculation of the number of minutes that you can afford to devote to each question.

It is at this point that your attention is drawn to the opening remarks of this section, *i.e.* that none but the most gifted student can hope to score full marks. If you score sixty you will be sure of passing. Are you capable of scoring sixty? Do the questions appear to give you that hope? Can you answer four of the five well? Or only three? These questions can only be answered by the candidate with the examination paper in front of him. If the answer is favourable then re-allocate the time per question before settling down to work. But remember that if, for example, you answer four questions out of five, your sixty marks must be earned from a total of, perhaps, eighty possible marks only. It would be wise therefore, to leave half an hour at the end for going on to another question to earn a few bonus marks and for "polishing up" your answers.

By adopting this technique quite a lot of the "pressure" will be eased. The result will almost certainly be that a far better paper will be handed in than would otherwise be the case.

EXAMINATION QUESTIONS

Suggested answers to these questions are given in Appendix III.

1. Oaken Ltd issued £100,000 6% debentures at par in 1957 redeemable at 101 on 31st December 1967. Under the terms of a Debenture Trust Deed a Sinking Fund had been built up by annual appropriations out of profits which were invested, together with any income which had arisen on the fund, in gilt-edged investments on 31st December in each year. The trustees have power to purchase, for immediate cancellation, any debentures available at a market price below par and to realise sinking fund investments for this purpose.

On 1st January 1967 there were the following balances:

(1) Debentures outstanding £80,000.
(2) Sinking Fund Account £79,350 represented by an equivalent amount of gilt-edged securities standing in the books at cost.

During the twelve months ended 31st December 1967, the undernoted transactions took place:

(1) On 30th June the half-year's debenture interest to date was paid.
(2) On 1st July £5000 debentures were purchased in the market at 99 and cancelled. To provide funds for this purchase investments costing £5650 were sold and realised £5500.
(3) Interest was received on the sinking fund investments amounting to £3850 which was not invested in view of the impending sale of the investments of the fund.
(4) On 28th December £72,100 was received representing the proceeds of sale of the remaining investments of the sinking fund.
(5) On 31st December the debentures were repaid together with the half-year's interest thereon.

You are required to write up the following ledger accounts for the twelve months ended 31st December 1967:

(a) 6% Debentures,
(b) Sinking Fund, and
(c) Sinking Fund Investments.

Ignore income tax.

(*Chartered Accountants—16 marks*)

2. On 1st August 1967 a company had in issue £82,000 5% debentures, out of an original total issue of £100,000. The Debenture Trust Deed provided that:

(1) interest was payable on 31st January and 31st July;
(2) a sinking fund for redemption of debentures was to be built up by an annual appropriation of:

  (a) £1000, and
  (b) 5% of the total nominal amount of debentures already purchased and cancelled at the preceding 31st July

which, together with any interest received on the investments of the sinking fund, were to be invested on 31st July in each year;
(3) sinking fund investments could be realised at any time to purchase debentures in the open market at or below par for immediate cancellation.

You ascertain that:

(1) the sinking fund balance on 1st August 1967, was £8000;
(2) sinking fund investments were realised on 31st May 1968 for £815 (cost £790) and the proceeds were used to purchase debentures of a nominal value of £840; and
(3) interest on sinking fund investments for the year ended 31st July 1968 amounted to £325, on which date the available funds were duly invested.

You are required to write up the following accounts for the year ended 31st July 1968:

(a) Sinking Fund Investments,
(b) Sinking Fund, and
(c) Redemption of Debentures.

(Chartered Accountants—16 marks)

3. On 30th April 1966 the summarised Balance Sheet of Croft Limited showed the following position:

Share Capital:			Fixed assets	£429,000
7% redeemable pre-			Current assets	200,000
ference shares of			Balance at bank	204,000
£1 each	£120,000			
Ordinary shares of				
£1 each	280,000			
		£400,000		
General reserve		80,000		
Profit and Loss A/c		226,000		
		706,000		
Current liabilities		127,000		
		£833,000		£833,000

On 1st May 1966 the following transactions took place:

(1) The redeemable preference shares were repaid at a premium of 2s. per share; and
(2) £150,000 7½% debentures 1980–82 were issued at £98 per cent.

You are required to show:

(a) the necessary ledger accounts (including cash) to record the above transactions; and
(b) the summarised Balance Sheet of the company as it would appear immediately after completion.

(Chartered Accountants—14 marks)

4. Prospects Ltd was formed with an authorised capital of £150,000 consisting of 100,000 ordinary shares of £1 each and 50,000 7½% preference shares of £1 each, to acquire, on 1st July 1967, the business of James Wilson.

Wilson's Balance Sheet as on 30th June 1967 was as follows:

Capital Account—		Land and buildings	£40,000
James Wilson	£78,290	Plant and machinery	24,000
Trade creditors	16,580	Stock	15,960
Overdraft at Midtown		Debtors	23,860
Bank	8,950		
	£103,820		£103,820

The company took over all the assets and assumed all the liabilities and the consideration was fixed at £110,000. In computing this figure land and buildings were valued at £60,000, plant and machinery at £20,000, stock at £15,000 and the debtors at book value subject to an allowance of 5% to cover doubtful debts. The transfer of the bank overdraft to the company was agreed by Midtown Bank on condition that a debenture for £10,000, secured on the land and buildings, was issued to the bank.

The purchase price was settled by the issue at par to Wilson of 30,000 ordinary shares and 25,000 preference shares; the balance being paid in cash. Active Securities Ltd agreed to subscribe for 70,000 ordinary shares in Prospects Ltd at par and these were issued fully paid for cash on 1st July 1967. Prospects Ltd paid the formation expenses of £1875.

You are required to prepare:

(a) journal entries, including those relating to cash, to close the books of James Wilson; and

(b) the Balance Sheet of Prospects Ltd immediately after the completion of the above transactions.

(Chartered Accountants—20 marks)

5. Rose Limited has an authorised share capital of £75,000 made up of ordinary shares of £1 each. On 30th June 1966 the following balances were extracted from the books:

Ordinary shares, fully paid	£50,000
General reserve	40,000
Plant replacement reserve	30,000
Leasehold land and buildings, at cost	65,500
Motor vehicles, at cost	10,650
Plant and machinery, at cost	54,400
Sundry creditors	32,400
Balance in hand at bank	89,210
Stock on hand, 1st July 1965	10,640
Sales	272,520
Purchases	182,530
Overhead expenses	19,456
Selling expenses	16,428
Administration expenses	22,392
Profit and Loss Account, balances as on 1st July 1965	29,246
Taxation Account	7,000
Trade debtors	56,750
Interim dividend paid (net)	2,500
Provision for depreciation to 1st July 1965:	
Leasehold land and buildings	32,750
Plant and machinery	30,290
Motor vehicles	6,420
Provision for doubtful debts, 1st July 1965	1,030
Cash in hand	1,200

The following is relevant:

(1) Stock on hand on 30th June 1966 amounted to £11,450.

(2) Administration expenses include an amount of £6000 for directors' salaries. Benefits in kind received by the directors have been valued at £459 for the year.

(3) Provision for doubtful debts is to be adjusted to 2% of the outstanding trade debtors as on 30th June 1966.

(4) Provision is to be made for:

    (*a*) audit fee of £315 (fixed by directors);
    (*b*) depreciation on leasehold land and buildings at 5% on
        cost, plant and machinery at $12\frac{1}{2}$% on cost and motor
        vehicles at 20% on cost; and
    (*c*) directors' fees of £1000.

(5) The balance on Taxation Account represents the provision
made on 30th June 1965 for Corporation Tax at 35%, and
not yet paid. This is to be increased in order to provide for
Corporation Tax at the rate of 40%. The Corporation Tax
for the year ended 30th June 1966 is estimated at £7600
based on a rate of 40%.

(6) The directors wish to transfer £10,000 to general reserve,
and recommend a final dividend of 10%. The company is
allowed to retain the income tax deducted from the interim
dividend paid in December 1965, but must account for the
income tax deducted from the final dividend. The standard
rate of income tax is to be assumed to be 10*s*. in the £.

You are required to prepare in a form suitable for publication,
to comply with the minimum requirements of the *Companies Act*,
1948, the Profit and Loss Account for the year ended 30th June
1966, and the Balance Sheet as on that date.

    The auditors' report and corresponding figures are not required.
                        (*Chartered Accountants—30 marks*)

    6. The summarised balance sheets of Grasshoppers Ltd at 31st
March 1964, and 31st March 1965, are given below.

BALANCE SHEETS

	1964	1965		1964	1965
Issued share capital			Freehold properties at		
(shares of £1 each)	£150,000	£175,000	cost	£10,000	£8,000
Capital reserves:			Plant and machinery		
Share premium		5,000	at cost, less depre-		
Profit of sale of free-			ciation	143,000	154,000
holds		1,450	Preliminary expenses	800	400
Revenue reserve:			Current assets	69,200	83,050
Profit and Loss A/c	16,000	30,000			
$5\frac{1}{2}$% debentures	25,000				
Current liabilities	32,000	34,000			
	£223,000	£245,450		£223,000	£245,450

The whole share capital of the company was issued for cash.
Depreciation of plant and machinery written off during the year to
31st March 1965 amounted to £14,000. During the same year, the
company paid a dividend of £7,500.

You are required to prepare a statement showing:

(a) the net increase in working capital during the year to 31st March 1965; and
(b) the sources and application of working capital during that year.

Ignore taxation.

(Chartered Institute of Secretaries—20 marks)

7. The following are the summarised balance sheets of N.V.N. Ltd as on 31st December 1966, and 31st December 1967:

BALANCE SHEETS

	1966	1967		1966	1967
Issued share capital	£60,000	£75,000	Freehold properties, at cost	£33,000	£24,000
Share Premium A/c	—	5,000	Plant and machinery at cost, less depreciation	20,800	60,300
Capital reserve (profit on sale of freehold property)	—	17,000	Preliminary expenses	1,200	600
Profit and Loss A/c	21,500	21,200	Stock in trade	30,350	32,850
Trade creditors	27,200	32,600	Debtors	20,100	24,750
Proposed dividend	6,000	8,500	Balance at bank	9,250	16,800
	£114,700	£159,300		£114,700	£159,300

The following is a summary of the Profit and Loss Account for the year 1967:

Profit and Loss Account

Proposed dividend	£8,500	Net profit for year	£8,200
Balance, carried forward	21,200	Balance from 1966	21,500
	£29,700		£29,700

No plant and machinery was sold during 1967.

The net profit, £8200, is the amount after charging £7500 for depreciation of plant and machinery and after writing off preliminary expenses, £600.

You are required to prepare a statement showing:

(a) the net increase in working capital (*i.e.* current assets less current liabilities) during the year 1967; and
(b) the sources and application of working capital during that year.

Ignore taxation.

(Chartered Institute of Secretaries—20 marks)

8. The following is the summarised Balance Sheet as on June 30th 1966 of J. Moore Ltd, a private company:

Share Capital: Authorised issued and fully paid 50,000 6% cumulative preference shares of £1 each		£50,000	*Fixed Assets* Goodwill		£150,000 20,000
120,000 ordinary shares of £1 each		120,000	*Current Assets:* Stock	£10,900	
			Debtors	6,000	
		170,000	Balance at bank	100	
Less Profit and Loss Account —Adverse balance		25,000			17,000
			Preliminary expenses		3,000
		145,000			
5% debentures	£20,000				
Interest thereon in arrear	1,000				
		21,000			
Creditors		24,000			
		£190,000			£190,000

NOTE: The dividend on the preference shares is £9,000 in arrear.

The following scheme of reconstruction was agreed by all parties and the necessary sanctions obtained.

A new company, J. Moore (1966) Ltd, was to be registered, with a capital of 250,000 shares of 10s. each, to acquire as from 1st July 1966 the undertaking and assets of the old company for a consideration to be satisfied partly in cash and partly in the new company's shares and debentures sufficient to implement the following agreed terms:

(1) The new company to assume the old company's debenture liability by issuing to the holders corresponding debentures in the new company, together with two fully-paid shares in the new company for every £1 of interest in arrear.

(2) The creditors of the old company to accept, for every £1 due to them, 5s. in cash (to be provided by the new company) and two fully paid shares in the new company.

(3) The preference shareholders in the old company to receive two fully paid shares in the new company for each share held in the old company; further, the arrears of preference dividend to be satisfied by the issue of one fully paid share in the new company for every £1 due.

(4) The ordinary shareholders in the old company to receive one fully paid share in the new company for every three shares held.

(5) Costs amounting to £3600 to be borne by the new company and regarded as part of the purchase consideration.

It was agreed that current assets should be taken into the new company's books at the values in the old company's books (except that stock was to be reduced by £1000); goodwill was to be eliminated and the balance of the purchase consideration was to be attributed to the fixed assets.

The balance of shares in the new company was issued at par and paid for in full by certain of the old shareholders.

You are required to give:

(a) in the old company's books:
(i) the Realisation and Reconstruction Accounts;
(ii) the account with the new company; and

(b) in respect of the new company:
(i) the Cash Account; and
(ii) a summarised opening Balance Sheet.

(Chartered Accountants—30 marks)

9. The summarised balance sheet of D.G.L. Ltd on 31st March 1967 was as follows:

BALANCE SHEET

Issued share capital:			Goodwill, at cost	£25,000
9,000 ordinary shares			Fixed assets	49,500
of £1 each	£9,000		Preliminary expenses	190
42,000 6% cumulative			Current assets:	
preference shares of			Stock in trade	£10,500
£1 each	42,000		Debtors	24,060
		£51,000		34,560
Profit and Loss Account		3,500		
Debenture redemption reserve		2,500		
5% debentures		15,000		
Bank overdraft		2,250		
Trade creditors		35,000		
		£109,250		£109,250

The following scheme of reconstruction was accepted by all parties and was completed on 1st April 1967.

A new company, D.G.L. (1967) Ltd, with an authorised capital of 60,000 ordinary shares of £1 each, took over all the assets of D.G.L. Ltd and assumed responsibility for all the current liabilities. The purchase consideration was satisfied by the issue, at par, of shares and debentures in the new company, in accordance with the following arrangements:

(1) The holders of the 5% debentures in the old company were satisfied by the issue, at par, of 100 5% debentures of £100 each, and 5500 fully paid shares in the company.
(2) The holders of preference shares in the old company received one fully-paid share in the new company for every two preference shares in the old company.

(3) The ordinary shareholders of the old company received one fully-paid share in the new company for every ten ordinary shares in the old company.

(4) The balance of the authorised caital of the new company was issued at par for cash and was fully paid on 1st April 1967. The preliminary expenses of the new company, £625, were paid on the same date.

(5) The goodwill was valued at £2500, the stock in trade at £9,500, and the debtors at the amounts at which they appeared in the books of the old company. The balance of the purchase consideration represented the agreed value of the fixed assets.

Before the decision to proceed with the above scheme had been taken, an alternative proposal had been considered. Under the latter, the old company was to continue to carry on the business and was to issue for cash, at par, 32,500 ordinary shares of £1 each; there were to be no other changes.

You are required:

(a) to show your calculation of (i) the purchase consideration for the assets and (ii) the agreed value of the fixed assets and to set out the summarised balance sheet of D.G.L. (1967) Ltd on 1st April 1967, as it would appear after the completion of the reconstruction scheme;

(b) to compare the relative advantages of the reconstruction scheme and the alternative proposal, and to suggest reasons why the latter was not adopted.

(Chartered Institute of Secretaries—24 marks)

10. Black Ltd agreed to acquire the goodwill and assets, other than the balance at the bank, of White Ltd on 31st March 1967.

As on that date the summarised Balance Sheet of White Ltd was as follows:

Share Capital in £1		Goodwill	£12,000
shares	£90,000	Land, buildings and	
General Reserve	15,000	plant	90,000
Profit and Loss A/c	3,700	Stock	24,000
6% debentures	20,000	Debtors	5,200
Creditors	7,000	Balance at bank	4,500
	£135,700		£135,700

The consideration payable by Black Ltd was agreed as follows:

(1) A cash payment equivalent to 2s. per share for every £1 share in White Ltd.
(2) The issue of 150,000 £1 shares, fully paid, in Black Ltd having an agreed value of 24s. per share.
(3) The issue of such an amount of fully paid 5% debentures of Black Ltd, at a discount of 10%, as is sufficient to discharge at 6% debentures of White Ltd at a premium of 8%. All the debenture holders of White Ltd agreed to the exchange.

The liabilities of White Ltd, other than the debentures, were to be discharged by that company.

When computing the consideration, the directors of Black Ltd valued the land, buildings and plant at £130,000, the stock at £21,000 and the debtors at their value subject to an allowance of 5% to cover doubtful debts.

You are required to draft journal entries, including those relating to cash,

(a) in the books of Black Ltd—to record the acquisition; and
(b) in the books of White Ltd—to close the books, assuming that the company is liquidated and the assets distributed *pro rata* to the shareholders.

(Chartered Accountants—20 marks)

11. X Ltd and Y Ltd are two independent companies engaged respectively in the manufacture and distribution of a certain commodity.

X LTD BALANCE SHEET AS AT 31ST MARCH 1968

Capital, issued and fully paid:			Fixed assets		
			Patent rights		£20,000
50,000 8% preference			Land and buildings		60,000
shares of £1 each	£50,000		Plant and		
150,000 ordinary			machinery		155,000
shares of £1 each	150,000				
	200,000				235,000
General Reserve	80,000		Current assets		
Profit and Loss Account	9,000		Stocks	£35,000	
	———		Debtors	8,000	
	289,000		Bank balance	16,000	
Current liabilities				———	59,000
Creditors	5,000				
	———				———
	£294,000				£294,000

Y LTD BALANCE SHEET AS AT 31ST MARCH 1968

Capital, issued and fully paid:		Fixed assets		
40,000 shares of £1 each	£40,000	Goodwill		£7,000
		Motor vehicles		4,000
Profit and Loss Account	3,200	Furniture and fittings		2,500
	43,200			13,500
Current liabilities		Current assets		
Creditors	2,100	Stocks	£23,900	
		Debtors	6,200	
		Bank balance	1,700	
				31,800
	£45,300			£45,300

It has been agreed that both companies should be wound up and a new company, Z Ltd, should be formed to acquire the assets of both companies on the following terms:

(1) Z Ltd is to have an authorised capital of £300,000, all in £1 shares.

(2) Z Ltd is to purchase the whole of the assets of X Ltd (except the bank balance) for £279,500, to be settled as to £54,500 in cash and as to the balance by the issue of 180,000 ordinary shares, credited as fully paid, to be treated as of a value of 25s. each.

(3) Z Ltd is to purchase the whole of the assets of Y Ltd (except the bank balance) for £38,100, to be settled as to £600 in cash and as to the balance by the issue of 30,000 ordinary shares, credited as fully paid, to be treated as of a value of 25s. each.

(4) Z Ltd is to make a public issue of 50,000 5% preference shares at par and 30,000 ordinary shares at the issue price of 25s. per share, all payable in full on application.

(5) X Ltd and Y Ltd are both to be wound up, the two liquidators distributing the shares in Z Ltd in kind among the ordinary shareholders of the respective companies.

(6) The liquidator of X Ltd is to pay the preference shareholders £1 in cash for every share held, in full satisfaction of their claims.

The costs of liquidation, including the liquidators' remuneration, were £500 in the case of X Ltd and £200 in the case of Y Ltd. The preliminary expenses of Z Ltd amounted to £1800. In addition, the underwriting commission payable on the public

L

issue was at the rate of 6*d*. per share for the preference shares and 3*d*. per share for the ordinary shares.

You are required:

(a) to set out the closing entries in the books of X Ltd in the form of journal entries, together with the closing cash book entries;

(b) to state what the holders of 100 ordinary shares in X Ltd and Y Ltd would respectively receive; and

(c) to draw up the initial balance sheet of Z Ltd on the basis that all assets other than goodwill are taken over at book value.

(Chartered Accountants, Intermediate—30 marks)

12. The summarised balance sheets of E.C.Y. Ltd and its subsidiary companies, N.R.S. Ltd and W.F.D. Ltd at 31st December 1967 were as under:

E.C.Y. LTD

Issued share capital (150,000 shares of £1 each)	£150,000	Fixed assets	£39,000
		65,000 shares in N.R.S. Ltd at cost	96,000
Profit and Loss A/c (including the dividend received from W.F.D. Ltd)	37,600	24,000 shares in W.F.D. Ltd at cost	35,000
		Current assets	60,800
Creditors	43,200		
	£230,800		£230,800

N.R.S. LTD

Issued share capital (65,000 shares of £1 each)	£65,000	Fixed assets	£75,000
		Current assets	51,000
Profit and Loss A/c at 31st December 1966	27,300		
Add Net profit, 1967	9,500		
	36,800		
Creditors	24,200		
	£126,000		£126,000

W.F.D. LTD

Issued share capital (32,000 shares of £1 each)		£32,000	Fixed assets	£30,000
			Current assets	23,200
Profit and Loss A/c at 31st December 1966	£6,100			
Add Net profit, 1967	4,800			
	10,900			
Less proposed dividend	3,200			
		7,700		
Proposed dividend		3,200		
Creditors		10,300		
		£53,200		£53,200

E.C.Y. Ltd acquired the shares in both subsidiaries on 31st December 1966.

N.R.S. Ltd paid no dividend for 1966, and none is proposed for 1967.

The Profit and Loss Account of W.F.D. Ltd for 1966 was debited with a proposed dividend of £1600 which was paid in 1967.

The fixed assets of N.R.S. Ltd, include £1800 representing a motor vehicle purchased for that price, on 31st December 1967 from E.C.Y. Ltd. N.R.S. Ltd has not paid for the vehicle and the price is included in the creditors in the balance sheet of N.R.S. Ltd, shown above. No entries for this transaction have been made in the books of E.C.Y. Ltd and the van is included in the fixed assets in the balance sheet of E.C.Y., shown above, at an amount of £2000. It has been decided that, for purposes of the consolidated accounts, the van should be valued at £1800.

You are required to prepare the consolidated balance sheet of the group at 31st December 1967.

You are to show your calculations of the items.

Ignore taxation.

(Chartered Institute of Secretaries—22 marks)

13. The summarised Balance Sheets of West Ltd and its subsidiary companies, East Ltd and South Ltd, at 31st December 1966, were as follows:

WEST LTD

Issued share capital		Fixed assets	£88,000
200,000 £1 ordinary shares	£200,000	Shares in subsidiary	
Profit and Loss A/c (including		companies at cost:	
dividend from South Ltd)	31,000	75,000 ordinary shares	
Current liabilities	24,800	in East Ltd	£93,400
		15,000 ordinary shares	
		in South Ltd	£21,600
			115,000
		Current assets	52,800
	£255,800		£255,800

EAST LTD

Issued share capital		Fixed assets	£69,000
75,000 £1 ordinary shares	£75,000	Current assets	38,000
Profit and Loss A/c at			
31/12/65	£9,250		
Add net profit for 1966	7,000		
	16,250		
Current liabilities	15,750		
	£107,000		£107,000

SOUTH LTD

Issued share capital		Fixed assets	£18,000
20,000 £1 ordinary shares	£20,000	Current assets	26,000
4,000 6% preference shares	4,000		
	24,000		
Profit and Loss A/c	4,560		
Proposed dividends	2,240		
Current liabilities	13,200		
	£44,000		£44,000

The following is a summary of the Profit and Loss Account of South Ltd:

Proposed dividends:		Net profit, 1966	£2,800
Ordinary	£2,000	Balance at 31/12/65	4,000
Preference	240		
	2,240		
Balance c/d	4,560		
	£6,800		£6,800

West Ltd acquired the shares in both subsidiaries on 31st December 1965.

East Ltd paid no dividend for 1965 and none is proposed for 1966.

The Profit and Loss Account of South Ltd for 1965 was debited with a proposed ordinary dividend of £1600 and a proposed preference dividend of £240. Both of these dividends were paid early in 1966.

You are required to prepare a consolidated balance sheet as on 31st December 1966.

Show your calculations.

Ignore income tax.

(Chartered Institute of Secretaries—25 marks)

14. The final sections of the Profit and Loss Accounts of Green Ltd, Pink Ltd and Blue Ltd for the year to 31st December 1965 are as follows:

GREEN LTD

Proposed dividend	£20,000	Net profit for 1965	£24,600
Balance carried forward	14,000	Balance at 31st December 1964	9,400
	£34,000		£34,000

PINK LTD

Balance carried forward	£10,000	Net profit for 1965	£8,000
		Balance at 31st December 1964	2,000
	£10,000		£10,000

BLUE LTD

Net loss for 1965	£1,400	Balance at 31st December 1964	£1,700
Balance carried forward	300		
	£1,700		£1,700

Green Ltd acquired the whole share capital of Blue Ltd on 31st December 1964, and three-quarters of the share capital of Pink Ltd on 31st December 1963.

The balance of £2000 on the Profit and Loss Account of Pink Ltd at 31st December 1964 represents a credit balance of £1200 brought forward from 1963, and a net profit of £800 in 1964.

No dividend has been paid by either Pink Ltd or Blue Ltd since the holding company acquired the shares.

You are required to prepare the final section of the Consolidated Profit and Loss Account for the year to 31st December 1965.

(Chartered Institute of Secretaries—14 marks)

15. The following are summaries of the Profit and Loss Accounts for the year ended 31st December 1966, of D.V.N. Ltd and its

three subsidiary companies, A.B.Y. Ltd, C.M.L Ltd and L.G.T. Ltd.

D.V.N. LTD

Proposed dividend	£16,000	Net trading profit for	
Balance, c/f	23,480	the year	£23,480
		Dividends received	3,500
		Balance from 1965	12,500
	£39,480		£39,480

A.B.Y. LTD

Interim preference divi-		Net profit for the year	£460
dend paid	£180	Balance from 1965	100
Balance, c/f	380		
	£560		£560

C.M.L. LTD

Interim dividend paid	£3,000	Net profit for the year	£8,000
Proposed final dividend	3,000	Balance from 1965	5,400
Balance, c/f	7,400		
	£13,400		£13,400

L.G.T. LTD

Net loss for the year	£1,825	Balance from 1965 (after debiting a proposed dividend of £1,250)	£1,275
		Balance, c/f	550
	£1,825		£1,825

The issued share capital of the subsidiaries is as follows:

	A.B.Y.	C.M.L.	L.G.T.
Ordinary: Total	15,000	40,000	25,000
Held by D.V.N.	12,000	30,000	25,000
6% cumulative preference:			
Total	6,000	—	—
Held by D.V.N.	Nil	—	—

All shares are of £1 each and all are fully paid.

D.V.N. Ltd acquired the shares in A.B.Y. Ltd and L.G.T. Ltd on 31st December 1965. The shares in C.M.L. Ltd were acquired on 31st December 1964, when the credit balance on the Profit and Loss Account of that company was £2100. The net profit of C.M.L. Ltd for the year 1965 was £3300.

In February 1966 LG.T. Ltd paid a final dividend of £1250 for the year 1965.

In December 1966 D.V.N. Ltd sold goods to L.G.T. Ltd for £640. These goods were still held by L.G.T. Ltd on 31st December 1966, and were brought into that company's accounts at a valuation of £640. The cost of these goods to D.V.N. Ltd was £480.

You are required to prepare a Consolidated Profit and Loss Account for the year 1966.

Show calculations.

Ignore taxation.

(Chartered Institute of Secretaries—20 marks)

SUGGESTED ANSWERS
TO EXAMINATION QUESTIONS

Question 1

OAKEN LTD

6% Debenture Account

1967			1967		
July 1	Bank A/c (£5000 debentures purchased at 99 for cancellation)	£4,950	Jan. 1	Balance b/d	£80,000
1	Sinking Fund A/c (profit on cancellation of debentures)	50	Dec. 31	Sinking Fund A/c (premium on redemption of £75,000 debentures)	750
Dec. 31	£75,000 debentures (repaid at 101)	75,750			
		£80,750			£80,750

Sinking Fund Account

1967				1967		
July 1	Sinking Fund Investment A/c (loss on sale of investments)		£150	Jan. 1	Balance b/d	£79,350
Dec. 28	Sinking Fund Investment A/c (loss on sale of investments)		1,600	July 1	Debentures A/c (profit on cancellation of debentures)	50
31	Debentures A/c (premium on £75,000 debentures repaid)		750	1	Bank A/c (interest on sinking fund investments)	3,850
31	General Reserve: Debentures redeemed during year	£80,000				
	Balance of fund no longer required	750				
			80,750			
			£83,250			£83,250

Sinking Fund Investment Account

1967			1967		
Jan. 1	Balance b/d	£79,350	July 1	Bank A/c (proceeds of sale of investments which had cost £5650)	£5,500
			1	Sinking Fund A/c (loss on sale of investments)	150
			Dec. 28	Bank A/c (proceeds of sale of investments which had cost £73,700)	72,100
			28	Sinking Fund A/c (loss on sale of investments)	1,600
		£79,350			£79,350

Question 2

Sinking Fund Investment Account

1967			1968		
Aug. 1	Balance b/d	£8,000	May 31	Cash, proceeds of sale	£815
1968			July 31	Balance carried forward	9,449
May 31	Sinking Fund A/c (profit on sale)	25			
July 31	Cash (£1900 + £325 + £14)	2,239			
		£10,264			£10,264

Sinking Fund Account

1968			1967			
July 31	General Reserve	£840	Aug. 1	Balance b/d		£8,000
	Balance c/f	9,449	1968			
			May 31	Sinking Fund Investment A/c		25
				Redemption of Debentures A/c		39
			July 31	Cash, interest on investments		325
				Profit and Loss A/c:		
				Annual appropriation	£1,000	
				5% on £18,000	900	
						1,900
		£10,289				£10,289

Redemption of Debentures Account

1968			1968			
May 31	Cash	£815	May 31	Debentures A/c		£840
	Sinking Fund A/c (profit on redemption)	39		Debenture Interest A/c (£840 at 5% for four months)		14
		£854				£854

Question 3

CROFT LTD
7% Redeemable Preference Share Capital

1966			1966		
May 1	Preference Share Redemption A/c	£120,000	April 30	Balance	£120,000

Preference Share Redemption Account

1966			1966		
May 1	Bank A/c	£132,000	May 1	7% Redeemable Preference Share Capital A/c	£120,000
				Profit and Loss A/c	12,000
		£132,000			£132,000

Profit and Loss Account

1966			1966		
May 1	Preference Share Redemption A/c	£12,000	April 30	Balance	£226,000
	Capital Redemption Reserve Fund	120,000			
	Balance c/f	94,000			
		£226,000			£226,000

Bank Account

1966			1966		
April 30	Balance	£204,000	May 1	Preference Share Redemption A/c	£132,000
May 1	7½% Debentures	147,000		Balance c/f	219,000
		£351,000			£351,000

Capital Redemption Reserve Fund

1966			1966		
May 1	Balance c/f	£120,000	May 1	Profit and Loss A/c	£120,000

7½% Debentures Account

1966		1966	
May 1 Balance c/f	£150,000	May 1 Bank A/c	£147,000
		Discount on Debentures A/c	3,000
	£150,000		£150,000

Discount on Debentures Account

1966		1966	
May 1 7½% Debentures A/c	£3,000	May 1 Balance c/f	£3,000

CROFT LTD—BALANCE SHEET AS AT 1ST MAY 1966

			Fixed assets	£429,000
Share Capital				
Ordinary shares of £1 each		£280,000		
Capital Reserve			*Current assets*	200,000
Capital Redemption Reserve Fund		120,000	*Balance at bank*	219,000
Revenue Reserves				
General Reserve	£80,000			
Profit and Loss Account	94,000			
		174,000		
		574,000		
Less: Debenture discount		3,000		
Shareholders Equity		571,000		
Loan Capital				
7½% Debentures 1980–82		150,000		
Current Liabilities		127,000		
		£848,000		£848,000

NOTE: As an alternative the balance of £80,000 standing to the credit of General Reserve could have been transferred to Capital Redemption Reserve Fund and only £40,000 from Profit and Loss Account.

Question 4

JAMES WILSON—JOURNAL

Realisation A/c	Dr.	£103,820	
To Land and Buildings A/c			£40,000
To Plant and Machinery A/c			24,000
To Stock A/c			15,960
To Debtors A/c			23,860
Trade Creditors A/c	Dr.	16,580	
Bank A/c		8,950	
To Realisation A/c			25,530
Prospects Ltd A/c	Dr.	110,000	
To Realisation A/c			110,000
Bank A/c	Dr.	55,000	
Ordinary shares in Prospects Ltd A/c		30,000	
Preference shares in Prospects Ltd A/c		25,000	
To Prospects Ltd A/c			110,000
Realisation A/c	Dr.	31,710	
To Capital A/c (James Wilson)			31,710
Capital A/c (James Wilson)	Dr.	110,000	
To Bank A/c			55,000
To Ordinary shares in Prospects Ltd A/c			33,000
To Preference shares in Prospects Ltd A/c			25,000

WORKINGS

(1) Purchase consideration			£110,000
Deduct: Assets taken over —			
Property		£60,000	
Plant		20,000	
Stock		15,000	
Debtors	£23,860		
Less: 5%	1,193		
		22,667	
		117,667	
Less: Liabilities assumed (including Bank overdraft)		25,530	
			92,137
Value of Goodwill			£17,863

(2) Cash at bank			
Received from Active Securities Ltd			£70,000
Less: Paid to J. Wilson		£55,000	
Formation expenses		1,875	
			56,875
Balance at bank			£13,125

PROSPECTS LTD—BALANCE SHEET, 1ST JULY 1967

Share Capital	*Authorised*	*Issued*	*Fixed Assets*		
£1 ordinary shares fully paid	£100,000	£100,000	Land and buildings at cost		£60,000
7½% preference shares fully paid	50,000	25,000	Plant and machinery at cost		20,000
			Goodwill at cost		17,863
	£150,000	£125,000			£97,863
Current Liabilities			*Current Assets*		
Trade creditors	£16,580		Stock at cost	£15,000	
Bank overdraft	8,950		Debtors less provision	22,667	
		25,530	Balance at bank	13,125	
					50,792
			Preliminary expenses		1,875
		£150,530			£150,530

NOTE: A debenture of £10,000 secured on the company's assets is in issue to the Bank.

Question 5

Trading and Profit and Loss Account for year ended 30th June 1966

Opening Stock	£10,640	Sales	£272,520
Purchases	182,530		
	193,170		
Less Closing stock	11,450		
	181,720		
Gross profit	90,800		
	£272,520		£272,520

Overhead expenses		£19,456	Gross profit	£90,800
Administration expenses		22,392		
Selling expenses		16,428		
Depreciation:				
Leasehold property	£3,275			
Plant and machinery	6,800			
Motor vehicles	2,130			
		12,205		
Directors' fees		1,000		
Audit fee		315		
Doubtful debts—increase in provision		105		
		71,901		
Net profit on trading, *i.e.* before taxation		18,899		
		£90,800		£90,800

Having prepared the Trading and Profit and Loss Account in the normal manner we will now produce, in vertical form, a Profit and Loss Account suitable for publication:

Profit before taxation			£18,899
After charging:			
Depreciation		£12,205	
Directors emoluments:			
Fees	£1,000		
Salaries	6,000		
Benefits in kind	459		
		7,459	
Auditors' fees		315	
Less: Corporation Tax at 40%			7,600
Profit after Taxation			11,299
Balance brought forward at 1st July 1965		£29,246	
Less Underprovision in previous year		1,000	
			28,246
			39,545
Deduct:			
Transfer to General Reserve		10,000	
Dividend paid (net)	£2,500		
Dividend proposed	5,000		
		7,500	
			17,500
Balance carried forward to next account			£22,045

BALANCE SHEET AS AT 30TH JUNE 1966

			Cost	Depreci-ation	Balance
Share Capital					
Authorised:			*Fixed Assets*		
75,000 ordinary £1 shares		£75,000	Leasehold land and buildings	£65,500	£36,025	£29,475
Issued:			Plant and machinery	54,400	37,090	17,310
50,000 ordinary shares of £1 each fully paid		£50,000	Motor vehicles	10,650	8,550	2,100
Revenue Reserves					
Plant replacement reserve	£30,000			£130,550	£81,665	£48,885
General reserve	50,000					
Profit and Loss A/c	22,045					
		102,045				
		152,045				
Corporation Tax (payable 1st January 1968)		7,600	*Current Assets*			
Current Liabilities			Stock		£11,450	
Creditors and accrued expenses	33,715		Debtors (net)		55,615	
Corporation Tax	8,000		Cash at bank and in hand		90,410	
Income tax on proposed dividends	2,500					157,475
Dividend (net)	2,500					
		46,715				
		£206,360				£206,360

NOTE: The provision for depreciation in respect of the fixed assets shown above has been calculated as follows:

Leasehold land and buildings:		
Provision at 1st July 1965		£32,750
Add: 5% of £65,500	=	3,275
Balance c/f		£36,025

Plant and machinery:		
Provision at 1st July 1965		£30,290
Add: 12½% of £54,400	=	6,800
Balance c/f		£37,090

Motor vehicles:		
Provision at 1st July 1965		£6,420
Add: 20% of £10,650	=	2,130
Balance c/f		£8,550

Question 6

(*a*) Working capital at 31st March 1965 (£83,050
    less £34,000)   £49,050
    Working capital at 31st March 1964 (£69,200
    less £32,000)   37,200

        Increase during 1964/65   £11,850

(*b*) Working capital at 31st March 1964   £37,200
    Add: Cash received:
            from issue of share   £25,000
            from premium on share issue   5,000
            from sale of freehold property   3,450

                                                    33,450
            Net Profit for the year (see below)   21,500
            Charges in Profit and Loss
                Account:
            Depreciation   £14,000
            Preliminary Expenses
                written off   400
                                      ———————
                                                    14,400
                                                   ———————   69,350

                                                                   106,550
    Less: Cash payments:
            Redemption of debentures   25,000
            New plant   25,000
            Dividend   7,500
                                                 ———————
                                                                    57,500

    Working capital at 31st March 1965   £49,050

Reconciliation

(*c*) Additions to working capital during year as shown
    above   £69,350
    Less: Special cash payments as shown above   57,500

    Increase for the year per (*a*) *above*   £11,850

M

NOTES: The following accounts may be of help:

Profit and Loss Appropriation Account

Dividend paid	£7,500	Balance brought forward	
Balance carried forward		at 1st April 1964	£16,000
(as per Balance Sheet)	30,000	Net Profit on trading	
		after charging depre-	
		ciation and amount	
		written off Prelimin-	
		ary Expenses	?
	£37,500		£37,500

The opening and closing balances shown above are those given in the Balance Sheet. We are told that a dividend of £7500 was paid during the year and this must, therefore, be debited above. The remainder, which amounts to £21,500, *must* be the Net Profit. This sum is shown on the Statement at (*b*) above.

Freehold Property Account

Balance b/d	£10,000	Bank A/c	£3,450
Capital reserve (per		Balance c/d	8,000
Balance Sheet)	1,450		
	£11,450		£11,450

Plant and Machinery Account

Balance b/d	£143,000	Depreciation	£14,000
Bank A/c	25,000	Balance c/d	154,000
	£168,000		£168,000

Question 7

(a) Working capital at 31st December 1966 (£74,000 less £41,100) £33,300
Working capital at 31st December 1965 (£59,700 less £33,200) 26,500

Increase during year 1966 .... £6,800

Statement of Sources and Application of Funds

(b) Working capital at 31st December 1965 .... £26,500

    Add: Net profit for the year £8,200

        Charges in Profit and Loss Account:

        Depreciation £7,500

        Preliminary Expenses written off 600

                 8,100

    Cash received from:

        Issue of shares 15,000

        Share premium 5,000

        Sale of property 26,000

                 46,000

                 62,300

                 88,800

    Less: Cash payment:

        Plant and machinery 47,000

        Proposed dividend 8,500

                 55,500

Working capital at 31st December 1966 .... £33,300

Reconciliation

(c) Additions to working capital during year as shown above £62,300

    Less: Special payment and provision as shown above 55,500

Increase in working capital during year £6,800

Question 8

Entries in the books of J. Moore Ltd

J. Moore (1966) Ltd

Realisation A/c	£129,100	Debenture Holders A/c	
		New debentures £20,000	
		10s. shares 1,000	
			£21,000
		Creditors A/c	
		Cash 6,000	
		10s. shares 24,000	
			30,000
		Preference Shareholders A/c	
		10s. shares:	
		for capital 50,000	
		for dividend arrears 4,500	
			54,500
		Ordinary Shareholders A/c	
		10s. shares	20,000
		Reconstruction A/c Costs	**3,600**
	£129,100		£129,100

Realisation Account

Fixed assets	£150,000	J. Moore (1966) Ltd (purchase consideration)	£129,100
Goodwill	20,000		
Current assets	17,000	Reconstruction A/c (loss on realisation)	**57,900**
	£187,000		£187,000

Reconstruction Account

Realisation A/c—Loss	**£57,900**	Ordinary Shareholders	
Preliminary expenses		A/c	£100,000
written off	3,000		
Profit and Loss A/c—			
debit balance written			
off	25,000		
Creditors A/c	6,000		
J. Moore (1966) Ltd—			
Costs	**3,600**		
Preference Shareholders			
A/c	4,500		
	£100,000		£100,000

Entries in the books of J. Moore (1966) Ltd

Bank Account

Balance at bank taken		Creditors of J. Moore	
over	£100	Ltd	£6,000
Share Capital A/c		J. Moore Ltd—Costs	3,600
(51,000 shares of 10s.)	25,500	Balance c/d	16,000
	£25,600		£25,600

BALANCE SHEET AS AT 1ST JULY 1966

Share capital		Fixed assets		£113,100
250,000 shares of		Current assets		
10s. each	£125,000	Stock	£9,900	
5% debentures	20,000	Debtors	6,000	
		Bank	16,000	
				31,900
	£145,000			£145,000

NOTE: The purchase consideration of £129,100 has been allocated as follows:

Current Assets of J. Moore Ltd (per Balance Sheet)		£17,000
Less: Amount written off stock		1,000
		16,000
Balance being the remainder which is to be considered as being the value of the fixed assets		113,100
		£129,100

Question 9
Stage 1

(a)   *D.G.L. (1967) Ltd*

Realisation A/c	**£37,400**	5% Debentures A/c		
		New debentures	£10,000	
		Shares	5,500	
				£15,500
		Preference Shares A/c		
		Shares (one for two)		21,000
		Ordinary Shares A/c		
		Shares (one for ten)		900
	£37,400			**£37,400**

Realisation Account

Goodwill A/c	£2,500	D.G.L. (1967) Ltd A/c	**£37,400**
Stock A/c	9,500	Bank A/c (overdraft	
Debtors A/c	24,060	taken over)	2,250
	36,060	Creditors A/c (taken	
Balance c/d	38,590	over)	35,000
	£74,650		£74,650
		Balance b/d	£38,590

Reconstruction Account

	£		£
Debentures A/c (bonus given to debenture holders)	500	Ordinary Share Capital A/c	8,100
Goodwill A/c	22,500	Preference Share Capital A/c	21,000
Stock A/c	1,000	Profit and Loss A/c (credit balance made available)	3,500
Preliminary Expenses A/c	190	Debenture Redemption Reserve (credit balance made available)	2,500
	24,190		
Balance c/d	10,910		
	£35,100		£35,100
		Balance b/d	£10,910

Stage 2

We must now close off the Reconstruction Account and transfer the amount made available to the credit of Fixed Assets Account.

Reconstruction Account

	£		£
Fixed Assets A/c	**10,910**	Balance b/d (from *Stage 1*)	10,910

Fixed Assets Account

	£		£
Balance b/d	49,500	**Reconstruction A/c**	**10,910**
		Balance b/d	38,590
	£49,500		£49,500
Balance b/d	£38,590		

Stage 3

The adjusted value of the fixed assets will now be transferred to the Realisation Account, thus closing it off.

Fixed Assets Account

Balance b/d (per *Stage 2*)	£38,590	**Realisation A/c**	**£38,590**

Realisation Account

Fixed Assets A/c	£38,590	Balance b/d (per *Stage 1*)	£38,590

BALANCE SHEET

Issued share capital	£60,000	Goodwill	£2,500
5% debentures	10,000	Fixed assets	38,590
Trade creditors	35,000	Current assets	
		Stock	£9,500
		Debtors	24,060
		Bank	29,725
			63,285
		Preliminary expenses	625
	£105,000		**£105,000**

(*b*) The alternative proposal would have provided almost exactly the same amount of fresh working capital as the scheme which was adopted. It would have had the advantage of saving the expense of forming a new company and would have been much more advantageous to both the preference and ordinary shareholders of the old company. In addition, the balance of £3500 on Profit and Loss Account and the balance of £2500 on the Debenture Redemption Reserve would have remained as revenue reserves legally available for dividend.

It appears unlikely, however, that the alternative proposal could have been put into effect. The old company was very highly geared and the proposed issue of ordinary shares might appear very unattractive to potential subscribers. Under the alternative proposal it would have been necessary to find £750 *per annum* for debenture interest and £2520 *per annum* for preference dividend before any profit was available for ordinary dividend. Under the scheme of reconstruction which has been adopted, the only prior claim on income is for £500 *per annum* as debenture interest, and a profit (before charging debenture interest) of £4100 will be sufficient to permit the payment of an ordinary dividend of 6%. Under the alternative proposal, the amount of profit required is £5760.

Without additional working capital the company was liable to collapse. On a forced sale the fixed assets would probably have produced considerably less than the amount at which they were transferred to the new company. In the event of liquidation the ordinary shareholders would have received nothing and there might have been very little available for the preference shareholders. If 32,500 new ordinary shares were issued without any other changes the capital of the new subscribers would be represented, in large measure, by goodwill and fixed assets, both of which are heavily overvalued. Both as regards income and capital rights the alternative proposal would be most unfavourable to new investors.

Question 10

Black Ltd—Journal

Land, buildings and plant	Dr.	£130,000	
Stock		21,000	
Debtors		5,200	
Goodwill		54,660	
To White Ltd			£210,600
Provision for doubtful debts			260
		£210,860	£210,860
White Ltd	Dr.	210,600	
Discount on debentures		2,400	
To Share Capital Account			150,000
Share Premium Account			30,000
5% Debentures Account			24,000
Bank Account			9,000
		£213,000	£213,000
Share Premium Account	Dr.	2,400	
To Discount on Debentures (assuming that the debenture discount is being written off)			2,400

White Ltd—Journal

Realisation Account	Dr.	£131,200	
To Goodwill			£12,000
Land, buildings and plant			90,000
Stock			24,000
Debtors			5,200
Realisation Account	Dr.	1,600	
To Debenture Account			1,600
Black Ltd	Dr.	210,600	
To Realisation Account			210,600
Bank	Dr.	9,000	
Shares in Black Ltd (150,000 £1 shares at 24s. per share)		180,000	
Debentures of Black Ltd Account (£24,000 debentures at a discount of 10%)		21,600	
To Black Ltd Account			210,600
Creditors Account	Dr.	7,000	
To Bank Account			7,000
Share Capital Account	Dr.	90,000	
General Reserve		15,000	
Profit and Loss Account		3,700	
Realisation Account—Profit on sale		77,800	
To Sundry Members Account			186,500
Sundry Members Account	Dr.	186,500	
To Shares in Black Ltd Account			180,000
Bank Account			6,500

Question 11

NOTE: Although the question does not ask for the ledger accounts of X Ltd it is felt that the more important ones should be shown in order to make it easier for the student to see how the journal entries are compiled.

Realisation Account

	£		£
Patent Rights A/c	20,000	Z Ltd A/c	279,500
Land and Buildings A/c	60,000		
Plant and Machinery			
A/c	155,000		
Stock A/c	35,000		
Debtors A/c	8,000		
	278,000		
Bank A/c—Costs	500		
Ordinary Shareholders			
A/c (profit on realisa-			
tion)	1,000		
	£279,500		£279,500

Z Ltd Account

	£		£
Realisation A/c	279,500	Bank A/c	54,500
		Shares in Z Ltd A/c	
		(180,000 shares at	
		25s. per share)	225,000
	£279,500		£279,500

Shares in Z Ltd Account

	£		£
Z Ltd A/c	225,000	Ordinary Shareholders A/c	225,000

Bank Account

Balance b/d	£16,000	Realisation A/c—Costs	£500
Z Ltd A/c	54,500	Creditors A/c	5,000
		Preference Shareholders	
		A/c	50,000
		Ordinary Shareholders	
		A/c	15,000
	£70,500		£70,500

Preference Shareholders Account

Bank A/c	£50,000	Preference Share Capital A/c	£50,000

Ordinary Shareholders Account

Bank A/c	£15,000	Ordinary Share Capital	
Shares in Z Ltd A/c	225,000	A/c	£150,000
		General Reserve A/c	80,000
		Profit and Loss A/c	9,000
		Realisation A/c—profit	1,000
	£240,000		£240,000

Converting into Journal entries we would have:

JOURNAL

Realisation A/c	Dr.	£278,000	
To Patent Rights A/c			£20,000
Land and Buildings A/c			60,000
Plant and Machinery A/c			155,000
Stock A/c			35,000
Debtors A/c			8,000
		£278,000	£278,000
Z Ltd A/c	Dr.	£279,500	
To Realisation A/c			£279,500
Shares in Z Ltd A/c	Dr.	225,000	
To Z Ltd A/c			225,000
Sundries	Dr.		
Ordinary Share Capital A/c		150,000	
General Reserve A/c		80,000	
Profit and Loss A/c		9,000	
Realisation A/c (profit)		1,000	
To Ordinary Shareholders A/c			240,000
		£240,000	£240,000
Preference Share Capital A/c	Dr.	£50,000	
To Preference Shareholders A/c			£50,000

The Balance Sheet of X Ltd shows that the company had originally issued 150,000 £1 ordinary shares.

As can be seen from the Ordinary Shareholders Account these shareholders were due to receive a total of £240,000. When the preference shareholders had been paid £1 for each share they held there remained a balance of £15,000 in cash which was paid to the ordinary shareholders. This left a balance of £225,000 to be satisfied by the issue of shares in Z Ltd.

These shares were issued at a premium of 5s. per share which leaves us with a nominal value of £180,000 for the shares, i.e. 5s. 4d. × £180,000 = £225,000.

This means that 150,000 shares in X Ltd were to be replaced by 180,000 shares in Z Ltd. Therefore, the holder of 100 shares in X Ltd would receive 120 shares in Z Ltd. In addition he would receive £10 in cash, *i.e.* £15,000 was paid to the holders of 150,000 shares which amounts to £1 for every 10 shares held, or £10 for every 100 held.

The shareholders of Y Ltd owned 40,000 £1 shares. They are to receive 30,000 shares in Z Ltd. Therefore, the holder of 100 shares in Y Ltd will receive 75 shares in Z Ltd.

BALANCE SHEET OF Z LTD

Share Capital		*Fixed Assets*	
Authorised	£300,000	Land and buildings	£60,000
		Plant and Machinery	155,000
Issued:		Motor vehicles	4,000
50,000 5% preference shares of £1 each	£50,000	Furniture and fittings	2,500
		Patent rights	20,000
		Goodwill	3,000
240,000 ordinary shares of £1 each	240,000		244,500
	290,000	*Current Assets*	
		Stocks £58,900	
		Debtors 14,200	
Capital Reserve		Bank balance 28,975	
Share Premium Account	60,000		102,075
		Preliminary Expenses (including Underwriting Commission)	3,425
	£350,000		£350,000

Question 12

Cost of Control Account—N.R.S. Ltd (*100% subsidiary*)

Cost of shares	£96,000	Share Capital A/c	£65,000
		Profit and Loss A/c (31/12/66)	27,300
		Goodwill A/c	3,700
	£96,000		£96,000

Cost of Control Account—W.F.D. Ltd (*75% subsidiary*)

Cost of shares	£35,000	Share Capital A/c (¾ × £32,000)	£24,000
		Profit and Loss A/c at 31/12/66	
		(¾ × £6100)	4,575
		Balance c/d	6,425
	£35,000		£35,000
Balance b/d	£6,425	Dividend ex pre-acquisition profits	£1,200
		Goodwill A/c	5,225
	£6,425		£6,425

Goodwill Account

Cost of Control A/c:		
N.R.S. Ltd	£3,700	
W.F.D. Ltd	5,225	
	£8,925	

Minority Interest Account

	Share Capital A/c ($\frac{1}{4}$ × £32,000)	£8,000
	Profit and Loss A/c ($\frac{1}{4}$ × £7,700)	1,925
	Proposed dividend ($\frac{1}{4}$ × £3,200)	800
		£10,725

Profit and Loss Account (E.C.Y. Ltd)

Cost of Control A/c (W.E.D.)	£1,200	Per Balance Sheet	£37,600
Loss on sale of motor vehicle	200	Profit and Loss A/c (N.R.S.) (Net	
Balance c/d	49,300	profit for 1967)	9,500
		Profit and Loss A/c (W.F.D.)	
		($\frac{3}{4}$ of net profit for 1967, *i.e.*	
		$\frac{3}{4}$ of £4800)	3,600
	£50,700		£50,700

CONSOLIDATED BALANCE SHEET

Share capital	£150,000	Goodwill	£8,925
Profit and Loss A/c	49,300	Fixed assets	142,000
Minority interest	10,725	Current assets	135,000
Creditors	75,900		
	£285,925		£285,925

Question 13

Cost of Control Account—East Ltd (100% subsidiary)

Cost of shares (West		Share Capital A/c	£75,000
Ltd)	£93,400	Profit and Loss A/c	9,250
		Goodwill A/c	9,150
	£93,400		£93,400

Cost of Control Account—South Ltd (75% subsidiary)

Cost of shares (West Ltd)	£21,600	Share Capital A/c	£15,000
		Profit and Loss A/c	3,000
		Goodwill A/c	3,600
	£21,600		£21,600

Minority Interest Account—South Ltd

	Share Capital A/c:	
	Ordinary shares	£5,000
	Preference shares	4,000
	Profit and Loss A/c— 1965	1,000
	Proposed dividends:	
	Ordinary £500	
	Preference 240	
		740
	Profit and Loss A/c— 1966	140
		£10,880

Goodwill Account

Cost of Control A/c:		Profit and Loss A/c West Ltd (dividend from pre-acquisition profits)	£1,200
East Ltd	£9,150	Balance c/d	11,550
South Ltd	3,600		
	£12,750		£12,750
Balance b/d	£11,550		

Profit and Loss Account—South Ltd.

Proposed Dividend A/c:			Balance b/d (31/12/65)	£5,840
Ordinary	£1,600			
Preference	240			
		£1,840		
Cost of Control A/c		3,000		
Minority Interest A/c		1,000		
		£5,840		£5,840
Proposed Dividend A/c:			Net profit for the year	
Ordinary	£2,000		1966	£2,800
Preference	240			
		£2,240		
Balance c/d		560		
		£2,800		£2,800
Minority Interest A/c		140	Balance b/d	560
Balance c/d		1,920	Proposed Dividend A/c	1,500
		£2,060		£2,060
			Balance b/d	£1,920

Proposed Dividend Account—South Ltd

Cash paid during 1966	£1,840	Profit and Loss A/c 1965:		
		Ordinary	£1,600	
		Preference	240	
				£1,840
	£1,840			£1,840
Profit and Loss A/c 1966		Profit and Loss A/c 1966:		
(Dividend written		Ordinary		£2,000
back)	£1,500	Preference		240
Minority Interest A/c	740			
	£2,240			£2,240

CONSOLIDATED BALANCE SHEET

Issued Share Capital		£200,000	*Fixed assets*			
Profit and Loss Account			West Ltd	£88,000		
West Ltd	£29,800		East Ltd	69,000		
East Ltd	7,000		South Ltd	18,000		
South Ltd	1,920				£175,000	
		38,720	*Goodwill*		11,550	
Current Liabilities			*Current assets*			
West Ltd	£24,800		West Ltd	£52,800		
East Ltd	15,750		East Ltd	38,000		
South Ltd	13,200		South Ltd	26,000		
		53,750			116,800	
Minority interest		10,880				
		£303,350			£303,350	

Question 14

Consolidated Profit and Loss Account

Proposed dividend	£20,000	Net profit for year ended			
		31st December 1965:			
		Green Ltd	£24,600		
		Pink Ltd	6,000		
				30,600	
		Less:			
		Net loss—			
		Blue Ltd	1,400		
				£29,200	
Balance c/f	19,200	Balance brought for-			
		ward from 1964:			
		Green Ltd	£9,400		
		Pink Ltd	600		
				10,000	
	£39,200			£39,200	

Question 15

Consolidated Profit and Loss Account

Minority interest:			Net profit for the year 1966:			
A.B.Y. Ltd (preference			D.V.N. Ltd		£23,480	
dividend)	£360		A.B.Y. Ltd		460	
A.B.Y. Ltd (⅕ of £100, *i.e.*			C.M.L. Ltd		8,000	
£460 less £360)	20				———	
	——				31,940	
	380		*Less:* L.G.T. Ltd			
C.M.L. Ltd (¼ of £8000)	2,000		Net loss		1,825	
C.M.L. Ltd (¼ of £3300,					——— £30,115	
the 1965 profit)	825		Undistributed profit of			
	——	£3,205	earlier years:			
L.G.T. Ltd—Stock A/c (un-			D.V.N. Ltd		12,500	
realised profit in goods sold			C.M.L. Ltd	£5,400		
to L.G.T. Ltd by D.V.N. Ltd,			*Less:* Pre-			
i.e. £640 less £480)		160	acquisition			
Proposed dividend		16,000	profit	2,100		
		———		——	3,300	
		19,365			———	15,800
Balance c/d		26,550				
		———				———
		£45,915				£45,915
		═══				═══

NOTE:

(*i*) In calculating the amount of the interest of the minority shareholders we must allow for a full year's preference dividend for A.B.Y. Ltd, *i.e.* 6% on £6000, £360. Since A.B.Y. Ltd made a profit of only £460 and as £360 of it is absorbed by the preference dividend there remains only £100 to apportion. The minority interest is entitled to one-fifth, *i.e.* £20.

(*ii*) The dividend paid by L.G.T. Ltd in February 1966 is paid entirely out of *pre-acquisition profits* and must, therefore, be excluded. This has been shown as a *deduction* on the credit side. The reason for this, of course, is that it should have been credited to Cost of Control Account instead of Profit and Loss Account.

CERTAIN REQUIREMENTS
OF THE *COMPANIES ACT*, 1967

Certain matters relating to the *Companies Act*, 1967, which could not conveniently be incorporated in Chapter VI (Published Accounts) are set out in this Appendix.

1. United Kingdom taxation. A company is required to show:

(*a*) *Corporation Tax:*

    (*i*) the amount of the liability for Corporation Tax on the profits;

    (*ii*) if the company is entitled to any *relief from double taxation* the gross amount due in respect of Corporation Tax, *i.e. before* deduction of such relief;

    (*iii*) the **basis of computation** of the charge to Corporation Tax.

(*b*) *Income Tax:*

    (*i*) the charge for United Kingdom Income Tax (*see* Chapter XVII);

    (*ii*) the **basis of computation** of the charge to Income Tax.

(*c*) *Overseas Taxation:*

    (*i*) the charge for overseas taxation of profits and income;

    (*ii*) the charge for overseas taxation in respect of capital gains so far as this has been *charged to revenue.*

(*d*) *Special circumstances.* Any special circumstances which affect the liability in respect of the taxation of profits, income or capital gains for (*i*) the financial year, or (*ii*) succeeding financial years, must be stated.

2. Appropriations of profit.

(*a*) *Renewal of assets.* If, *in addition to* the ordinary provision for depreciation, an amount is set aside for the **renewal** of an asset, this amount must be stated separately. (p. 45 *above.*)

(b) *Reserves, i.e.* any *additional amount* to be transferred to the credit of General Reserve. If, for any reason, the company wishes to transfer a sum *from* General Reserve to Profit and Loss Appropriation Account (credit side) this, too, must be shown.

(c) *Provisions.* Similar regulations are laid down in respect of "provisions," other than provisions for depreciation. This requirement, however, seems likely to apply to revenue items in the trading section of the Profit and Loss Account as well as to the Appropriation Account. Exemption from disclosure may be obtained if the fact that transfers have been made is stated.

(d) *Any portion of the trading profit* which is to be set aside for the purpose of:

(i) *the redemption of preference shares;* or

(ii) *the redemption of debentures* or other loans, must be shown.

The accounts which will be credited are, respectively, Capital Redemption Reserve and Debenture Redemption Reserve.

(e) *Dividends,* paid or proposed. These amounts must be shown **gross.**

NOTE: It is by no means uncommon for a company to write off preliminary expenses and discount on an issue of shares or debentures as well as goodwill. If any of these items are being written off it is customary to write them off in the appropriation section.

3. Loans made to a company. The following information must be disclosed :

(a) Debentures of the company held for the company by nominees or trustees stating nominal and book amounts.

(b) Debentures of the company held by subsidiaries.

(c) Redeemed debentures which may be re-issued.

(d) Liabilities secured on assets of the company.

It is not necessary to specify the assets involved.

Borrowings, *other than bank loans and overdrafts*, which are repayable either wholly or in part more than five years from the date of the balance sheet, must be stated in aggregate.

4. Current liabilities. The 1967 Act requires that inter-group indebtedness must be shown, stating separately aggregate amounts owing to subsidiaries, including loans. In addition, there must be shown the aggregate amounts owing to holding and fellow subsidiary companies distinguishing between debentures and other indebtedness.

Movements on provisions other than those for depreciation, etc., are to be stated together with the source of any increase and the application of any decrease, in the aggregate.

5. Fixed assets. Under each fixed asset heading the aggregates of the following amounts must be shown:

(a) Cost or valuation, as shown in the company's books.
(b) Aggregate amount provided for depreciation,
(c) The difference between (a) and (b) above.

Exceptions to the above requirements are made in the case of the following fixed assets:

(a) Quoted investments.
(b) Unquoted investments.
(c) Goodwill, patents and trade-marks.
(d) Investments in subsidiary companies.
(e) Assets, the replacement of which is provided:

    (i) by making provisions for renewals and charging the cost of replacement against the provision, or
    (ii) by charging the cost of replacement direct to revenue,

but in such cases there shall be stated:

    (iii) the means by which their replacement is provided for, and
    (iv) the aggregate amount of provision (if any) made for renewals and not used.

6. Fixed assets included at a valuation. Where any fixed asset, with the exception of *unquoted* investments, has been included at a valuation there must be shown (by way of a note or statement) *for each separate valuation*:

(a) the year of valuation if known, and
(b) the amount of the valuation.

For each asset which has been *valued* during the financial year under review there must be stated:

(a) *either:*

    (i) the names of the valuers, or
    (ii) particulars of their qualifications; *and*

(b) the bases of the valuation used.

7. Movements on fixed assets. Where any fixed assets have been purchased or disposed of, with the exception of investments, there must be stated (by way of a note or statement) the aggregate amounts of:

(a) assets acquired, and
(b) assets disposed of or scrapped during the period.

8. Land held as fixed assets. The following classes of land must be shown *separately* by way of note or in a statement:

(*a*) freehold land;

(*b*) land held on a long lease; and

(*c*) land held on a short lease.

NOTE:

(*i*) A lease having more than fifty years to run is regarded as a long lease.

(*ii*) All other leases are short leases.

(*iii*) Interests in land are regarded as including any buildings thereon.

9. Goodwill, patents and trade-marks. These assets need not be stated separately; the aggregate may, therefore, be shown as a single item.

The amount to be shown is that which is ascertainable from the company's books and relevant documents, so far as not written off.

10. Unquoted investments in equity share capital. Where the directors' estimate of the value of such shares is not shown, there must be stated:

(*a*) the aggregate income for the year from such investments;

(*b*) the amount of the company's share *before* taxation, and the amount *after* taxation, of the net aggregate amount of the profits less losses of the bodies in which the investments are held;

(*c*) the amount *owing to* the company in respect of undistributed profits;

(*d*) the manner in which losses, made by the company invested in, have been dealt with.

NOTE: Subsidiary companies are excluded from the provisions set out in **9** and **10** above.

11. Subsidiary companies. Information relating to shares in and aggregate amounts owing from subsidiaries must be set out separately from all other assets. Details of all loans must be given, and shares must be distinguished from indebtedness.

The aggregate of shares in fellow-subsidiaries must also be stated.

Debentures in and amounts owing to the company by holding and fellow-subsidiaries must be shown separately. Debentures must be distinguished from other debts.

GROUP ACCOUNTS

12. Additional information. The following information must be given:

    (*a*) A subsidiary company must disclose the name of its holding company.

    (*b*) Where a company has a subsidiary or owns more than one-tenth in nominal value of its issued capital, the name and country of registration must be stated together with details of the shares held.

13. Other relevant factors. The following matters apply:

    (*a*) A true and fair view must be given.

    (*b*) Group accounts may be presented in varied forms at the discretion of the directors.

    (*c*) The accounts must comply with the requirements of the Eighth Schedule (1948 Act) as amended.

    (*d*) The accounts shall combine the information contained in the separate accounts of the holding and subsidiary companies but need not give:

        (*i*) details of directors' emoluments;

       (*ii*) particulars of loans to officers;

     (*iii*) information regarding certain investments;

     (*iv*) details of employees' emoluments which exceed £10,000 per annum.

    (*e*) Omission of a subsidiary from group accounts is permitted in certain circumstances (1948 Act, *s*.150). Section 15 of the Second Schedule, 1967, requires the company to provide explanations on some points.

14. Directors' report. A company is now required to provide information relating to the following matters:

    (*a*) Directors' names.

    (*b*) The principal activities of the company (or group), noting any significant changes during the year.

    (*c*) Any important changes in fixed assets during the year.

    (*d*) Whether the market-value of the company's interests in land held as fixed assets differs materially from the book value at the year end.

    (*e*) Details of any issues of shares or debentures during the year.

    (*f*) The interest of any director in any contracts the company has entered into.

    (*g*) Directors' rights to acquire shares or debentures in the company.

(*h*) Directors' interests in shares or debentures of the company at the year end.

(*i*) Any other matters which may be material to enable the members to appreciate the state of the company's affairs.

(*j*) An analysis of the company's turnover and profit or loss before taxation.

(*k*) The average number of employees per week if this exceeds one hundred.

(*l*) The aggregate remuneration paid or payable to employees for the year if the numbers exceed one hundred.

(*m*) Political and charitable contributions made during the year.

(*n*) The value of the company's exports during the year.

15. Special classes of companies. Board of Trade recognition is required in respect of:

(*a*) Banking and discount companies.

(*b*) Shipping companies.

The exemptions granted to an insurance company may be revoked or restricted by the Board of Trade if its business is substantially other than insurance business.

INDEX